NASTY BUSINESS

PETER PARADIS

NASTY
BUSINESS

One Biker Gang's Bloody War
Against the Hells Angels

HarperCollins*Publishers*Ltd

Nasty Business: One Biker Gang's
Bloody War Against the Hells Angels
Copyright © 2002 by Peter Paradis
and John Kal.

Photographs courtesy of *Allô Police!* and
Peter Paradis. Reprinted by permission.

HarperCollins books may be purchased for
educational, business, or sales promotional use.
For information please write:
Special Markets Department,
HarperCollins Canada,
55 Avenue Road, Suite 2900,
Toronto, Ontario, Canada M5R 3L2

First edition

National Library of Canada Cataloguing in
Publication

Paradis, Peter
Nasty business : one biker gang's bloody war
against the Hells Angels / Peter Paradis.

ISBN 0-00-200099-7

1. Paradis, Peter. 2. Rock Machine (Gang)
3. Hells Angels. 4. Motorcycle gangs—Quebec
(Province)—History. 5. Gang members—
Quebec (Province)—Biography. I. Title.

HV6491.C32Q8 2002   364.1'092
C2002-902419-6

HC 9 8 7 6 5 4 3 2 1

Printed and bound in the United States
Set in Sabon

CONTENTS

NASTY BUSINESS

CHAPTER 1

I left the apartment intending to commit a crime. I dressed the part, wearing an overcoat, the kind that makes it easy to hide weapons underneath. As I approached the grocery store, the automatic doors swooshed open. My fingers undid a few buttons on my coat, but not all.

Down the aisles I walked, getting progressively more nervous. I knew where to go since I had already picked my target. Looking around, I tried not to appear too guilty. Nobody should be able to recognize me here as one of the leaders of the Rock Machine, a gang that was battling the Hells Angels for control of Quebec's billion-dollar drug trade, leaving bombed ruins and corpses in our wake.

I reached the meat shelves, and saw staff and customers milling around. Then my eyes scanned for the target. I found it.

Swiftly, I reached down into the meat freezer, grabbed two T-bone steaks, and walked away with them in my hands. In an empty aisle, I stuffed the meat into hidden pockets in my mustard coat.

I was stealing my food about three times a week because I was broke. My biggest fear wasn't being assassinated by the Hells Angels, but being caught and seeing the next day's jeering headline, "Full-patch biker caught shoplifting $10 in beef." The shame would have tortured me. I sauntered over to the cigarette counter and calmly bought some smokes to camouflage the real purpose of my trip.

Back home, I cooked up the steaks. They were fine, but I didn't feel the same way.

The war with the Angels had taken its toll, leaving 170 dead and just as many injured by bullets or bombs. It was the bloodiest biker war in the world. As one news program put it, we even outdid Al Capone and his bloodthirsty gangsters. I was one of the people who had been shot, aerated four times by bullets from an Angels hit team.

As I ate my steak, I ruminated about recent events. Police had raided my drug network a few months back and put me out of business. Serious charges were hanging over me. I couldn't carry a gun because if police found one on me they would revoke my bail. Meanwhile, all my bodyguards were behind bars, the Angels were trying to finish me off, and my fellow gang leaders were avoiding me because of all the police attention.

In time, I had had enough of the fear and empty pockets. I needed a safe place that would feed me. So I asked my lawyer, Marion Burelle, to deliberately get my bail revoked. In jail, at least I would be taken care of. My lawyer told the judge I no longer had a permanent address, which is a prerequisite for being let out while awaiting trial.

Another gang member did the same thing. We smoked some hash the night before going behind bars, and he stuffed more of it up his butt to have something to use in jail.

At my preliminary hearing, ten of us stood accused of gangster-ism, a new federal charge designed to fight biker gangs. I was the boss. Alongside me were my enforcers, dealers, and those who stashed the drugs.

As I sat in the prisoner's box listening to the evidence against us, I decided to end this life. I'd gotten offers to turn informant, but always refused them out of hand. But now I kept thinking about the two anti-gang police officers I had gotten to know as they stalked my gang. Det. Sgt. Clement Rose looked more like Howdy Doody than a cop. Young and friendly, he had warned me a few times about contracts taken out on me by the Hells Angels. Word of the contracts had been picked up by police surveillance and Rose made sure to tell me to keep my eyes open. I didn't know why he did that, because, to a cop, a dead biker is better than a live one. I didn't trust him at the time, thinking it was some sort of ploy. He looked middle class, not like a street cop. His partner, Claude Lambert, was a bit older and looked like the typical hard-nosed street cop, gruff and a man of few words. Maybe I could trust them now.

But I was behind bars, and it would be hard to contact police without the entire jail wing getting wind of it when the plainclothes officers showed up to talk to me. A month into the preliminary hearing, my lawyer told me he could get me out on bail again. "Do it," I said, but didn't explain why.

I was released that same night, a Thursday. At a cousin's place, I popped open a few beers to celebrate, letting my years in crime run like a film through my mind. At 35, half my life had been spent pushing drugs. Everything was so confused.

I got drunk and convinced myself that what I was about to do was the right thing. I passed out with that thought in my mind, and that's how I woke up the next day. I was staggering about from the alcohol, but I still believed it was the right thing to do.

The debate in my head continued all day; but the more I thought about it, the more I realized my brothers in the Rock Machine, for whom I had been willing to give my life, didn't care about me. After years of giving thousands of dollars to help those in jail or other members on hard times, no one stood by me. So screw them.

But what about my family? My mother had lived through my shooting and that of my younger brother Robert. My brother was still involved with the Rock Machine, having followed in my footsteps. I spoke to him many times during the day, but could not bring myself to tell him what I was going to do. He would have tried to change my mind.

I called my Uncle Jimmy from my mother's side of the family. He showed up 20 minutes later and told me I was doing the right thing.

Finally, I got up the nerve to call Det. Sgt. Rose. I knew his pager number by heart since he had been getting in my face for the last year. But mental exhaustion erased it from my mind. I sat at the kitchen table for half an hour trying to remember it, until I noticed the *Journal de Montréal* in front of me. The crime tabloid had been running little ads telling the public to call a 1-800 number if they had information to give police on the gang war. I dialed and asked to be patched through to Rose. As I waited, I could hear my heart pounding. I was about to hang up when Rose identified himself.

"It's Peter," I said hoarsely.

"What can I do for you?" the Montreal police officer asked in his usual polite way.

"I gotta see you."

I told him where I was and he promised to be at my place in 45 minutes.

As I sat down to wait, I took out a piece of paper and a pen and wrote in French: "Who do I talk to, you or the RCMP?"

To that I added: "*Pas de crosse.*" It means "don't screw me." I was putting my life in his hands, and I guess it was a plaintive cry for him to be fair.

I wrote it all down because I didn't want to say anything and risk my voice being captured by a hidden microphone on Rose. Then, I sat and stared into space, thinking of the consequences. All my thoughts were in a whirl.

The phone rang.

"Come on out," Rose said. "We are in front of your apartment building."

Once on the street, I saw a car slowly making its way toward me. I joined Rose and his partner inside.

A puzzled Clement looked at me. He had no idea what I wanted. "How are you doing?"

"OK, I guess."

"What is it you want to talk to me about?"

I showed him the paper. I had added two names to it in brackets: Simard and Quesnel.

To cops and bikers, those names were well known. Aimé Simard was a gay biker with the Angels who turned stool, even against his own biker lover. Serge Quesnel was another infamous informant, a ruthless cold-blooded man who killed five people for the Angels before going to police. Putting their names on the paper left no doubt about what I wanted.

Clement's jaw was hanging. Usually, low-level underlings like Simard and Quesnel become informants. Here he had someone at the highest level of the Rock Machine willing to squeal—the first full-patch member.

"I've had enough of this life and shit," I said with a force that surprised even me. "I've got no more gas to keep going and I am fed up."

Clement recovered quickly.

"Let's go. We'll go somewhere where we can talk. I'm just going to tell the other car that everything is all right and they can leave."

"What other car?" I asked, looking around.

"I didn't know why you wanted to see me, so I had to take precautions."

I realized he must have thought I was laying a trap to kill him as payback for busting my network. It wasn't a far-fetched thought. The Angels had randomly chosen two prison guards and killed them as part of a campaign to destabilize the justice system.

We drove around looking for somewhere to talk. Clement's first question about my past was very direct.

"Have you killed anyone?"

"No," I said, and then qualified the answer. "But I was involved in four murders, a couple of attempted murders, bombings, arsons."

"We'll talk about that later in detail," he said, "but I have to know if you killed anyone with your own hands."

"No," I repeated aggressively, getting mad at him for not accepting my first answer.

"OK," he said to mollify me. "What is it you want to know?"

"I want to know how the witness-protection program works, and what I could receive by cooperating."

Clement spent an hour explaining the program, how an informant is paid, and the change of identity that leads to a new life. I would also be relocated by the government to wherever I wanted. He wanted to take me into custody right away, worried I'd change my mind or get killed if word leaked out. I knew the danger of staying free, but I refused. I wanted to get laid.

Since I had just gotten out of Rivieres-des-Prairies detention center the day before, I hadn't had a chance to see my girlfriend Chantal. But I didn't tell them that, just that I needed to do some things.

Finally, Lambert asked to speak to Rose outside the car. For ten minutes they talked, glancing at me. As they got back in the car, Lambert was laughing as he said he had explained to the clueless Rose why nature called so strongly.

The two cops agreed to give me another day. I held out for two, until Sunday.

"I won't change my mind," I assured them. "I told you I'm fed up."

When I got back to my cousin's place, I called Chantal in Ottawa and she took a bus straight to Montreal. Knowing I had just gotten out of jail and was about to go back for a number of years, I didn't waste any time with her.

The weekend went quickly. I didn't change my mind, but thoughts of how others would react kept creeping in. What kept me strong was knowing I would start a new life. Sunday at noon, Rose phoned.

"How are you holding up?" he asked. "Did you change your mind?"

"No."

He said he'd pick me up in two hours. I then called my Uncle

Jimmy to say goodbye. He came round in person. Tears were rolling down his face as he walked into the apartment.

"You're doing the right thing. You don't need this shit anymore. You are still young and you have a lot of good years to live so you might as well live them in peace."

My cousin was also there. Both she and my girlfriend were crying. I was pretty close, too.

"OK," I said. "That's enough of this crying bullshit. You're supposed to be happy for me."

They started to laugh, thankfully, or I would have started bawling. At 2 p.m. the phone rang. Rose asked me to go outside. I hugged everyone as they started crying again.

Walking outside, I saw Rose and Lambert standing by their car. They were not alone. A minivan was in front with a few heavily armed SWAT officers in it. An unmarked Econoline van was at the rear, with more SWAT officers inside. Two stood outside with submachine guns. As we took off, I realized my police escort was identical to how I travelled through Verdun when I still had my gang enforcers and bodyguards.

We made a stop where my mother worked at a department store to say goodbye. Rose asked me if I had my leather biker vest, known as my colors, and my Rock Machine ring. I said they were hidden at my mother's home and I would get the key from her. At the store, the SWAT team stayed outside. My mother saw me, dressed in an adidas exercise outfit, arrive with two men in suits. Her eyes were bulging and showed concern, but she remained calm.

The cops introduced themselves. Then I spoke.

"It's finished. It's over for me."

She knew what I meant.

As I left, she turned to Rose.

"*Y va être correct?*"

She wanted to know if I would be safe.

"*Oui, madame,*" Rose reassured her. "*Ça va aller. Inquiètez-vous pas. Il est entre bonnes mains.*"

Don't worry, he told her. I was in good hands.

We headed to my mother's house to pick up the Rock Machine leather vest and ring. I warned the detectives to have the SWAT team on the lookout because I had gotten word the Angels had rented an apartment across the street to shoot me if I came to visit.

I handed over the colors with remorse. I had worked so hard to get them, and dedicated so many years to the war. You are supposed to protect the vest with your life. Giving them so easily to a cop seemed wrong.

There was one last stop to make—my brother's place. I had to pick up a list of people who, in total, owed me $150,000 in bad debts. The list could end up being important in court because one name was Gilles Nolet, a friend killed by one of my henchmen a month earlier over a $15,000 drug debt.

"Don't take an hour," Rose told me as he and the SWAT team waited around the corner to avoid being seen. My brother was surprised to see me. It hurt to do it but I kept the truth from him.

"I'm not going to court tomorrow," I told him. "I'm going to hide in Ottawa."

I grabbed some clothes I had kept at his place. Puzzled, he gave me the list of drug debts, but kept asking me to stay awhile.

"I gotta go. My ride to Ottawa is waiting."

I walked out of his life, feeling sick to my stomach as I handed Rose the list. He noticed my anguish and assured me I'd talk to Robert again on the phone.

I was subdued as the detectives took me to a hotel room and ordered pizza. Then came hours of dissecting the Rock Machine from top to bottom. Both Lambert and Rose had spent years on the outside trying to look in. They were fascinated to finally get past the wall of silence.

Two detectives stood guard all night. The next day was Monday, and I was supposed to be in court for my preliminary hearing with the rest of my gang, but Rose figured the best thing to do was for me to go missing for a day or two, even if the judge swore out a warrant for my arrest.

I spent the day being questioned. It felt weird talking to cops—they had been the enemy for so long. We went back to the beginning, in the mid-1990s, when the Angels started the war by muscling in on drug trafficking in Montreal. The Rock Machine fought back. And the killing began. Police originally bet on us to win because we had such strong allies among independent drug dealers in the city. But so many on our side were quickly arrested and killed that the Angels gained the upper hand and kept it.

The war quickly spread throughout Quebec, already known for bloodthirsty bikers. The deaths occurred over such a drawn-out period that it became nothing special. Car bombings, attacks on biker clubhouses, and hit teams took care of thinning out the outlaw ranks. But then a car bomb under a Jeep sent deadly shards of burning metal into an 11-year-old boy playing nearby, snuffing out his life. And the Angels started targeting law officials, putting bombs at police stations, and later shooting a crime reporter. Outrage grew. After a lot of biker talk, we switched to sports.

I was finally taken to court the next day. Rose wanted to do this in style so he brought back the SWAT team. Their leader went up the stairs first, stopping and crouching at each corner. He peered around quickly, instantly retracting his head. A hand signal told us to proceed.

I was the only one without a bulletproof vest, a bit ironic considering it was my life at risk. We walked that way up four flights, and then I waited in a tiny cubicle for my turn to enter the courtroom.

"Ready to go?" one SWAT officer asked.

"I'm just trying to catch my breath after all those stairs," I lied. I needed some time to pull myself together.

"OK. I'm ready."

I walked in surrounded by police and headed to the witness

stand, resting my hands on the back of the bench. The police, guns in hand, took positions in all corners.

I kept my eyes on the judge, but I could see my lawyer out of the corner of my eye. He was staring at me. Another defense lawyer, Jacques Bouchard, threw his pen on the desk with disgust.

Prosecutor Jean-Claude Boyer announced I wanted to plead guilty to all charges. He turned to me and asked if I wanted a lawyer.

"No."

My gang members were shaking their heads, sitting there with their jaws hanging. Cheeky, one of my bodyguards, lowered his head. He knew I'd witnessed him kill a man in broad daylight. Others stared directly at me, leaving no doubt I was now their enemy.

The judge accepted my guilty plea but seemed a bit disbelieving, asking me three times if I had been promised anything or threatened.

"Your honour, I'm 35 years old and I am old enough to know what I am doing."

I walked out, surrounded by my new protectors. One of my old protectors spit out a word as I went by.

"*Cochon*," Beluga said. He had earned his nickname because he's as fat as a baby whale.

In English, *cochon* means pig. But in biker slang, it really refers to a rat, a stool pigeon. I didn't look back.

CHAPTER 2

My parents married in September 1964, while my mother was two months shy of giving birth to me. As youngsters, they had lived across the street from each other near the downtown railway yards of Montreal. My mother fell head over heels in love soon after she met my dad at the age of 14. He was kind to her, but it didn't last. As they courted and she worked, she would give him pocket money from her work in an insurance office since he was jobless. That should have been her first clue of things to come, she would say years later.

My mother still remembers her father saying they would marry over his dead body. He had seen something unsavory in Pierre Paradis. In the end, her father did die before the union he so desperately tried to prevent.

Once married, Pierre went on nightly drinking binges, but my 21-year-old mother said nothing to those around her since she had been brought up in a traditional Italian family. When I was two and my brother Robert was just a few months old, my father was the passenger in a car accident. The driver was killed but my father suffered only a concussion. Still, the insurance payoff allowed my parents to buy a convenience store in the middle of a bustling industrial area in Point St. Charles. My father also used the insurance to buy Robert and I about four hundred dollars' worth of presents that Christmas.

The convenience store, which cost $8,000, was at a great location at the corner of Wellington and Bridge streets. Workers from the nearby CN workshops and the Redpath sugar refinery were constantly in and out for soft drinks, hamburgers, and snacks. As well, the traffic over the nearby Victoria Bridge from the south shore of Montreal made it a moneymaker.

But there was also a bar next door where my father spent most of his time. He would get angry at my mother and neglect her. He'd also neglect the store, either closing up early to go next door or hiring staff who would steal more than they sold. With two young children to take care of, my mother was in a panic. She finally got our father's sister to babysit us for $25 a week while she worked and her mother helped out.

My mother would get up at 4:30 a.m. to open the store an hour later for the factory workers to get their breakfast toast and coffee. My father would start his shift around 6 p.m. and supposedly stay until around 11 p.m. If he was too hung over or had decided to start drinking in the afternoon, our grandmother would take a shift.

One time, my mother came home to find my father had a woman sitting at the kitchen table with him and another man. She had suspected he was cheating on her, and she got the impression this strange woman was one of his conquests.

"Take that and get out," she told him, pointing at the woman. Instead, my father tossed us out. After our father threw our clothes out on the tiny lawn in front of our apartment, we went to our Granna's until they reconciled.

My mother continued to work long hours and our father continued to drink. One night, a family member invited my mother out to dinner, saying she deserved a break from the store. A babysitter took care of Robert and me as our father did his night shift. We were asleep in the room we shared next to the kitchen when he walked in carrying some takeout cartons of rigatoni from an Italian place. He'd also stopped off for a few drinks.

My father's rage upon finding his wife missing from the home woke both Robert and me instantly. Swearing, our father began throwing the rigatoni against the kitchen walls. Quivering noodles flew through the open door of our bedroom, sticking to our flannel pyjamas and bedsheets. I was terrified. This wasn't the first time Robert and I saw him unleash his anger upon arriving home. We'd await that nightly moment with equal parts dread and happiness, since he did show a softer side sometimes. We'd usually be relieved if he just passed out.

It is hard to remember, but I think our father gave us a swat or two on the backside the night of the raining rigatoni. It wouldn't have been the first time. But it was one of the last, because my mother left him a month later. I was five and a half.

Now my mother was running the corner store alone since it had been in her name. To work, she had to put Robert and me in a boarding school at a convent in northern Montreal. We cried when she left us with the nuns the first time. We'd come home for the weekends and be happy, but then the crying would start again on the trip back every Sunday. The store had been in trouble because of my father's drinking, and now things got worse. He'd walk in to the place almost every day while a woman waited for him in the car.

"Give me some money," he demanded. My mother would hand over $25 or $30. He'd also take whatever he could carry—soft drinks, cakes, cigarettes, and chips.

"Make me some hamburgers," he'd then order his estranged wife. And she'd do it. My father would take the food my mother prepared and share it with his girlfriend in the car.

Eight months after they separated in 1970, my mother lost the store by racking up $10,000 in debts. A man offered to pay off what she owed and took the place over. She had $4.67 in the bank and two kids to care for so she went on welfare. But Robert and I were happy because she took us out of the convent. We lived in Verdun, a suburb of Montreal that had seen better days. Our apartment was on the bottom floor of a triplex. Like most area buildings, legacies to the need for cheap housing for workers in the bygone glory days of industrial Montreal, it was as thin as possible, squeezed against other homes on both sides so the only windows were in the front and back. Robert and I shared bunk beds in the back, but my mother had to make do with a windowless enclosure off the front living room. That space was known as a "chambre double," and allowed landlords to charge for an extra room even though the only things that separated it from the living room were curtains.

One Mother's Day, Robert and I organized a thank you. As she pretended to sleep in, we cooked. The tray we brought her in bed contained blackened eggs, burnt toast, a plastic flower, and a cup of coffee. She thanked us.

"Mommy, I put six teaspoons of sugar in your coffee. That's how you like it," I said with authority.

My mother tried not to recoil. She took coffee black.

"Yes, Peter," she answered, completely hiding her distaste of our offering. "But you boys are going to help me eat all this, aren't you?"

I imperiously turned to Robert.

"Now Robert, you don't touch nothing. This is all Mommy's."

I never felt I missed anything as a child, even though times were tough. Robert and I were brought up Catholics, and we attended St. Willibrord's regularly.

Welfare regulations allowed my mother to work a bit, so she'd waitress in restaurants. Babysitting was expensive until a family friend who lived a few blocks away agreed to take care of Robert and me. I loved this friend because he was always ready with candy and treats, but it was his tropical fish that really drew me there. The neighbor had several large aquariums and I could watch the exotic fish for hours.

He would sit me on his lap so I could see the fish better. After I got comfortable with him, he asked for a kiss every time he gave me candy. I thought nothing of it. After a while, he stuffed his tongue in my mouth and held me so hard I couldn't get away. Then he wanted more. He would take out my penis and play with it while kissing me.

"If you don't share our secret with anyone, I'll give you a big bowl and a goldfish just for you," he said once. He kept that promise. I loved that fish so much I would take his bowl for walks outside, all proud, not realizing or caring how foolish it looked.

At that age, I had no idea I was being molested. After a year or so, he tried to kiss my penis, and he attempted to get me to touch and kiss his. I refused. I began to dread baths at his house because they gave him a chance to touch me, always trying to make it a game. I told no one.

My father stayed away, though my mother heard he had had four other children with a woman he started seeing when she was 17.

I learned to make money at a young age. Like other Verdun boys, I'd shovel snow off stoops in the winter, but I'd still hassle my mother for candy money. She'd always tell me to go return empty bottles for the refunds. One day at the local Steinberg's grocery store when I was 11, I was doing just that when I saw an older boy politely asking customers if he could help them carry their groceries. I couldn't understand why he was being so nice until I noticed one person give him a dollar as he carried three bags of groceries to a wagon. They walked away together. I raced home and hounded my mother for a wagon. She was fed up with my demands on our small budget and kept refusing until I told her I would never bug her for money again. I got my wagon.

Every Thursday and Friday evening after school I was at the supermarket, hauling groceries and making between $15 and $25 a day. I was rich for a boy in the mid-70s. On Saturdays, I'd spend half the day with my wagon and the other half wasting my fortune on candy and toys. My mother remembers me constantly buying little gifts for her. In wintertime, I'd switch to a sled for my delivery business and the heavy snows brought even more clients.

On Sundays, I'd go to church and help Father Cameron as an altar boy, making $5 sometimes when I'd perform at a funeral.

Around the same time, my mother met a guy named Ronnie while waitressing. After a year of dating, they got married. Ronnie was the opposite of my father. He was calm, steady, and had a good job at a bottling plant. My mother kept working but got off welfare, even sending the government a letter of thanks for their help over the years. She got no reply.

I was a good student and athlete. When I played for various football and hockey teams, I could always count on my stepfather and my mother being in the stands, cheering me on. I was getting spoiled, thinking I had it so much better than friends with deadbeat fathers.

My experience with alcohol began in church. I would arrive early for mass at St. Willibrord's and shrug on my altar-boy gown. One time, I noticed the little carafe used by Father Cameron to recite mass. I looked around, saw no one looking, and took a drink. I thought I'd puke. That progressed to hounding people at my mother's parties to let me taste their drinks, getting laughs from people who would see my face sour after a sip. I'd also sneak tastes from forgotten glasses of vodka, rum, Bloody Caesars, whatever I could find.

At 14, I began going to local Saturday dances set up for teens where the cool thing was to go behind the hall to smoke hash or drink beer. Since I couldn't afford any of that, I would take an empty milk carton and fill it from different types of hard liquor in the house while my mother was at work, always replacing my theft with water. I called the resulting concoction jungle juice. I felt cool drinking it and then puking my innards out while the other teens were just taking in beer. I wanted attention.

At the dance hall, I met my first love, Guylaine. We did everything together, including karate lessons. But something happened to me in the last year of high school: I was thrown off the hockey team for fighting. My marks had always been good but they slipped as I stopped caring. I dropped out before Christmas in my final year. The arguments started with my mother.

"You are not going to sit around the house doing nothing," my mother said. "Either work or go back to school."

"Aww, Mom."

"Better get a job now while you are young because without your high-school diploma, no one will hire you in the future."

"Stop telling me what to do."

"If you live here," she said angrily, "you will do what I say."

I looked at her defiantly.

"Yeah, maybe for now. But when I turn 18 . . ."

"You are not going to turn out like your father!"

At 18 I moved out, carrying my hockey bag full of clothes. I hooked up with another guy and we rented a bachelor apartment together. Both of us were on welfare and got $166 each a month, the amount given youths under 30 with no dependants. But we still had a hard time making ends meet.

I was spending lots of time in local pool halls, where the dealers would set up headquarters during the winter months. Since I was always there, people assumed I was selling. I wasn't, but it gave me an idea. I went to the guy I bought from when I had a bit of money and got a quarter pound of hash for $800. I didn't have the money, of course, so he fronted it to me, something called "on the arm" in Quebec.

A quarter pound gave me 112 grams, which I sold for $15 each. That made me more than $800 profit on the package. After selling it in two weeks, I went back to the dealer, gave him his money, and got more on credit. To lessen my chance for arrest while loitering inside the pool halls, I'd keep just a few grams wrapped in aluminum foil in my pockets. The rest of my nightly needs were hidden outside behind a loose brick in the elderly buildings or under a wooden step of a nearby house. I made it a rule to only sell to people I knew.

When summer came, I told my clients I'd be out on the boardwalk. It was a line of greenspace on top of a long hill that separated the crowded tenements of Verdun from the St. Lawrence River. Though the boardwalk was mostly known as a place to skateboard, bicycle, drink an illicit beer, or just enjoy the sun, a six-block area was the hangout of about 40 pot and hash dealers. It was safer than the pool halls because you could see the cops before they could make it up the hill.

Dealers used every trick they could to hide their stash from shakedowns. Some stuffed their goods in potato-chip bags scattered around. Others, in the bushes. I started by putting my hash inside the steel handlebars of my bicycle, an old trick shown to me by other dealers. A twist of the rubber grips and it was hidden beyond the imagination of any cop. But they soon got wind.

So I switched to beer-bottle caps. A gram of hash covered in foil or plastic wrap went inside a cap before I would twist it shut like a gnocchi noodle.

When I walked up to the boardwalk every afternoon—drug dealers and users are mostly late-risers—I'd toss the caps throughout the territory I staked out near the sand horseshoe ring. But I also threw down some rubbish so the hash-filled caps wouldn't look out of place. Anyway, the area was usually strewn with lots of bottles and caps because police generally tolerated a little outside drinking to diffuse tensions in the working-class area.

There was one cop named Agnessi who made it his business to give us a hard time.

Whenever he approached, one dealer would pass a warning down the line. I'd grab the hash in my pockets and stuff it in my mouth until he left. Agnessi did what he could, but he usually ended up just telling the guys to pour out their beers or giving tickets for drinking in public. As he walked by one time, he kept stepping on my bottle caps. He knew the drugs were somewhere, but had no idea how close. I smirked, as did other guys near me.

"You think this is all a joke," he told us. "You will get into serious trouble someday."

When he left, I roared so hard tears came out.

Another day, a guy next to me grunted a message. A dealer had noticed someone watching us from the top of a high-rise with binoculars. It was Agnessi. We waved, which pissed him off, and he came down. He did that stunt other times but could never get close enough to nab us.

My profits were making it easy to pay the rent and eat well. Only 19, I was still seeing Guylaine, who had finished school and was working at a bank, but she had no idea what I was doing. She also didn't know I was relaxing many nights at strip clubs. One time, I was at the Filles d'Eve strip club on Montreal's main street, Ste. Catherine, when a man walked in and greeted everyone by name, waving fingers fat with diamond rings. He was led to a reserved table.

The girls flocked to the table and he enjoyed their company, looking hungrily at their bodies or handing them $20 instead of the usual $5 for stripping at his table. I want that, I kept thinking on my way home.

Back at the club the next day, the man waved me over. His name was Pierre Beauchamp, better known as Ti-Bum, Quebec slang for Little Bum. He was known as a big cocaine dealer.

"What are you drinking?" were his first words. He gestured for a waitress. "Give him a Grand Marnier with ice, a double," he spoke with a confidence that came from money.

He didn't introduce himself or ask who I was. (I later found out he knew of my hash sales.) When the first round came, I went for my pocket. He stopped me.

"Don't worry about that," he said with a laugh. "There's no problem. Money's meant to be spent."

A waitress moved her barely concealed breasts toward our table.

"Watch her face," Ti-Bum said, having fun.

"For what?"

He just waved his arm in the air.

"Hey, Honey, bring me two bottles of champagne."

Her face lit up from the expected fat tip on such an expensive order.

"Why two bottles?" I had to ask.

"One for me and one for you," he said, and then yelled after the waitress. "Bring four glasses with that!"

"Why four glasses?" I must have sounded like an idiot with my questions.

"You'll see," he said, laughing mockingly.

Before the champagne arrived, Ti-Bum got up abruptly and headed to the men's room. "Follow me."

In the washroom, Ti-Bum went into a stall and took out a pack of cigarettes and a little bag of white powder. He spread three lines on the cigarette package and then reached into his pocket and took out the biggest roll of cash I'd ever seen. My eyes bugged out more about the cash than the cocaine.

He took a $100 bill, rolled it up, and used it to snort a line.

"Ahh," he said and looked at me. "Do one."

The feeling was instant. I felt a little blizzard going through my nose and down my throat. It was my first hit of cocaine.

"Who's the third line for?" I asked, puzzled.

"For the house," he said, brushing it down the toilet bowl.

If that was meant to impress me, it worked. He then handed me the little bag of cocaine.

"What's this for?"

"For the girls," Ti-Bum said.

Those words were music to my ears and explained the two extra champagne glasses. Back at the table, we sat down while one stripper called over another.

"Dance for my friend," Ti-Bum told one.

I was delirious with happiness but tried to keep a straight face to show I was not impressed. The rest of the night went by so fast with these beautiful creatures treating us like gods. When I heard someone announce last call, I looked at Ti-Bum, feeling like a kid who had lost his puppy. He laughed.

"Don't worry, the night's not over yet. Finish your drink and I will meet you outside."

My eyes lit up when I saw Ti-Bum waiting in a Cadillac with the two dancers in the back seat. We ended up in a hotel room where one of the girls stripped and sat down in the jacuzzi while the other shed her clothes before spreading out on the waterbed.

I sat at a table and fixed lines of cocaine for all of us. The key was the cocaine. The more I gave the girls, the more sex Ti-Bum and I got. When I got home a few hours later, I kept thinking that was the life I wanted. And I knew I wouldn't get it from selling pot and hash.

As soon as I awoke the next afternoon, I called Ti-Bum.

"I gotta see you," I said.

"I was expecting you to call," he said cheerfully. "Come see me in a couple of days."

CHAPTER 3

A few days later, I rang Ti-Bum's doorbell. He lived just a few kilometers from my place in Verdun. When he opened the door, I stepped in but stopped abruptly. I'd never been in such a beautiful home. I leaned down and removed my sneakers, the first time I'd done that in anybody's home.

"Follow me," he said. "Don't worry about the floors. My old lady will clean it up."

"Your what?" I was in shock. Hadn't he just been screwing a stripper alongside me a few days earlier? "Are you serious?"

"No shit," he answered with a laugh.

We walked to the living room.

"Here," he said, tossing me a bag of white powder. "Now listen. I'm only going to tell you once. Don't fuck up."

His gaze was serious, almost menacing. "Make sure you pay me and don't bother showing up until you do."

"I won't," I assured him. I wanted to show him I was also serious. "You have my word."

"Your word means nothing to me right now."

I left a bit scared but also exhilarated. My customers in the pool halls and boardwalk began to get a choice—hash or coke. I also got others to sell for me. I kept my word to Ti-Bum, never missing a payment, so he started to respect me. With my new profits, I moved into a much bigger apartment. I also began hanging out full-time at strip clubs, where I noticed there was big money to be made among the dancers. They often paid back their gratitude for good coke with a screw. I became heavily into the bar scene, hanging out with strippers at P.J.'s, a disco in downtown Montreal that featured hilarious transvestite shows.

I'd be out all night sniffing coke before staggering to my mother's place to sleep it off at 5:30 a.m. Even though I didn't live there anymore, she'd let me stay for a few hours while she put my grimy clothes through the wash. When she'd leave for work, she'd wake me because she saw I was changing and she didn't feel she could trust me alone in her home.

Some of the strippers suggested I try dancing myself. I figured I would have a ball and it was a good way to get inside the clubs to supply coke. I loved dancing in discos but I was fearful of making a fool of myself in front of so many women. A stripper friend suggested I do like most go-go boys.

"Start in gay bars," she said. "They don't care how you dance. They just want to see you naked. It is a good place to practice and perfect your dancing."

Beyond my belief, I took her advice. One night, I sniffed a few lines of blow for courage and walked into the Tropical Bar on Ste. Catherine Street.

I was carrying a white overcoat like singer George Michael used to wear, with the sleeves rolled up to the elbows. With that went white pants, white cowboy boots, and a tiny thong. The club was almost pitch black, but I was able to see men kissing and holding hands while watching the act on stage.

"Are you hiring?" I asked the manager, my face red.

"Turn around," he ordered, wanting to see my ass. I guess he liked it.

"OK, go backstage and get undressed. We'll see what you can do."

I found a dressing room and changed while the guy on stage finished off.

I had three songs to do. For the first, I went out and danced around, but kept everything on. They only got a hint of my muscled chest and stomach through the coat. I tried to tease. For the second song, I took off the overcoat and unbuckled my pants before walking off the stage.

For the third song, you have to strip completely. I wanted to be naked as little as possible so I found a song on the jukebox that was just 45 seconds long. Backstage, I shed everything except my thong and did what was expected. I masturbated. Considering the circumstances, I was almost surprised to get an erection. I guess when you're a teenager, a stiff dick is never far away.

I walked onstage and the applause began as I kept my back to the room as much as possible. While that hid my privates, it also titillated the crowd. I also didn't stand in one spot for long. Movement was a good thing.

I faced the crowd, the thong came off, and my face was red again though nobody could see it because of the dim lights or because that wasn't the body part they were there to watch. I guess the customers liked their boys timid because they egged me on. Finally, the song ended. I grabbed my thong and ran backstage.

The manager met me with a smile. "You're hired. You can start right away."

He introduced me to a dozen other dancers, of which only two or three were gay. That made me feel less stupid.

"Hey buddy, you want some of this?"

I turned around to see one of the guys standing there with a mirror lined with coke. "It will take your mind off dancing for men."

I snorted some.

"Your first time dancing?"

"Yes," I replied.

"Don't worry. You'll make good money here. Just go parade around the club and it won't be long before you get your first table dance."

So out I went in my thong and cowboy boots, taking drink orders from customers. I felt confident until I was asked for a $5 dance by a customer. I made my way backstage and sat down, staring at the floor.

"What's wrong?" asked the guy who had offered me the coke.

"Somebody just asked me to dance for him."

"So?"

"I don't feel right dancing in front of a man, a gay man to boot."

"You'll be all right after the first dance."

"I don't think so."

"Why not?"

I stood up and glumly showed him my penis, which had been scared into hibernation. "This is why."

He roared with laughter.

"Here," he said while still chuckling. "Take this. It should help you."

A *Playboy* magazine was thrust into my hand.

"Go give it a shake. You'll be fine."

I found a corner and started flipping through the pages. I thought I was OK as soon as I was partially erect. I made my way to the customer's table but had to turn around because my little turtle had returned to its shell.

"What's wrong now?" said the same dancer as I skulked backstage. I showed him the evidence.

"OK." He handed me an elastic. "Try this."

"What do I do with that?"

"Get your dick back up and then wrap the elastic two times around your testicles and the base of your dick."

"Are you serious?" my voice squeaked out.

"Ask anybody here. They'll tell you. Once you are semi-erect, wrap the elastic around like I told you and it will cut off the blood circulation. That way, you can keep your length. It is a little uncomfortable but it works."

He laughed. "You now know the go-go boys' secret."

I went back to my corner with the *Playboy* and did exactly what he said before heading to the customer's table. This time, I made it there intact.

I got through the dance, but couldn't make myself look at the client's face or even talk to him. I felt sick to my stomach. I spent the rest of the night sitting backstage earning my minimum wage for doing stage dances.

At home that night, a girl I was screwing behind my girlfriend's back was waiting for me. I told her I couldn't go through with this.

"Dance for me," she said.

"What?"

"You heard me. This song should suit you." It was "Mama" by Genesis.

I started to gyrate and I could tell she was getting hot.

"You are doing fine," she said as her eyes stared with obvious intent.

"Ya, but you are a woman."

I went back to dancing in gay clubs for a few months. Then the time came to try out for women at a place called New York-New York. I was in good shape, visiting the tanning salons often, and my baby face and smile seemed to excite the customers. My coke sales were great, too.

I also met a 17-year-old girl named Brigitte who was dancing underage. I was still 19 at the time, and we hit it off. That relationship quickly put an end to my five-year romance with my teenage love. Guylaine's parents caught Brigitte and me holding hands one night, and obviously told their daughter. The next day, I went to Guylaine's home to beg forgiveness, but she told me to get out. We were already heading separate ways.

One night, I was dancing for a table when I spotted Brigitte heading to a nearby chair. She had heard from a female friend there was a hot stripper named Peter at the New York. She realized the friend was talking about me, making her curious to see my act. But her being there made me uncomfortable. I unconsciously danced farther away from the woman at my table. When I finished, I went to see Brigitte, who had ordered me a Grand Marnier and then handed me a rose.

"How's it going?" she asked with a mischievous smile.

"Great," I said, wearing only my thong.

"I heard that you were becoming popular here."

"Yeah, I already have a hundred and twenty-five dollars and it is not even midnight yet."

She acted coquettish as she pulled out a $10 bill.

"Now you made a hundred and thirty-five. Go get your little box and dance the next slow song for me."

"Are you serious?"

"Yes. I see you naked every night but here I can't touch you."

When the song was over, she told me to hurry home when my shift finished.

After that, we almost always worked together in clubs that featured both male and female strippers, which let us keep an eye on each other. Brigitte found out I had been seeing her on the side while still dating my first girlfriend, so watching me was necessary. Since most of these male/female clubs were outside Montreal, I put friends in charge of my drug business and grabbed a few ounces to sell as we hit the road for two weeks at a time.

Things went fine, though it was difficult to tolerate male customers ogling Brigitte. I knew what they were thinking. The worst was when Brigitte and I would have to dance at the same table for a couple. We'd give each other daggered looks that said the other was dancing too close to a client. When the tension became too much, we decided to keep working at the same clubs but to find ones where the male and female shows were on different floors. The adulation I was getting from dancing, and the power of the coke, was going to my head.

"One day," I kept telling Brigitte, "I'm going to go to the top." I kept envisaging a huge drug empire. She was impressed at first, but after hearing me say it hundreds of times, she responded with, "Yeah, yeah. I know."

On the road, I'd cheat on Brigitte almost every night with customers in the bathroom, a car, or even outside the club. We worked for more than a year at a club called the Mints, in Niagara

Falls, where my cheating got worse after Brigitte told me she was pregnant. I would stagger home drunk, coked up, and smelling of perfume. One morning, I returned to our room and she was gone. I was so high on coke it didn't register. It just made screwing around much easier.

My stripping routine was automatic so the coke didn't hurt. It helped dull the pain of losing Brigitte and my unborn child. In Niagara Falls, I was sniffing about five times more a day than I used to, and I was no longer using my own supply from Montreal. I started buying pure coke from Sam, an Ontario member of the Outlaws biker gang, racking up a $400 debt. I didn't bother paying it back promptly since it was such a small amount.

Every few weeks I'd call Brigitte in Montreal to see how she was doing. When she told me she would give birth soon I felt guilty, knowing I had screwed up my life with the screwing around, and would not be there for my child. That sent me into an alcohol haze for two days. Constant snorting kept me from passing out from the booze. No one tried to stop me. The only one who came to see me was Sam. He pulled out a gun and let me know he was collecting from everyone. I ignored him, kept sniffing his coke and drinking beer with Jack Daniels chasers. When I finally hit bottom, I laid down in my room and stared at the ceiling, thinking about Brigitte, my screwed-up life, cocaine, and women in general. Then paranoia took over. Why did Sam show me a gun if he didn't plan to use it?

Without telling anyone, I grabbed my things and headed straight to the bus terminal to catch the first ride back to Montreal.

The first call I made upon arriving in Montreal was to Brigitte, begging her to see me. She finally met me at her mother's home. She was in her last month of pregnancy and very big. I promised numerous times not to cheat anymore. We ended up making love as well as we could considering her condition. That caused the contractions to start, and we raced off to the hospital. It was February 1986, and my son was born.

I was 21 years old. Brigitte was 19. No parents were ever less prepared. We were both still using cocaine. Although I was happy, I had no idea what to do. I would hold my son like a football and feel scared. But I was the perfect gentleman for a few months, doing all the errands that come with parenthood except changing diapers because that turned my stomach. I had quit dancing and stopped selling drugs.

I tried to keep an honest job, the first time since my teen years, signing up with an agency that sent people door-to-door selling memberships for health clubs and discount packages at beauty salons. It meant getting up at 6:30 a.m. I gave it up after a few months and borrowed money to buy some drugs and resume selling.

A few months after my son was born, Brigitte said she wanted to return to dancing. We left the baby for a few weeks with my brother Robert and his wife Suzanne while we headed out to small towns. We were making good money and Brigitte was happy I was no longer disappearing every so often.

During a stop in Granby, I got a shock when a woman named Nathalie, whom I'd partied with in Niagara Falls, arrived to dance at the Studio Sex. I couldn't take my eyes off her, and she was staring right back. Brigitte was eyeing both of us.

"Who's that?" she asked.

"It is just someone I worked with in Niagara Falls," I answered, hoping that would satisfy her.

"I'm a woman and I know that look," she said. "I think it is a little more than that."

I kept lying.

One night, Brigitte and I went to an afterhours club following our shifts. They served us Grand Marnier in coffee cups as we sniffed cocaine until dawn.

"We're out of coke," I told Brigitte, standing up. "Wait here. I'm going back to the room to get more."

As I was putting the hotel key in the lock, I heard a door open down the hallway. When I looked, I saw Nathalie standing there in a tiny negligee.

"You got any coke?" she asked. "Can you sell me a bit so I can party a bit by myself?"

I got some blow and walked into her room. I knew it was dangerous considering I was half drunk and very high, but I couldn't stop myself.

"How much you want?"

She came close and put a $100 bill on the nightstand. Before I could move, she dropped to her knees and had my dick in her mouth. I lost track of time.

I was screwing her when Brigitte kicked the door open and went straight for Nathalie. She grabbed her by the hair, punching and slapping her around with a fury that gave her blows more power than you'd expect from such a small person. She looked so scary I didn't even try to step in.

Brigitte punched her so hard that Nathalie fell backwards over the bed and hit the floor while trying to deflect the blows. Brigitte went after her.

"Slut," she yelled. "Bitch."

A slew of obscenities were also being thrown my way.

"You prick!"

Another slap to Nathalie.

"Fucker."

Slap.

"Son of a bitch."

Smack.

"Asshole."

When her rage subsided, Brigitte left and I followed her back to our room. When I woke up the next morning, she was gone.

CHAPTER 4

I returned to Montreal a few days later, but I couldn't bring myself to call Brigitte. That episode ended my dancing career and I went back full-time to drugs, both taking and selling.

Brigitte called me a few months later, but not to reconcile. She wanted me to go see our son, the first of many calls to make sure I was a presence, however intermittent, in his life. I'd see my son at my mother's place because she took him almost every second weekend to give Brigitte a break.

I concentrated on business, trying to drum up more by heading to Montreal's most notorious corner—Ste. Catherine Street and St. Laurent Boulevard. For decades, it has been known as hooker headquarters, teeming with overused women, their pimps, middle-aged clients, and teenage boys. Police also made their presence known without making a dent in the corner's historical vocation. Behind the sidewalk action were the sex shops, strip clubs, 25-cent peep shows and some of Montreal's best hot-dog and french-fry places. I had gotten to know many strippers and their friends, so it was a good spot to provide them with blow.

Some of the hookers would also get coke from me before their pimps could take their cash. They'd take a break for a few hours, get high, come back to the corner for a slap across the face from their man before going back to work.

One night, I was doing my walk up and down the street when a Harley roared up. On it was the biggest man I've ever seen. He was about six-foot-four and must have weighed 500 pounds.

"That's Sasquatch," a pimp told me.

Sasquatch seemed to be keeping an eye on the action on the street. We'd kept crossing paths for the next two weeks until we stood, staring at traffic, next to each other by the Frites Doré, a fry shop on St. Laurent.

"What exactly are you up to?" he asked.

He looked scary and I knew he was somebody.

"Business."

"Well, you just better keep your business among your friends."

I agreed. Anyway, I wasn't going to take a chance selling to strangers who might be cops.

"You want to work my corner, you are going to have to make a donation."

That surprised me. Montreal's drug business at the time was open, no boundaries. You could buy your drugs from anybody and you could sell them anywhere you wanted except for some clubs run by organized crime. My expression turned serious.

"Look," I said with resolve, "if you don't like it, I'll just tell my customers to meet me on another street."

"Relax," he said, laughing, his whole body moving. "Just throw me a dollar once in a while."

"That's it?"

"Yeah, you seem all right."

An hour later, we crossed paths and I flipped him a dollar coin. He caught it and laughed. Every two hours, I'd flip him another. I think I flipped him maybe $100 in the months I did the corner until I got bored.

I'd motivate myself by taking blow and renting *Scarface*. I saw the movie so many times I knew the script by heart. The story of a poor Cuban crook played by Al Pacino who grabs power and riches in Miami by pushing cocaine really struck home with me. I ignored how it all went wrong later in the film.

Brigitte would call once in a while for some coke, and we'd use that as an excuse to hit the sheets together. We did try to reconcile, but it never worked.

After leaving the street, I concentrated on selling coke from my apartment and making the rounds of the strip clubs. But I didn't want to stay away from home too long and miss business, so I didn't linger. I would leave ten packets of cocaine with a stripper at each club. She'd distribute the powder and collect the money. I'd go back the next day, pick up my cash, and restock the girls. Each quarter-gram package would sell for $25, and I'd give each girl $5 of that.

While taking taxis from club to club, I learned that many cabbies used coke, either because they were hooked or to help them stay awake during long shifts behind the wheel. One cabbie named Denis started selling my product to other drivers to make extra money. I got him a pager so he could take over the deliveries to the strippers because I no longer wanted to run around with drugs in my pockets. I introduced him to each of my girls, who would page him when they needed more with a special code identifying their club.

Denis was using so much blow that he would get mixed up and deliver my coke to the wrong girl, and I'd have to go down and get what remained back or work out a payment plan if they had snorted their windfall away. Those mistakes didn't bother me much because it meant the girls would feel obligated to provide some sex or just suck up to me and make me feel big.

Denis would call me up almost every morning when the clubs were closing to ask if he could bring some of the girls to my place to party. I was screwing so many girls that I began using cocaine to stay erect longer. And the more coke I gave out, the more open-minded the girls became.

Business kept growing, and people, especially strippers, were streaming through my place at all hours to buy and do coke. I was worried the cops would notice, so I asked everyone to be discreet. The heavy volume also meant I was getting no sleep. So a second cabbie was hired for those clients, and the number of visitors to my place dropped to a manageable number.

During this time, four-day binges without sleep were common. During one of these, my home was full of friends and customers when I pulled out a gun. A customer had traded it to me a while back for $200 to $300 worth of coke.

"What you doing, man?" one drunk guy asked, his stoned voice not able to mask a bit of anxiety. No one tried to do anything because I had become very aggressive when high. The rage masked growing feelings of worthlessness that came with the lows of my drug habit, and the underlying guilt of abandoning Brigitte and my son, who was now two years old. Though I felt powerful and important from all the cash I was making on the street, I was not whole.

That night, I had a large bag of coke on the table before me as well as a beer and a bottle of Jack Daniels. But the pistol had my attention.

"I want to see Brigitte now!" I stuttered. I don't know why I asked for her.

I then spun the gun barrel, put it up to my head, and pulled the trigger.

The place went silent. Everyone heard the click as the firing pin hit empty air in the chamber.

"Put the gun down," a friend said. "You're drunk and fucked up."

"That's right," I said with a near hysterical laugh. "I won't feel a thing."

He didn't find that funny, and he started to come toward me. I pointed the barrel at his face.

"You asshole," he said and shrank back.

I went back to snorting and drinking, always with the gun in my hand. Those at the party kept throwing nervous glances at me, but that was all. I didn't care: I hardly knew them and they were just there to get high off my drugs. An hour later, the doorbell rang. Brigitte walked in and sat down across the table from me. Two friends had gone to pick her up.

"What's wrong?" she said, her blue eyes looking concerned.

"Nothing. I guess I'm a little fucked up right now."

"What's the gun for?"

"Nothing in particular."

"Why don't you put it away if you don't need it?"

People were looking at her because her tone would usually have set me off like a rocket. She continued, though.

"You don't need the gun while I'm here so just put it away or give it to me before you do something you will regret."

"I won't hurt anybody."

When a friend told her I had put the revolver to my head and pulled the trigger, Brigitte leaned across the table and put out her hand.

"Give me the gun."

I let it go. She took it, opened the barrel, and let the two bullets inside fall to the floor.

"Are you losing your fucking mind?" she yelled, realizing I'd had a one in three chance of dying.

"Who gives a fuck what I do?" I yelled back.

"I do." Those words felt good to hear but I said nothing.

"Why don't you get these people out of here and get some sleep?"

"Only if you stay," I shot back.

"I can't sleep here," she said. "But I'll stay until you fall asleep."

The next day, my life was back to drugs and alcohol. The more cocaine I sold, the more I could afford to use and give away. I was going through one ounce of coke a day—some for me, some for women I was screwing, and some for those who partied with me.

I kept trying other things to improve business. Early on, while I was still dancing, I had become a silent partner in a take-out pizza place called Le Roi de la Pizza with two guys. It was my only legal business, and the only one to lose money. To cut costs, my mother would make the pizza and spaghetti sauces using traditional Italian recipes. She'd cook up a huge batch at home and I'd drive her over to the eatery. It was an ugly place and thankfully most customers never saw it because they had their food delivered.

One of the partners did the deliveries at first, the second answered the phone and handled the cash, while I was in the kitchen flipping dough. I had a stack of menus made up and gave local kids $20 to distribute them door-to-door. The calls started coming in and we got a delivery boy named Mario Jolicoeur. I knew him because he'd buy coke from me once in a while.

Money from pizza sales grew but it was never enough to make our expenses. Even after we cut down on the quality of the cheese and pepperoni, and put less on the pies, it still didn't work. A month after the place opened, I went up to Mario, who was unhappy about making meager tips from our few customers, and asked him if he'd like to help me move coke. He'd get $5 off each quarter gram I sold for $25 and delivered through him. He agreed and I bought him a beeper.

I called up my cocaine customers and told them if they called the restaurant for a pizza I could deliver their coke at the same time and they'd get the coke a little bit cheaper. My partners didn't mind. One was by now a major cokehead and alcoholic, and the other was spending all his cash, and some of our receipts I realized later, on the horses at Blue Bonnets racetrack.

My coke customers would page Mario with their code so he knew where to go. If clients spent $100 on blow, they'd get a free child-sized pizza—what we called the bambino. I'd just throw a bit more cut into the coke to cover the freebie.

Mario was able to deliver cocaine until 3 a.m. without anybody getting suspicious. He did get pulled over a few times by cops, but all they ever found were barely edible pizzas.

After several months, Mario was stabbed to death in a bar fight after he finished doing his deliveries. Business dropped as I scrambled to find someone to keep serving my drug clients. It took a while for the new guy to learn the codes, and I lost thousands of dollars because my customers kept saying they had paid off their drug debts the very night Mario was killed. I couldn't prove otherwise. The pizza place closed its doors soon afterwards.

But that debacle didn't stop me. After the cabbies were working fine, I met with a friend who did deliveries for a corner store that remained open until 11 p.m. I also knew the store owner, who used my coke sometimes. He didn't object when I had my day customers transferred to his delivery boy. People called for coke, but had to buy something like toilet paper, bread, or milk from the store to cover up the real transaction.

A guy named Ian who had played football with my brother on the local team during high school approached me one day. He was already buying a quarter ounce of hash off me every once in a while.

"I'd like to try and sell some coke," he said in his quiet way.

I fronted him a quarter ounce.

Within two days, he showed up with my money and asked for half an ounce. I gave it to him. Two days later, Ian paid back his debt and bought an ounce, paying for it on the spot. For eight months he continued doubling his order every time until he reached the kilogram stage.

With clients like that, business exploded, and so did my spending. I'd head out to a downtown strip club and pick up a few girls. I passed them coke in a rolled-up bill while paying for $90 bottles of champagne. So I could sniff coke constantly in public, I grew the pinky nail long on my right hand. I would sit at a table and take my bag of coke out of my pocket, depositing it in my lap. Then I'd reach in with my pinky nail, grab about a quarter of a gram, put it up to my nose and sniff. About every 20 minutes, I'd repeat the action. I also got into crack cocaine, doing it for years until I realized it was doing me major harm. Then I just stuck to coke.

The drugs I was using and selling were still coming from Ti-Bum, though he was now selling them to me through an intermediary named J.P. Financing my partying was expensive. But Ian, the former football player, made it easy. He was selling a kilo of my coke every three weeks. And he was paying upfront instead of taking it "on the arm." Since I bought the coke for $32,000 or $33,000 and sold it to him for $37,000 or $38,000 after diluting it with some cut, Ian was worth an extra $10,000 in my pocket at every sale.

Ian didn't party or indulge in his product and he looked down on those who did, always quick with a snotty, "Are ye fried, Petey?" when we met and he saw my condition. He was fascinated by watching people get high, sometimes for hours, alternately intrigued by what they did and disgusted by how much was wasted on their habits. What got him excited was money. To save as much as possible, he didn't hire runners to deliver his coke. I got word the street was laughing at him because he was doing dropoffs on his ten-speed bike. He only had one pair of jeans, and he didn't buy another until the first pair wore out. He saved his money, bought an apartment building, and moved into the top floor. People on the street stopped laughing at him when they noticed the $30,000 Harley-Davidson he was riding. He even spent another $8,000 getting it gold-plated.

On one rare occasion he took a taxi instead of his ten-speed and police pulled him over and caught him with a quarter pound. He got a weekend sentence, finished it, and was caught again. This time he did real time. But his business kept running, and he was responsible at one point for most of my profits.

A few months after his last prison sentence, he was in his third-floor apartment when the police showed up outside for a disturbance. Ian panicked and started swallowing the cocaine he had at his place to avoid another arrest. But it fucked him up, and he was rushed to hospital that night. He survived but suffered serious mental and physical damage. Ian's crew of pushers scattered, and my profits dropped drastically.

I had no close friends, though I attracted lots of hangers-on who stroked my ego in exchange for the coke I'd throw around like confetti and a chance to bed the girls who hovered around. I'd rent a limousine and driver for $175 an hour, and we'd all pile in. Often, the girls would pop their heads out the sunroof and flash their tits along packed Ste. Catherine Street. Sometimes, I ordered the driver to head to my Verdun haunts along Wellington Street, about ten minutes away. He'd stop in front of the pool hall where I used to sell hash and now it was my turn to stick my head out and bask as people pointed and waved. That was my kick, making them drool. Then we'd just drive around, sniffing coke and laughing. The limo was also good for some moving sex. If the ride lasted longer than expected, I'd use the car phone to call the driver—who was both a friend and customer—to tell him to lower the tinted window between us and just toss him enough coke to cover the difference. I also used the same limo company to take my mother and her husband for rides on Mother's Day.

Though I was only 28, I had dark bags under my eyes, and my muscles had disappeared along with 40 pounds. My haunts remained strip joints, but many of the beautiful dancers started to shun me. I settled for the bar sluts who had no problem having sex with anyone who had coke. Anyway, the sex was no longer interesting. I was happy to finish so I could get back to snorting.

For three years I had been living with Sylvie, a simple country girl I'd met at the Venus in Ville LaSalle. As soon as we got serious, I ordered her to stop dancing. We, and her young daughter, lived off the income from the drugs. We moved in together, though that didn't stop me from screwing around.

I was moving about a quarter pound of coke every three days. I still used the corner stores and cabbies, but the place I shared with Sylvie on Evelyn Street had become a major attraction for my neighbors. Between 50 and 100 people would visit every day for drugs, and the only reason no one in the area complained to the cops was because most were buying from me.

We'd keep the child in the living room while I'd do the sales in the kitchen, but the girl ended up getting to know many of the regulars and greeting them like friends. My binges got worse, and Sylvie would sometimes have to weigh out my product to clients as

I locked myself in a bedroom with a bag of coke, just sitting in the dark. I was doing so much that I was extremely paranoid, as well as embarrassed to be seen so screwed up. To spare me that shame, Sylvie would tell people I was asleep.

During this period, my mind would often flash back to the abuse I suffered at the hands of my neighbor with the aquariums. Many times while high, I would try to find him, to exact revenge. I went back to his home once, but he'd moved. Then I'd get word he was sighted at different places, and I would detour by them often, hoping to cause some harm. I never found him.

The number of visitors at my place looking for blow was again getting too heavy. So I rented an apartment for $350 a month on Gordon Street and put a guy named Daniel in it to sell for me 24 hours a day. Then he needed a roommate to handle the night calls so he could sleep.

My partying led me to hang out in many afterhours clubs because I didn't want to go home at 3 a.m. when the bars closed in Montreal. At one place, I was drinking straight cognac out of a coffee cup with a few women when the police barged in. I immediately tossed a couple of grams of hash I was carrying on the floor. But an officer saw me doing it and I was arrested for possession. That came with a $240 fine. Until then, I'd accumulated few arrests in my life. Breaking into a house with two acquaintances started it all in 1984. The judge ordered me to serve 20 weekends at Bordeaux jail. The old place was so crowded I never did an entire weekend. I'd check in, wait around for a few hours, and then be let out. In 1989, I was arrested for armed assault. But all the drugs I was taking at the time made it impossible for me to remember what for. That arrest came with a $400 fine and a year on probation.

My first afterhours arrest was in 1991. The second followed a year later at the same place. Some strippers from the club across the street and I were having fun when the cops broke in again. My brother stood up to complain and when the cops grabbed him, I went to his defense. High and drunk as usual, I ended up with my face against the floor, being cuffed. That obstructing-justice arrest led to a suspended sentence.

One night at my drug den on Gordon Street, I was alone so I snorted my way through about seven grams of coke. Most people could get three or four lines out of a quarter-gram package worth $25. I made one fat line out of each package. It didn't take long before $700 worth of blow disappeared.

I was alone in the morning as my head came off the buzz, and depression took over as I sat in the living room, thoughts centered around how much I, at the age of 28, hated my life. I was just sick of how things were going. I kept trying to get rich; my goals were a great car, big house, and even bigger bank account. But my nose was robbing my pockets the minute I put a roll of cash in them.

I went to the kitchen and grabbed a steak knife. Back in the living room, I sat on the floor. A quick swipe and I cut my left wrist from side to side. The escaping blood was surprisingly reassuring. A few sleeping pills went down my throat and I lay back on the floor, waiting. I was already weak from the coke and lack of sleep so it didn't take long for me to go into some sort of trance. How much time went by I don't know, but a friend found me there. She ripped up an old T-shirt and wrapped it around my wrist, stopping the blood.

I needed a change, so I scraped up some money for a trip to Acapulco with Sylvie. My brother ended up paying for the rest. While I was getting lost in cocaine, his business was flourishing. He had fancy cars and even bought a sex boutique at one time. He and his wife came along to Mexico, as did a guy in the Irish mob who sometimes sold me coke during dry spells. We lazed around and did some deep-sea fishing. I felt far from my problems back in Montreal, especially when I landed a 145-pound sailfish after a two-hour fight. I stayed away from coke, and vowed to keep far from it upon returning to Montreal. That lasted a few days.

Sylvie sometimes told me to slow down. My swift explosions made that rare.

"What are you fucking talking about?" I would yell. "I know what I'm fucking doing."

I was either verbally abusive while high on coke or a raging mess when coming down the next day. One afternoon, Sylvie's daughter was at school when something set me off while weighing my coke. I threw a chair off our second-storey balcony at our new apartment on Evelyn Street. Then the living-room table, some lamps. I kept going.

Sylvie was in tears, imploring me to stop. Without thinking, I gave her a quick slap to the face. The tears intensified.

We ended up on the street among our smashed belongings as a police car rolled up. A male and female cop emerged.

The female cop looked at the debris.

"What are you doing?" she asked me.

"None of your fucking business," I said with anger. I then walked a few feet away.

The officers looked at Sylvie, noticing the red mark on her cheek.

"Why is your face red?" one asked.

Sylvie said nothing.

"Did he hit you?"

"No, I've been crying," she finally spoke in her tiny voice.

The police officers looked at each other, not believing her but unable to do anything about it.

"Get the furniture off the street," one ordered.

Sylvie and I went inside. I apologized, wracked with guilt.

Not long after, she left me. My cocaine haze didn't let that register for a few weeks. Then she took me back, telling me to join her in the quiet suburb of Châteauguay, away from Verdun. Other than a client or two, none of my party friends came to visit. Since we were living off Sylvie's welfare check, a meal for us and her daughter was often a few hot dogs and a box of macaroni and cheese.

A decade had passed since I'd started selling Ti-Bum's cocaine, six years since my son was born. Despite all the work I'd put into my business, it was all gone. Since I couldn't afford cocaine for my habit, I quickly went into withdrawal. No cold sweats, but it wasn't pleasant. I was constantly irritated and cranky, but my anger tapered off. When Christmas of 1993 came around, I had no money to buy presents for Sylvie's child or my family. My mother bought stuff for under the tree and put my name on the wrapping.

CHAPTER 5

In the beginning of 1994, I walked into Ti-Bum's boot boutique and saw him with a guy I'd noticed before on the streets.

"This is Renaud," Ti-Bum told me by way of introduction. "He's the acting president of the Rock Machine."

My brother had mentioned something about that group in the past but I had not paid any attention. I took a good look at the guy.

Renaud was dressed in jeans with a denim shirt and black leather vest. He wore sunglasses. He spoke: "It's a new organization, but we are already established all over Montreal and Quebec City."

He didn't say what the organization did, but just him being there with Ti-Bum made it clear drugs were involved. I wasn't keeping up on happenings on the streets of Montreal, preferring to hide my poverty in Châteauguay with Sylvie. When I did get a lift into town, it was usually just to see my mother and my son.

Renaud scrutinized me before turning to Ti-Bum.

"Is this the guy you were talking about?"

"Yes," Ti-Bum said.

Renaud looked at me.

"Take down my pager number," he said, reciting it out loud. I scrambled to scribble it on my cigarette pack. "Call me tomorrow. I have a proposition for you."

"OK," I said.

I left, asking myself questions about what they wanted and about this group called the Rock Machine. The next day, I called Ti-Bum.

"What's going on? Why does this guy want me to call him?"

"Don't worry. I'll be there when you meet. I've known the guy all my life."

That calmed me down a bit. Then Ti-Bum continued, "Peter, I also want to talk to you about your brother."

"What about?"

"Let's just say he's in a bit of trouble."

That sent my brain racing. What had Robert done? Ti-Bum cut my thoughts short.

"Anyway, meet me at the boutique later and we'll sort all this out."

I hung up and called my brother.

"Are you in any trouble?"

"No. Why?"

I told him what Ti-Bum had said and about the coming meeting with this guy from the Rock Machine.

"I didn't do anything wrong," Robert said. "I just owe Ti-Bum a bit of money and that's it."

"What's a bit of money?"

"That is none of your business."

"For now it isn't," I said. "I have a meeting with them in a couple of hours. I'll call you back when I'm done to let you know what's going on."

I got a lift to Ti-Bum's boutique at de l'Eglise and Evelyn streets. Ti-Bum had numerous legitimate businesses on the side, including this shop that was trying to cash in on the popularity of the cowboy image, selling boots, buckles, belts, and other leather goods. Ti-Bum met me at the counter. He briefed me a bit on the Rock Machine, a loose group of independent drug dealers with big plans.

"The Rock Machine is moving in and will be taking over the whole southwest side of Montreal."

"What's that got to do with me? I don't have any business anymore."

"I know. But over the years, I kept telling Renaud who you were and about all the good business you did in the past. We'll talk about it when he gets here. Come. We'll wait in the office."

Renaud walked in, wearing almost the same things as the day before. The sunglasses never left his face despite the darkness of Ti-Bum's backroom office. He sat down beside me after saying hello.

"What have you been doing lately?"

He was the opposite of easygoing, gregarious Ti-Bum. Renaud spoke calmly, and wore only one ring, next to the pinky. It had the head of an eagle in the middle, sporting a red eye. On top was the word Rock and under the eagle was Machine. The whole thing was circled by diamonds. I pointed at the inscription.

"What's the business with all of this?"

"This," he said, tapping it, "this is the future. We are an independent organization."

"If you are independent, why are you called a gang?"

"Being a group gives us more power to expand and keeps us from being forced to work for the Hells."

In Quebec, the Hells Angels were not called Angels for short like in the rest of North America. It was much easier to say Les Hells in French than Angels.

"I know of them," I said.

The local Hells were well known as murderers who had no qualms about killing each other. In the mid-1980s, they had slaughtered five members of their Laval chapter who had spent too much time partying and using coke instead of selling it. The bodies were wrapped in sleeping bags, weighted down with cement blocks or weightlifting discs, and then tossed in the St. Lawrence River.

"I don't want to have anything to do with them," I told Renaud.

"That's why I'm here. I want you to join our organization."

"Why? I don't have a business anymore."

"I know," he replied calmly, almost fatherly. "But I think you have the potential to clean yourself up and make money like you never made before in your life. You know everybody in this town. I'm sure you will be able to clean house and control this area.

"But don't forget," he said with a seriousness that was almost scary. "I'll still be your boss." Then he laughed.

I looked at Ti-Bum. "What do you think?"

He chuckled. "I've been doing business with Renaud for years."

Ti-Bum said he wasn't a member of the Rock Machine, but he and Renaud already traded coke amongst each other depending on who had a good or cheap supply at the time. They even did legitimate business together, and Ti-Bum had just sold Renaud the boot boutique.

Renaud resumed his attack. Obviously Ti-Bum had told him about my drug problems.

"There are better things to do than get high and live in misery," he said.

He was convincing. My life was in a rut, completely boring and mindless. I had cleaned up my drug habit, but that didn't mean I wanted to stop dealing. I didn't want to miss this chance to get off Sylvie's welfare, but I wanted to make sure the Rock Machine wasn't going to be run like the Hells. With their reputation, I didn't trust anything that resembled a biker gang.

"We are not a motorcycle club," Renaud assured me. "The reason we are an independent organization is because we disagree with the Hells mentality, everything they do and how they do it."

With that out of the way, I turned to Ti-Bum.

"What's the deal about the trouble my brother's in?"

Ti-Bum looked at Renaud, and then me.

"He owes me forty thousand dollars."

My arms dropped and my mouth flew open.

For seconds, I tried to figure out how Robert got in so deep. As I pondered, Renaud spoke up.

"He also owes me money."

"How much?" I replied with a sinking feeling.

"About five thousand."

"I don't know what this is all about," I sputtered, "but it is all news to me."

"Peter," Ti-Bum replied, "that is a lot of money and your brother is going to repay me one way or another."

"What do you mean by that?" I snarled, jumping to my feet and pointing at Ti-Bum. "If anything happens to him, I'm coming after you, you son of a bitch."

He backed away and looked at Renaud for help. Renaud stood between us.

"Let's all calm down and we will try to work something out."

I turned to him, glad he was on my side. "Thank you. But if he has anything done to my brother, I'll kill him." I stared at Ti-Bum.

"Go home," Renaud responded. "Nobody's killing anybody."

Ti-Bum's look was defiant as I left.

I went straight to a phone booth near the metro station. My brother's wife answered.

"Where's Robert?"

"He took off to Miami." Suzanne was edgy. "After your last call, he was unsure what might happen."

I was fuming at Robert but tried to stay calm.

"Why didn't he tell me anything?"

"Try and do something," she said. "Please."

"If he dies, he won't die alone."

That comment didn't reassure her. So I tried again.

"I'll call you tomorrow night and let you know what's going on. In the meantime, if Robert calls, tell him to stay where he is until I sort all this out."

I swore as I hung up and headed back to Châteauguay. I'd left the meeting without finding out what I was supposed to do next. Did my blowup at Ti-Bum just ruin my chances with the Rock Machine?

The next day, my doorbell rang. A short, stocky guy was at the door. His receding hairline made it easy to see a tattoo of a straight flush across his forehead like a billboard. A mustache and goatee surrounded a mouth that didn't smile. Wrinkles stretching almost to his ears came off half-closed eyes that had a grim hold on me. He had biker written all over him.

"Renaud sent me."

The words were neutral but his voice was gruff, brusque, and lacking any warmth.

"Come in," I said, really wishing to say, "Go away." We walked to the kitchen and sat at the table.

"Listen," he started, "I'm not here to cause you any problems. But your brother fucked me for about five thousand two weeks ago."

This guy must have been Renaud's go-between with Robert, I thought.

"Where is he?" the guy asked.

"Forget him," I said. "He left the country."

That didn't make him happy. His adrenaline was going and his face turned red.

"So what happens now?" I asked him.

"He can't run forever," was his simple response.

He leaned over and untucked his sweater. My eyes went to the revolver crammed between his belt buckle and belly fat. The last time I'd seen a gun was when I had played Russian roulette with two bullets in the cylinder. I wish I'd still had the piece, I thought. But I'd sold it to buy coke.

"Maybe we can work something out," he finally said.

"What do you mean?"

"Renaud tells me you used to move a lot of coke in the past. And you could do it again and make a lot of money." He leaned over. "Serious money."

I saw where this was going.

"He also told me you had a reputation as a guy who did business straight and never fucked anybody over."

"What are you trying to say?"

"My point is I want you to be my partner. I will bring you up in the organization. You can't do this alone."

He pointed to the gun in his jeans. I could still see the handle.

"The way I see it, we need each other since we are both starting over from scratch."

His next words didn't come as a big surprise.

"I just got out of prison. I did four years. And you, well, you lost everything because of a bad habit."

He again pointed to his gun. "With my experience and knowing the ropes like I do, and with the business you will be able to get us, there is no reason we can't clean house in Verdun."

"Agreed," I said, "but what about my brother?"

"If you join our family," he said, "there is no reason why we should kill one of yours. You have my word on it."

"OK, but what about Ti-Bum? My brother owes him forty thousand."

"I know. But if I am not mistaken, Ti-Bum and Renaud sometimes roll on credit with each other for a lot more than that. You are now going to be one of us and I doubt very much Renaud will let Ti-Bum harm your brother knowing you decided to join his family."

"If he does hurt him, I'll kill him," I said. "I don't care who is friends with who."

The guy nodded, and gave me his phone number. We planned to set up a meeting the next day with Renaud to keep Ti-Bum at bay. I told the guy it wouldn't be easy because Ti-Bum was arrogant and cocky.

"I don't care," he said coldly. "If he fucks with me, I'll kill him myself."

We shook hands and he left.

I had just met Raymond Lareau, out of prison following a lengthy sentence on charges of attempted murder, extortion, and using firearms. His nickname was Mon-Mon, pronounced Mo-Mo.

When he was gone, the first thing I did was roll a huge joint of hash to calm my nerves.

CHAPTER 6

Mon-Mon was at my place the next morning. On our way into the city to meet with Renaud and Ti-Bum, he coached me on what to say. I was to tell Ti-Bum he would never get his money if he had Robert killed. If he was patient, I would make payments after I got back on my feet. Any good businessman would accept that, Mon-Mon reasoned. Ti-Bum would look like a fool if he didn't because he was the one who told the Rock Machine I could be trusted. If he wasn't willing to trust me on this, then how could he tell Renaud to have confidence in me.

At lunch, Ti-Bum glared at me after he realized he had no choice. When Mon-Mon dropped me off later, he shook my hand.

"It was a good day for you, eh?"

"Yup."

"This is only the beginning, *tabarnac*."

It became clear that Mon-Mon used most of his energy to swear. Whereas in English swear words are sexual, they are mostly of a religious nature in French. Using the word *tabarnac* is incredibly crass and refers to the tabernacle in church.

"Can you see what kind of fucking power you can actually possess, *tabarnac*?" he went on. "I'll be back tomorrow morning to explain to you how the family works and tell you of certain rules that have to be respected by everybody in the family. Everybody. No exceptions."

"OK." His last words worried me somewhat.

The next day he picked me up.

"Are you ready for your first day?"

"Sure, but why are you making this sound like a job?"

"Because it is," he said. "We will leave every morning and come back after the day is done for supper. Working this way five days a week should get the job done. Nobody works the weekend in the family. That's reserved for the wives and the kids."

He laughed. "We're going to have enough aggravation during the week. The last think we need is to have the fucking wives on our case on top of that."

I laughed.

"Hey, what are the rules you said that everybody had to follow?" I asked.

"I will let you know all of them as we go along. But I will tell you off the bat what is fucking forbidden and not tolerated when you are starting out.

"First of all, *tabarnac*, you take no drugs at all. The only exception is pot or hash. And even those, fuck, you don't take during our working day. Maybe you can on a rare day when we are in the city and have fucking nothing to do. Next, no lying to anyone in the family. And no fucking around with the wives or girlfriends of other members of the family."

"I can live with that," I responded, "but I won't lie off the bat. I am going to have a hard time with the no-cocaine deal."

"The only thing I can tell you, Christ," Mon-Mon said, chuckling, "is don't get caught."

"What's so funny?" I said, thinking he was making fun of me.

"Nothing," he answered before taking a small bag of white powder from his pocket.

"What's that? Don't tell me you fucking turn around and pull this out of your pocket after telling me not to do cocaine?"

"It is not coke, *tabarnac*," he said. "It's mescaline. Do you want a line?"

"What's the difference what it is? You said nothing but pot and hash."

"Yes, but I also told you not to get fucking caught by anybody in the family. Since both of us are doing a little something, neither will say anything to anybody since we would both be in deep fucking shit."

He laughed at my expression. As he drove, he rolled up a bill and stuffed it into the bag, sniffing deeply. Then he offered me the bag.

I thought he was testing me. So I took out some of the PCP, put it on my cigarette pack and also sniffed with a bill. I took just a little, enough to feel it, nothing like the amount his nose vacuumed up.

"I'm almost fifty fucking years old," he continued. "I told you I've been around the block. I've done lots of fucking things.

"This," he said, pointing to the bag, "is clean fun and will establish a trust between us. We are headed into some serious shit and I want to go into it with full trust in my partner. We need fucking loyalty to each other. We're heading into a war with the Hells, those fuckers."

"Renaud mentioned that. He said the Hells want to take over throughout Quebec."

"They can try, *tabarnac*. But a lot of people are against those suckers, and so are we. What those goddamn suckers want to do is a lot easier said than done. The Rock Machine has different plans. We don't fucking believe in dictatorships. We believe in brotherhood, *tabarnac*."

I was learning a bit about Mon-Mon. His non-stop swearing and voice like jagged nails made him seen very dangerous. By pairing me with him, Renaud made sure I was safe while learning the gang mentality. Mon-Mon had been a leader of the Black Spiders motorcycle club in his youth and his temper was legendary. He could explode, eyes bulging and face turning purple, over the smallest thing, whether it be the weather or an unpaid debt. Renaud gave him another nickname after a typical eruption, calling him Grognon, a French word for grumpy.

I told him about my past, even confessing my days as a go-go boy.

"Don't you dare tell anybody in the club," he said through tears of laughter. "You'll never hear the end of that."

The only other person I told was Renaud.

Renaud set up the two of us with some coke. Since I was low level, he didn't tell me where it came from. And I knew it wasn't polite in the crime world to ask. Mon-Mon and I hit the streets with an ounce or so, making the rounds of my old contacts. I'd used my previous reputation as a good supplier and friendly guy to talk up the Rock Machine. The Hells had their people doing the same.

At the beginning, Mon-Mon and I made only about $350 a week. But it grew quickly. Within a short time we were selling four ounces, a quarter pound, a week. Renaud would give us the quarter pound for between $4,800 and $5,000. We'd step on it, creating a fifth ounce by adding in some cut. Then each ounce would sell for between $1,400 and $1,500. We'd make a few hundred dollars on each ounce we bought, plus at least $1,400 from the extra fifth ounce created in our makeshift basement lab.

Renaud would point me to people he knew from growing up in Verdun, and tell Mon-Mon and I to either force them out or get them to sell for us. The Rock Machine's support and Mon-Mon's thundercloud demeanor as backup made me confident.

But Mon-Mon was riding my ass constantly.

One day, when I was supposed to talk to a potential dealer, I did some errands instead.

"Hey, Paradis, did you see that guy?"

"No."

"*Tabarnac!* What's your problem, Paradis? When you are supposed to do something, do it. Don't fuck around."

It was months before he called me by my first name.

We hired a guy named Gaetan to stash the drugs Mon-Mon and I were moving. He kept them in a VCR-sized safe in his room. Gaetan was also our runner, taking the small quantities to dealers on the street when they ran out.

Early on, I asked Renaud if I could go see J.P., a local guy who carried a lot of weight. I used to buy cocaine from him before hitting rock bottom.

"Who does he work for?" Renaud asked.

"Usually, he works with Ti-Bum, but I hear he's been buying from others."

Renaud thought for a minute. "Go ahead. Tell him he's only going to buy from one place now. He ain't going to roam around anymore."

I was alone when I ran into J.P. on the street the next day. He'd gotten rich in the years I'd been down, buying a house in the sub-urbs and wowing everyone with a Delorean, a stainless-steel car with gull-wing doors that opened upwards. The last he'd heard of me, I was a junkie.

"Come here," I told him. I was cocky—he was friendly.

"How are you?"

"A lot better."

"Oh ya? Why's that?"

" 'Cause I'm working with Renaud and the Rock Machine now."

I got down to business.

"There are not going to be any more independent dealers here."

I told him the Rock Machine was expanding into southwestern Montreal. He could join us and be supplied through me and Renaud, or he could go with some other crime families affiliated with us. But he could no longer roam from one to the other looking for the best price.

"I'll think about it." J.P. left, promising to get back to me.

But I never heard from him again. Gaetan, who had worked for J.P. in the past, broke the news to me a while later. J.P. had decided he had already made his fortune and was going to move away to Winnipeg instead of fight. I went after J.P.'s pushers, telling them they now worked for me.

If some dealers refused to come with me, I went after their cus-tomers, who usually owed money to their suppliers. I told the addicts that I would pay off their old debt and they would start with a clean slate if they bought from me. To recoup the debt pay-ments, I'd just put a little extra cut into the coke I gave those guys for a while. By doing that, I got what I wanted even if the dealers shunned my offer to join forces with me.

Mon-Mon and I were especially busy on the first of the month—welfare day. Many people would cash their checks and go on binges. So we always made sure we had a lot of stock by the end of the month. We'd also do collections from the dealers and customers who had bought on credit. I would park by a particularly troublesome client's home and wait for the mailman to come by. As soon as he passed, I would ring the doorbell before the client had a chance to spend anything.

As business improved, we moved the stash out of Gaetan's place, thinking it was too easy for police or the Hells to follow him home from his runner duties and grab the coke. The mother of one of our dealers took over and gave us keys to her place so we could get in while she worked. We gave her $100 a week in exchange for putting a safe the size of a small TV in her basement laundry room.

Mon-Mon and I had about 20 dealers buying from us after a few months. That meant we were getting into large amounts, about a pound a week. Renaud decided to insulate himself from possible arrest by handing us over to Martin (Frankie) Bourget, another full-patch member of the Rock Machine. As his share, Renaud still pocketed $100 from Frankie for each ounce we bought. So that meant he got $1,600 a week for doing nothing but being my sponsor and advising us.

When our stash was close to running out, I went to someone's home who had nothing to do with drugs to call Frankie on his pager. I left the phone number and the code 2025. That was the address of the Rock Machine's bunker on Huron Street in east-end Montreal. The code told Frankie someone in the gang wanted him.

"Go to Mario's tomorrow at five," he said when I told him we should meet.

I was on time the next day as I drove my car into the lot of Mario's eatery near the industrial port in Montreal's east end. My eyes scanned the area looking for anything out of place among the blue-collar workers stopping for steamed dogs and fries.

Since Mon-Mon and I were buying pounds now, the cost had dropped from $1,200 an ounce to a grand. So I'd brought $16,000 with me in small bills, divided into $1,000 lots and placed inside Playtex baby-bottle liners. When I handled the plastic liners, I wore latex gloves stolen by a friend who worked at the Verdun Hospital. I didn't want the cash, wherever it ended up, traced back to me by my fingerprints in a police database.

The money was on the seat next to me, inside the bag of a video-rental place; I preferred this bag because it was an opaque blue. The clump of money even looked like a few videos. I walked inside. Frankie was there, sitting in a booth with a hot dog and a drink. On the table was a folded-up *Journal de Montréal*, the local crime tabloid.

I walked by him to the empty washroom. Frankie came in a few seconds later with his newspaper. I gave him the video bag and he passed me the newspaper.

"Everything cool?" he asked.

"Yup. You?"

"Yeah."

I walked out of the toilet first. As I drove away, my eyes were on the mirror to see if anyone was paying any attention.

I was most nervous during those exchanges since being caught with such a large amount of blow could put me in prison for a couple of years. After a few months, I introduced Frankie to my runner. Gaetan then did the pickups, and I gave him $200 to $300 for each trip. He'd take the coke back to the stash house, where I'd be waiting to put the unopened package into the safe, hidden under some covers in a basement corner. I left it there for the night to see if police had followed Gaetan and would raid the place.

The next day, I filled up my gas tank and took a long drive, getting on and off highways ramps, to see if I was tailed. When I felt safe, I paged Mon-Mon with a code telling him to meet me at the stash house.

Mon-Mon was waiting for me in the basement. I went to the hidden safe and got the pound of coke. We sat at a workbench and unpacked the duct-tape wrapping and then the plastic wrap. The coke was in solid rock form.

Mon-Mon took a rolling pin to it on the table to crush it into smaller pieces. While I drank a beer, I used an empty bottle to crush the rocks into powder. I grabbed some cut we kept in the safe and put about 4 ounces into the pure 16 ounces of coke. That just upped profit by about $5,000.

In my early years, I had used powdered baby milk as cut. It was harmless, cheap, and legal to buy at any pharmacy. Anyone sniffing the coke with that lactose would not notice any difference unless their dealer got greedy. Too much powdered milk would make the coke taste sweet and leave cruds of crust in a sniffer's nose as the lactose mixes with the moisture in his nostrils and then dries. Though small amounts of lactose worked fine for sniffers, customers who shot up with syringes would notice the cut right away. They'd see cloudy white water in the spoon as the coke and water boiled into a liquid mixture. Those who smoked crack cocaine would also see the lactose. As soon as they cooked the coke, the lactose would bubble up and encrust the spoon. Other dealers used mannitol, or superflake, as we called it. It wasn't as gross as the lactose when cooked, but it was still detectable and left a bad taste.

I'd learned about a special cut as I became more experienced. It was tasteless and kept its volume when cooked. As well, it dissolved clear into water, not turning milky like lactose. It cost $150 an ounce under the counter at various drug-paraphernalia shops. After a few months with Renaud, I asked him if he knew were to get cheaper cut. He told me the Rock Machine had chemists who made it, and we could get it through Christian Deschenes, the gang's accountant. Christian gave it to us for $100 an ounce.

Once Mon-Mon and I had mixed our pound with the special cut, we had 20 or 21 ounces instead of the original 16.

"*Tabarnac*, I'm getting a buzz off this," Mon-Mon told me.

I looked at him. His mustache and beard were speckled with fine white powder thrown up by the rolling pin. So were his sweatshirt and jeans. I was also feeling high from the fumes. We looked like mad bakers.

The next step was getting the coke ready for our dealers. We gathered the powder into a pile on our table. We put two or three ounces into a plastic freezer bag and then wrapped it tight with duct tape. I grabbed a hammer and banged on the package for a while to compress it. Then we threw the package into the lady's freezer while we wrapped more.

After 20 minutes in the freezer, the hammered coke would lose its humidity and become rock hard. We did all this because cocaine in rock form was seen on the street as being of much higher quality. Dealers would believe, mistakenly, that our solid cocaine had just been broken straight off a shipment from Colombia without any cut added in.

In the beginning, we froze the coke in small packages, but it became tedious as business grew. So we had a welder at a car garage make us a special metal frame for a hydraulic jack we bought at the local Canadian Tire. We put a pound of coke in a four-sided steel box with a flat bottom. One of us would jack the box up toward a thick metal plate. The harder we jacked, the more the metal plate compressed the coke. The hammer and freezer were no longer needed.

Once compressed, Mon-Mon would set the coke in front of him. His kick was to chip off exactly the right amount of hard cocaine we needed. The size varied, depending if our dealers wanted quarter-ounce bags or full ounces. Mon-Mon weighed the coke and then stuffed it into Playtex baby-bottle liners. We used them because it was less suspicious than buying loads of sandwich baggies.

Mon-Mon handed me the plastic liners and I slid one under a

plastic heat sealer. I sealed the opening, put the bag inside a second liner, and sealed that, too. That double seal became our calling card on the street.

I rubbed at one of my itchy eyes.

"Fuck!" I yelled, grabbing my face as horrendous pain spread through it. I had inadvertently massaged my eye with cocaine residue.

Mon-Mon couldn't stop laughing.

Gaetan showed up. I weighed each package for him, showing him they were precise and making sure he saw everything was in rock form. If he tried to tamper with the seals or remove some coke from a bag for his personal use, it would be noted. He left with enough coke to service our dealers for three days.

Whatever small packages of coke remained went inside extra-large plastic freezer bags filled with rice to keep humidity away from the rocks. Humidity was worst in summer, when coke wrapped in thick plastic could turn to paste. That's why I preferred Playtex liners. They were thinner than cheaper ones.

We tossed the bags into the safe, for which only Mon-Mon and I had the combination. Then we slid a playing card across the work table to collect the coke residue. We left the residue for the lady who lived there and let ourselves out.

CHAPTER 7

A few weeks after I met Mon-Mon, he took me one evening to a strip club in northern Montreal. The place was owned by a crime family that was good friends of the Rock Machine. We didn't go for the dancers. While Mon-Mon and I were busy building up business, Renaud also wanted me to meet some of the gang.

"This is Norman Baker," Renaud said, pointing to a man with a ponytail and a beard that could have rivalled ZZ Top.

"Let's go outside," Norman said, walking away from my table.

He headed to the back door. My mind went wild. Why me? I thought back to my brother's debt, which had not been paid yet. I had threatened to kill Ti-Bum if he tried to hurt Robert. Did the Rock Machine see my threat as bravado that could not go unpunished? I believed I was being set up for a hit. But hadn't I gained Renaud's and Mon-Mon's confidence?

We stopped and faced each other in the dark parking lot beside the building. My eyes didn't leave his hands. For the moment, they were empty.

"Do you know what I want to talk to you about?" he asked.

"I'm not sure." My voice was small, nervous.

Norman whipped out a pistol. I thought my heart would stop. This is it.

But Norman didn't fire, at me or anything else. He'd heard a car parked around the corner start its engine and went to check it out.

"You can never be too sure," he said when back from the corner of the building. "It's OK."

He tucked the gun back into his leather jacket.

"Did Renaud explain to you what the deal is?" he asked.

I got my voice back.

"He told me the Rock Machine started up to make sure the Hells didn't take over the drug market."

Norman smiled.

"I'm going to tell you in plain English so you understand. We are preparing to go to war with them. They've already asked us to wear their colors, but Renaud and Gilles Lambert refused."

Like Renaud, Gilles was a founding member of the Rock Machine. They had started the Montreal chapter of the gang five years earlier, in 1989, with eight others. There was a second chapter in Quebec City as well. But the Rock Machine had been very low key until now. Norman told me that would change, as the Hells would soon realize.

"They don't know just how organized and how many we are," he said. "Boy, are they going to be in for a shock."

"Fuck them," I said, full of bravado. "I'm in."

Mon-Mon had been telling me bits about the Rock Machine's plans as we went about taking over the drug trade in Verdun. But my exposure to the gang was still minimal when its clubhouse in the seediest part of Montreal was raided by police on March 9, 1994.

Police officers had dressed up as firefighters and borrowed a ladder truck to climb in through a top-storey door, saying there was no other way to penetrate the building without risking a firefight.

"It's a fortress," one officer told the Montreal *Gazette* newspaper. "All the entrances are barricaded, so we decided to enter by the third floor, where a patio door was unlocked. That way, nobody was injured."

Cops found no drugs, just firearms, $49,000 in cash and motorcycles, but the media went crazy with the stunt. I was amazed that police feared my new friends so much.

"I'm in the big time now," I thought.

Both Renaud and Mon-Mon told me it was a good idea to get a gun. So I bought a .38 Special, a revolver I was familiar with. Mon-Mon badgered me about it as we sat in his living room on JFK Street in Ville LaSalle, a town next to Verdun.

"Paradis, a 9 mm shoots much faster than your fucking .38," he said.

"Yeah, but those things jam," I answered, trying not to show I knew nothing about the semi-automatics he favored.

Mon-Mon figured out I was embarrassed by my ignorance, so he whipped out his pistol.

"Look, *tabarnac*. You just take the safety off, crank the chamber by pulling it back, and let it go forward. That loads a bullet. Then you fire. It's that simple. Now you do it, *tabarnac*."

I took the 9 mm, and did it all, but very slowly. I put the safety lock back on, and passed him the gun with the barrel pointing straight at him. He looked disgusted.

"No, no, no, *tabarnac*. Paradis, never hand over a gun like that."

He took the gun, pointed the barrel downwards and held it by the stock, his fingers far from the trigger.

"That's how you do it. Now watch, I'll show you how to load the chamber again."

He did it expertly and handed the pistol back to me, properly.

"Just put it down," he ordered.

I dropped it on the table. A sharp blast startled us and we looked at each other. The pistol had gone off, mortally wounding a new 30-inch TV that Renaud had loaned to Mon-Mon.

"Are you fucking crazy?" Mon-Mon yelled at me, his eyes bulging. "Give me that gun before you kill both of us."

I took the gun, looked at it, and then at Mon-Mon.

"You're the one who forgot to put the fucking lock on," I said. We both laughed.

"What am I going to tell Renaud?" he asked, checking out the big hole in the plastic under the TV screen. "How am I going to explain that?"

In addition to being my boss, Renaud was a full patch in the Rock Machine and Mon-Mon's superior as well, since my partner was one notch down as a prospect. The stage under that was hangaround, and I hadn't even reached that. I was just known as an associate, with no standing in the Rock Machine at all. Shooting my boss's TV didn't help my chances of changing that.

"Relax," I told Mon-Mon. "I'll call a booster and get the same TV from him for a gram of coke."

I called a guy who knows where to find stolen stuff and gave him the make and size. A few days later, he showed up with one. In the end, it cost me one-and-three-quarter grams. When Mon-Mon and I confessed a week later, Renaud laughed so hard he had to hold his sides. He made sure I was teased by everyone in the gang.

As business had improved, I'd moved back to Montreal with Sylvie and her daughter. We rented a bottom-floor apartment in a duplex owned by Ti-Bum on De Montmagny Street. It had a huge backyard and a parking spot. I also bought expensive furniture from Ti-Bum for $8,000.

"Paradis," Mon-Mon said one day, "go grab some chips. Get big bags. Also some of those fucking big bottles of Coke and 7Up. Oh ya, if you don't want to do a lot of dishes, pick up styrofoam cups."

"Why?"

"We're having a meeting in your basement."

"Oh ya? Who?"

"The guys. Now get the stuff."

My basement had been chosen for a regular meeting of the lower ranks so they could discuss business and pay their monthly dues, usually about $100 for hangarounds and up to $500 for prospects. The full patches also had meetings—called mass—once a month, but they were off-limits to the lower ranks. The full patches paid $1,000 in dues a month. All that money went to pay lawyers, or take care of guys behind bars.

In my basement, I laid out all the junk food. About 15 men walked into my house and headed straight downstairs. Only two or three introduced themselves.

"OK, everybody's here," Mon-Mon told me. "Stay up here."

"What? This is my place. I bought all the fucking food and I can't come?"

"That's the rules. You ain't part of the family yet."

I sat at the kitchen table, fuming. From below me, I heard occasional laughter and some shouting. An hour later, everybody trooped up.

"Hey," one said to me as others asked the way to the washroom. "I'm J.P."

"Peter." I shook his hand.

J.P. turned to Mon-Mon, chiding him. "Why isn't he at the meetings? You hiding him? You not want to share with the family?"

"He's the guy I told you about. If he's a secret now, he won't be for fucking much longer."

Mon-Mon was building up his new partner. Most of the guys already knew I had some connection to Renaud because his souped-up 1979 Camaro was parked in my driveway. Renaud had sold it to me for $3,000, half of what it was worth.

A few weeks later, Mon-Mon and Renaud showed up at my door. They handed me an oval ring surrounded by diamonds. In the middle, on a stone of black onyx, were more diamonds in the shape of an A. The ring also had the initials A.L.V. A.L.M. They stood for the Alliance slogan *A la vie, à la mort*. For life, till death.

"You now have an official title," Renaud said, looking at me with pride.

It was an Alliance ring. That meant I was now seen as a part of an alliance against the Hells Angels. The Alliance was made up of dealers who worked with the Rock Machine. Some wanted to become part of the gang in the future, while others wanted to stay independent.

"There's more," Renaud said. "You are now a hangaround, too."

It was my first step toward being accepted into the Rock Machine. I smiled while trying the Alliance ring on my pinky. It was too small.

Renaud and Mon-Mon laughed and took it back. "We'll get you another one."

As a hangaround, I could now attend meetings such as the one in my basement. The rules were explained to me early on. I existed to serve the full patches. If I was paged by a full patch, I had half an hour to respond. If I didn't, I would be fined up to $100. Fines would also be leveled against anyone who didn't show up at meetings with a notepad to write down whatever information was passed around on our Hells adversaries. That could include their license plates, addresses, the type of vehicles they drove, and the habits of their wives.

If hangarounds or even prospects missed more than three meetings without a good excuse, they were out. If I complained about my punishment, whether it be a fine or some sort of task, it would double. And anything said at the meetings could not be repeated outside the gang.

A while later, Renaud and Mon-Mon came up with a ring that fit me at an Alliance hockey game. The games were Renaud's idea. It gave Rock Machine members and Alliance people a chance to know each other outside of business and to strengthen the bond necessary to back each other up. We'd usually bring the wives and kids for the games at the 4-Glaces skating rink in suburban Brossard, off the island of Montreal. In the dressing room, we'd have a few joints while suiting up. Few of the guys had played much as children, and they had put on a lot of weight since, but that didn't stop them from buying the most expensive equipment they could find. They also kept their heavy gold chains on while playing.

The best on skates were Frankie, my drug supplier, and Sylvain Pelletier, a rich drug dealer from the impoverished east end of Montreal. Sylvain was part of the Alliance, probably the most powerful member.

We played a semi-contact game, allowing some body checks, but not so rough that people would be losing their usually short tempers. The matches would always start with energy, the guys jumping over the boards when it came time to change shifts on the ice. By the second period, they'd use the door. By the middle of that period, some didn't want to go back on the ice. After that, out-of-breath players on the ice were constantly looking at the bench, hoping anyone would replace them. Numerous time-outs were needed to get water and a couple of puffs from pot and hash joints making the rounds.

The games reunited me with Paul Porter, better known as Sasquatch, from my days on the corner with the prostitutes and peep shows. He was a full patch in the Rock Machine, one of its founders. His hairline had receded a bit and he'd gained a bit of weight. Most guesses now put him at 550 pounds. Since the rink couldn't find a pair of skates for his feet, Sasquatch rented broomball shoes for the ice. He was actually a very good defenseman, parking himself on the blue line and waiting for anyone to come near. If he was checked, he'd just grab the person in his meaty arms and throw him to the ice.

As time went by, Renaud and I got closer. He'd often coach me on ways to handle problems, and tell me his philosophy on the best way to do business. We'd watch the movie *Braveheart* often, Renaud saw the warriors as good role models for the Rock Machine. Full of duty and purpose, fighting for principles and freedom.

Renaud also coached me on how to avoid police wiretaps.

"Use your hands instead of words," he said before going into what looked like a game of charades.

"Use this for hash," he said, pretending to smoke a cigarette.

"Coke." His finger went to the side of his nose.

"PCP." Renaud drew a line across his forehead, probably to show how the stuff screwed up your mind.

He put his fingers like a pistol. "Gun."

The pantomime continued. If I had the cash to pay for drugs right away, I should rub my fingers as if they held money. If I wanted to buy on credit—on the arm—I should tap my bicep. The Hells used identical gestures.

The top people in the Rock Machine had good contacts with

other crime groups like Montreal's Irish mob and the Montreal mafia. We ended up using some of the mafia's titles—the lower ranks in our gang had godfathers among the full patches, and the Rock Machine was "the family." Though some members had motorcycles worth the price of modest homes, we weren't a biker gang. We did, however, adopt the same hangaround/prospect/full-patch designations as the Hells, but we had no motorcycle jackets festooned with patches. We had rings and sweaters, much less conspicuous to police.

Renaud and I met almost every night to share information about who was selling for whom on the street. He took me to Kingston one time to do what we called public relations, meeting with Ontario independents to see how they felt about the Hells. As usual, booze, pot, and hash were everywhere at a party in some guy's home. Hard rock music bombarded the place, keeping conversations short. It became a bit boring being surrounded by just men.

"Renaud," I asked, "do these guys plan on getting any broads?"

Renaud laughed after hearing me ask a half-dozen times.

"You'll have more than your share," he said, chuckling mysteriously.

Finally, some women showed up, a bit cowed as the eyes of 30 drunk men looked at them. After a few beers, they began dancing a bit with each other and flirting with us. Renaud collected money from any of the guys interesting in screwing the girls. Luckily for the women, only about half the men wanted at them. Renaud went up to the women, showed them the cash, and told them to get going.

Two jumped on the pool table and started kissing, then fondling each other as clothes came off. They gave each other oral sex as the other women stripped and threw teasing looks at the guys.

Renaud walked up to me.

"Which one do you want?"

"Can I have all of them?"

He laughed. "Sure. But there's a catch."

"I don't care. Let's get it on."

Renaud went around to all the girls and yelled something in their ears over the music. The ones on the pool table beckoned me over. As I approached, the music died.

"Hey," Renaud yelled for everyone's attention. Then he looked at me.

"Are you a man of your word? Or will you not do what you said?"

"Sure I will."

Renaud was enjoying himself.

"Remember earlier? I told you you could have all of the women on one condition and that you didn't care what the catch was."

"Yes," I responded, starting to realize this could go badly.

"OK," Renaud said. "You are going to get what you asked for, but you will have to do this on the pool table in front of everybody."

The crowd cheered, egging me on.

"OK, OK," I said with a sheepish smile.

The music resumed its deafening beat. On the pool table, the two girls took care of my clothes as the guys gave me a beer for one hand and a joint for the other. Two other hookers joined in, keeping my body occupied and my mind off the spectators. Renaud came over after the show finished and the other guys went off to rooms with individual girls.

"You really have balls to go through something like that in front of everybody," Renaud said.

I laughed, thinking of my sore genitals. "I had balls."

For the rest of the night, the guys came over and slapped me on the back. As I got more and more drunk, I deliberately waited a few minutes after seeing one guy and a girl close the door behind them.

I walked in. "Hi. What are you doing?"

They were naked on the bed.

"What the fuck are you doing?" the guy responded.

I just walked around the small room.

"Don't be shy. Go about your business."

I did that all night.

Frequent meetings with Renaud allowed me to see how he did business. He didn't believe in gratuitous violence, preferring to negotiate.

"If you are right," he kept telling me, "I'll back you up 100 per cent against anyone. But you better be right."

I also spent a lot of time with Mon-Mon even when we were not working. We were watching the news at his place when an item came on about a guy who had been blown up in a Jeep Cherokee in the parking lot of his condo. The news report showed images of the mangled vehicle.

Mon-Mon recognized the Jeep. It belonged to Sylvain Pelletier, the powerful boss of the Alliance in the east end.

"Shit," Mon-Mon said, looking at me. "It's started, *tabarnac*."

From that day on, the hockey games stopped.

CHAPTER 8

Gang members later told me how Sylvain had died. The week before his death on October 29, 1994, Pelletier himself had ordered the death of a former drug ally who had gone over to the Hells. After that, the Rock Machine believed, Sylvain sent his truck off to be fitted with an alarm system since tensions were worsening. But another defector to the Hells used that as a heaven-sent opportunity to install a bomb instead.

The next to die among us was Daniel Bertrand, an associate who was peppered with bullets at the Sainte-4 bar he owned on east-end Ste. Catherine Street.

That December, I accompanied 30 guys in the gang to the Rolling Stones show at Montreal's Olympic Stadium. My job as hangaround that night was to shadow any members who separated from our large group, and to make sure nothing happened to them.

"I've got to take a piss," Bam-Bam told me before the show started. Richard Lagacé was very strict with lower ranks in the gang, often telling them their whole purpose was to serve full patches like him. I learned quickly never to answer back when he flipped his lid, which he did often, making the recipient of his anger feel stupid and ashamed. A few of us victims thought he was treating this too much like the army.

I followed Bam-Bam to the portable toilets at the edge of the field. He closed the door behind him and I went back to the group. I was talking with others when an enraged Richard stepped near me.

"You stupid fuck," he yelled. "You just left me alone. Are you retarded? What's the problem with this new guy?"

Early in the night, we ran into the Rockers, a puppet group that did the bidding of the Hells. We were wearing Rock Machine sweaters, so they knew who we were.

"Hold your ground," Norman Baker told everyone as we stood facing them in a line. We stared. They stared back. The tension mounted, and mounted. One of the Rockers was holding a red sweater over his hand, giving the impression he had a hidden pistol.

"What are you going to do, asshole?" I said to him, waving my hands in the air at the crowded stadium. "There are eighty thousand people here."

Security guards stepped between us, pushing our groups in opposite directions.

Skirmishes between the Rock Machine and the Hells had started slowly a few months before Pelletier was killed. It began when the Rock Machine saw its two kingpins jailed for long sentences. Salvatore Cazzetta and his younger brother, Giovanni, had built a huge drug empire along with the other original founders of the Rock Machine. They made a fortune before the war started, amassing houses, cars, and motorcycles. They'd also bought the $90,000 building on east-end Huron Street that became the gang's clubhouse. Renovations made it worth close to $1 million. Giovanni had gotten a hefty sentence for drug trafficking in 1993. And Salvatore was on the run from an extradition warrant sworn out by the United States on charges of exporting more than ten tons of cocaine. He was finally arrested in 1994, just before all the shooting began in Montreal. When the brothers were put away, the power went to Renaud and Gilles Lambert.

Meanwhile, the Hells were moving into Montreal. Their traditional space was in the regions and suburbs off the island, but Maurice Boucher, nicknamed Mom, had his headquarters in Montreal's east end and wanted to expand into areas controlled by crime families like the Pelletiers, Bertrands, and others in the Alliance. One of the stranger coincidences of the war is that Mom and Salvatore, leaders of two warring camps, had been members of the same biker gang—the SS—in their younger days.

Police mark the war's real beginning in July 1994, months before Pelletier's death. During two fateful days, Rock Machine soldiers planned hits on four targets to stop the Hells from encroaching on their territory. First, a Hells dealer was killed, and then an influential member named Normand Robitaille was shot. Third, five people tried to blow up the bunker of a Hells gang called the Evil Ones in suburban Saint-Basile-le-Grand, but were arrested before they could do it. Last, two guys were circling the garage Boucher used as an office when their suspicious movements were spotted by a cop coming off his shift. He followed them in his own car while radioing for a cruiser to check it out. In the suspicious car, police found submachine guns and realized it was an attempted hit on the Hells leader. I knew little of this at the time because I was too low in the gang to be trusted yet.

A month after the Rolling Stones concert, Norman Baker boarded a plane with his girlfriend for a vacation in Mexico. Also on the plane were more than a dozen Hells. They must have noticed him because a few days later, one Hells prospect walked into a restaurant and fatally shot Baker, who was eating dinner with his wife. Robert Léger, a Rock Machine prospect also there on vacation, was standing at the bar when the killer fired and then jumped out a window. Waiters ran after the Hells prospect and tackled him.

The night before he left, I'd seen Baker at the clubhouse and he'd told me to be careful. His funeral was my first in the gang. I walked into the funeral parlor while a cassette tape played "Wanted Dead or Alive" by Bon Jovi. When one side of the tape finished, it was flipped. And then flipped again, all day long.

Baker's death brought home that this wasn't a typical gang war, usually fought on the streets with chains, bats, and fists. I'd been in plenty of those fights as a teen when the French and the English would go at each other. Or blacks and whites. But this was serious.

Two weeks after Norman died, it was Dada's turn. Daniel Senesac of the Rock Machine was installing a bomb under an enemy's car while another gang member was not far away with the detonator. The bomb went off prematurely, killing Dada.

The last time I saw Dada I was also at the clubhouse, doing watch duty. Prospects and hangarounds had to do shifts keeping the place safe. At the beginning, we were paired off for the 24-hour shifts, but after the war started and fewer people could be spared that quickly dropped to one guy staying up an entire day.

The bunker was located near the Jacques Cartier Bridge in one of the seedier parts of town. The nearby streets would become clogged every afternoon as suburbanites fought their way across the span. Prostitutes also plied their trade there, sometimes getting into a commuter's car and heading to an alley for a quick blowjob before the motorist would get back in line, often losing little time.

Whenever I would approach the clubhouse at noon to begin my shift, I'd phone ahead.

"Check your cameras," I told the guy doing security inside. "I'm coming up."

I didn't want to wait long on the street, a perfect target for any killers. The guy inside glanced at one of the dozen surveillance cameras that surrounded the building, recognized my Camaro, and opened the gate to the parking lot by remote control.

Bandit sauntered over as I got out. The rottweiler, the size of a small pony and worth a few thousand dollars, jumped on me. He was in the parking lot to make sure no intruders tried to attach bombs to our cars or the clubhouse. Two other dogs, one of which was called Satan, patrolled a separate caged corridor that protected the back of the clubhouse. Those rottweilers weren't as ferocious and impressive as Bandit, but they still did the job. We were warned never to let Bandit near the others because of his temper.

I got Bandit off me and headed to the bunker as the big dog busied himself peeing on one of my tires. Doing watch wasn't the only task I had to do to show my worthiness for advancement. Running errands for full patches was another. A few times, I'd driven three hours to Quebec City and another three hours back to deliver pieces of paper between full patches who didn't want to risk communicating by phone.

At the bunker, I walked in through the main entrance, past the bulletproof windows beside the door, and into the bar. It contained a huge tavern-style fridge stocked with booze and soft drinks. On the wall behind the counter was the Rock Machine eagle in white neon lights. The rest of the room was filled with leather sofas and a pool table. We'd had a "Hells Angels Forever" icon on the wall but it was taken down when the war began.

I went to a steel-fortified door that was up a few steps and punched a code on the keypad. Behind the door was an immense living room with wall-to-wall carpeting, a fireplace, more leather sofas and a 50-inch TV screen. Off to one corner was the security room, filled with a dozen monitors. It had a bulletproof window looking out to the parking lot.

"How's it going?" I asked the guy. He was in a hurry to get home and sleep. "Everything cool?"

"Ya, nothing's up," he said.

"You clean up?"

"Yup."

At the end of a shift, the guy on watch is supposed to clean the wood and ceramic floors, empty the dishwasher, wipe off all the mirrors with Windex, wash the sheets if the beds had been used, take out the garbage, feed the dogs, and then pick up their shit. In the winter, they'd also have to shovel the walkway, parking lot, and roof.

I didn't take his word for it. I checked around because one guy I once replaced had lied and when a full patch came in later, I got shit for his sloppiness.

I went to the kitchen on the second floor. The costly appliances and dining table were spotless. I then checked out the five bedrooms, sometimes filled with snoring gang members sleeping off a booze-filled night. I glanced at the sauna and the whirlpool bath surrounded by mirrors on the wall and ceiling. On the third floor, I put my head in an empty room. It was supposed to become a con-ference area where we were planning to hang wall plaques com-memorating gang members or associates who died in the war. Through that room was a smaller one, where a tanning bed was set up with two video surveillance monitors on a chair so if a sentry was alone, he could tan on his stomach and check the cameras at the same time.

I didn't bother with the roof, which had a jacuzzi that could fit a dozen people. It also had a BBQ and a number of lawn sets. The edges of the roof had been built up a few feet to provide protection from any snipers. And there was a large crate at each corner to give shelter to anybody doing lookout duty. I did go to the basement, which contained a workout gym with numerous machines, a shower, and even a washer and dryer. Attached was a garage where gang members would park their motorcycles during the early stages of the war. When the killing began, they switched to cars.

I let the guard go and settled in, helping myself to a soda from the bar. We all chipped in to keep the fridges stocked up. Then I headed to the surveillance room to keep an eye on the cameras.

We were forbidden from leaving the place unless relieved. Imag-ine the embarrassment if the clubhouse was empty and the Hells broke in. How would we get it back? Call the police? We'd look like fools when that would hit the papers.

Strict rules forbid people from discussing business in the place. Signs saying "There are bugs in the walls" were plastered throughout.

Another day, Renaud called me and told me to replace the per-son on watch at the bunker. I went, asking no questions.

When I stepped into the bar, I noticed the pool table lying on its side, and the rest of the room in a shambles. I hope they don't want me to clean up, was my first thought. I went for the surveillance room, but a white refrigerator stood in the way.

Robert Léger opened the door to the surveillance room and came out to the bar with me. "Toute-Toute" was tall, very gentle, with a reputation as a good business guy. He was so disinterested in the gang part of the Rock Machine that he holds the record as the prospect who took the longest—seven years—to become full patch.

"Don't touch the fridge," he whispered. "Whatever you do, don't open it."

"What the hell is going on?"

"I don't know. But keep your eyes open."

Nothing made sense, I thought, as Toute-Toute left. I went to the surveillance cameras scratching my head. Most nights at the bunker, people would call or drop by. But this shift was deadly quiet. The fridge occupied my thoughts all night. Every time I went to the bar for a soft drink or bag of chips, I scrutinized the thing.

I decided to open it, and strode up to the door. But I lost my nerve and returned to the sofa. Are the guys testing me to see if I will follow orders? I finally decided to do nothing since the guys would have been able to verify my actions by looking at the surveillance tapes.

I handed over the clubhouse to another guy and went home. The next day, the fridge was taken away, and I never learned what was in it, though I once caught a few guys laughing about actually whacking a guy in the clubhouse.

A few weeks after the fridge left, Sasquatch walked in as my guard duty was finishing and I was waiting for the next guy in the bar. Sas looked at me.

"Your housecleaning done?"

"Yes," I answered. Sometimes I felt like a maid.

He left me at the bar and walked upstairs.

"Follow me," he said upon coming down.

He pointed out a mirror. It had a few specks of dust on it. Then he went to a washroom, showing me a bit of grime under the rim of the toilet bowl.

"Do the whole house over," he ordered as punishment.

I said nothing and got out the toilet brush.

Sasquatch reveled in his authority over the lower ranks, often sending me to a corner store to get him his favorite breakfast—

chocolate milk and a chocolate snack cake. I quickly learned his favorite lunch was a large pizza, though he limited himself to two Diet Pepsis to cut down the calories.

After numerous snowstorms, Sasquatch showed up with another full patch for a meeting at the bunker. He eyed me, another guy named Guy Langlois, and Tony Plescio. Tony, who had become a hangaround a few weeks before me, was the brother of a gang founder named Johnny, but that family link didn't save Tony from Sas's orders.

"Go shovel the side yard," he told us.

"But I did shovel it," I responded.

"Get rid of the snowbanks."

After several storms, everyone had just piled the snow up against the parking lot wall and the resulting hills were five feet high, and the width of a car.

"Are you serious?" I couldn't help myself from asking.

He gave me a stern look. "We have no place to park the fucking cars. Go."

We did it as fast as possible, tossing the snow out onto city streets. I feared being an easy target for any hit squad. After that time, Tony and I contacted a guy who worked for the city's snow-removal crew. We paid $100, and he used city equipment to haul our snow away when it got to be too much. The full patches slapped us on the backs for our ingenuity.

During the same winter, I was at the clubhouse with a few full patches when they got a craving for chicken. I brought them all the take-out flyers from local places. They wouldn't look at them.

"No, no, no," Alain Brunette told me. "We want Benny's."

"Where's Benny's?"

"Across the bridge in Longueuil."

"Are you fucking serious?"

That was a half-hour drive on a good day. Outside, a snowstorm raged.

"What's wrong with the chicken around here?" I continued.

"We want that chicken," Alain said firmly. He had just been named full patch and was testing his authority. The others nodded, checking if I would follow orders.

I got into my car and cursed all the way through the snowdrifts. When I got back, Renaud, Alain, Gilles, and Sas were cozy from the blaze in the fireplace.

"Thanks a lot," one said as he took the food from me. "I hope it's still hot?"

I gave them a killer look.

During another watch, this time in the summer, I finished my inside chores and headed outside to clean up the dog shit. While in the backyard with Satan and the third dog, I used the bunker's cordless phone to call Bam-Bam, telling him my replacement was late. As I got off the phone, I heard my cellphone ringing out in the parking lot. I hurried to answer it. When that call finished, I headed back to my shit-collection duties. I walked around the corner and got a shock.

Bandit was in a snarling match with Satan and the third dog. In my haste to answer my cell, I had left the door between their compounds open. Bandit had gone wandering, and was fighting off the other two dogs with sweeps of his fangs.

I didn't know what to do. I called Bam-Bam.

"You idiot," he said, telling me nothing new. "Get them apart."

"How?"

"Use your gun if you have to."

I hung up and took my piece out of my belt. By now, Satan and the other dog each had a mouthful of Bandit. Satan had him by the leg, the other by the throat. Bandit was looking to me with something I'd never seen before, an expression of despair.

I was pointing my gun at all of them, trying to line up a shot. Which one to kill? Bandit was worth the most, but, whatever I did, I knew the full patches would have my head.

Then Bandit gathered his strength with a roar, freeing his throat with a twist of the head. He used his fangs and strong jaws

79

to grab the third dog and throw him into the wire-mesh fence.

I put away my gun, grabbed the shit shovel, and went after Satan, who still chomped on Bandit's leg. The shovel came down on Satan's head. He held on. I hit again, harder. He felt it, but wouldn't give up the grip. Again and again I hit. He finally let go and ran off a bit, finding himself beside his partner.

I was now in between Bandit and his attackers.

Bandit was bleeding from his neck and mouth. I went after him, thinking one dog was easier to take on than two. He let out a huge growl from his slobbering mouth and I almost dropped the shovel in fright. I changed my mind, choosing one of the smaller dogs. I raised the shovel. Satan, remembering what that felt like, let out a whimper, turned and fled to the far wall. The third dog followed.

I dropped the shovel and ran to the gate. On the far side was Bandit's parking lot.

"Come, Bandit," I said in a soft voice, as if I were speaking to a puppy. "Come on. C'mon."

He followed me, and I locked the gate, relief on my face. I hosed down Bandit's bloody wounds and went inside to get some cold cuts from the fridge to make amends with the beast. I dreaded my next step—calling Bam-Bam. I barely got in a greeting before he exploded.

"You are going to do one straight week of guard duty," he roared. Extended periods of watch at the clubhouse were used to punish fuckups. You could get anywhere from three days to a full month.

"I'm sorry," I said, meekly.

He calmed down. "Which dog did you shoot?"

"None. I beat Satan over the head with a shovel."

"Are you serious?" Now he was laughing.

I told him what happened.

"OK, I won't discipline you," Bam-Bam said. "Just make sure this never happens again."

The clubhouse was often used by full patches who wanted to get away from their wives to screw prostitutes. Only the leaders could use the upstairs bedrooms or the jacuzzi for sex, but I always made sure I was invited along by bringing a few strippers with me and sharing. Johnny Plescio would often call two or three prostitutes, keep one for himself, and let us bed the others. Most of the time, Johnny wouldn't even have sex. He'd stay at the bar with his whore, get drunk, take coke, and call her nasty names all night. Not one whore walked out as long as Johnny was throwing money on the bar to keep her there.

We had many parties to get to know others in the underworld. One time, we invited the Irish mob as well as two busloads of Mohawks from the Kahnawake reserve. My brother Robert knew many, since his common-law wife was Native.

Benoit Roberge, a Montreal police officer who is an expert on biker gangs, was sitting outside the clubhouse in an unmarked car for that party. He must have gotten the surprise of his life seeing the Mohawks go in, thinking the Rock Machine had just started a new chapter.

Sasquatch saw the cop and his partner while checking the security cameras.

"Get a plate," Sas said to me. "Follow me."

We each loaded a plate of cold pizza and sandwiches from the buffet, grabbed a few soft drinks, and went up to their car.

"Here," Sas said to Roberge, pushing the plate in front of him. "Take this, a gesture of goodwill."

The cop politely refused.

"Come on," Sas continued, surprised anyone would refuse food. "Come on."

"That's OK," Roberge answered. Maybe he thought we would poison him.

As we walked away, I turned around and showed him the soft drink.

"At least take the drink? It hasn't been opened."

"No, thanks. I'm fine."

• • •

My cocaine business was growing despite the bloodshed. Most of the killing was in Montreal's east end. Since Verdun was separated from all that by Montreal's downtown, it was pretty calm for my business.

I was still with Sylvie, but instead of macaroni and hot dogs, we were now into prime beef roasts. I ended up meeting her ex-boyfriend, the man with whom she had conceived her daughter. Sylvie was from the Saguenay-Lac Saint-Jean area of Quebec, a region were the Hells had an iron grip. She'd always told me I could make a fortune there since an ounce of coke in Montreal would sell for $1,200 while the Hells were charging $500 more than that in her region for bad-quality stuff. Since I bought mine uncut in bulk now for between $900 and $1,000 when there was no shortage, I could cut it a bit and make even more.

Sylvie's ex wanted to sell my stuff up there, but he had no money.

"If you give me credit, you won't regret it," he said.

So I sold it to him for $1,600 an ounce, much more than in Montreal but less than the Hells in his region. I figured I deserved so much because I was the one taking the risk by fronting him coke. Even if I lost it, at least I'd be trying to expand the Rock Machine into Hells territory. Still, I wouldn't bet on this guy's life expectancy.

"Since you already sell their garbage for them, how do you expect to sell my stuff so they won't notice?" I asked.

"I'm going to cut it. Not as much as they do, but enough to fit in better."

He drove six hours to pick up the coke, and another six to return. The guy wanted half a pound, worth $12,800, to start. I refused. It was too much to risk losing to a guy I barely knew.

"I'll meet you about halfway." I gave him five ounces, putting him in my debt for $7,300. "If your business runs as well as you think, it should be enough to get you going," I told him.

I took four ounces of pure coke, put in another ounce of cut and pressed it into a solid rock. I made $600 on each ounce of real coke, plus the extra $1,600 for making an extra ounce out of cut, putting my profit at $4,000.

He bought the same amount again a few weeks later. Then I upped him to the half pound he originally asked for. Very quickly, I was making almost $10,000 a month off this guy. Half went to Mon-Mon since we were partners.

Sylvie's ex then asked me for a full pound. I gave him 13 ounces. That's when he stopped contacting me. I told Mon-Mon I had a feeling we had just been screwed.

"Paradis," he said after the swearing streak ended, "he's your customer. You are going to have to deal with it."

I paged the guy constantly. No response. Same at his home phone.

The guy probably thought I wouldn't drive into Hells territory to recoup my money. He was wrong. I had to do something or I would end up looking weak. I called up hangaround Stéphane Corbeil, better known as Bull due to his 300 pounds of bulk. He looked like a younger version of Mon-Mon.

"Anything for you," he said right away.

"Bring your gun," I told him. "This is Hells country. We need to be armed."

I warned Sylvie that her daughter might not have a father soon. I felt bad for the child.

Bull and I drove up one sunny June day in 1995. Despite the danger, we wore our black Rock Machine sweaters. When we got near Chicoutimi, we headed to a large shopping center. We wanted people to see the Rock Machine were in town. After we'd gotten plenty of stares, we left, not wanting to turn our walk into a suicide mission.

Sylvie had found out for us where her ex lived by calling some childhood friends. As we drove down his street, we saw him mowing his front lawn while his girlfriend lounged nearby.

I floored my Camaro, went over the curb, and came to a sliding stop on the lawn, right next to my startled prey. Bull jumped out with his pistol and went for the guy. The guy was paralyzed.

His girlfriend let out a squeak and ran for the house. I jumped out and went after her.

"Don't let fuckhead get away," I yelled to Bull as I went into the house.

The woman had the phone in her hand.

"Who are you trying to call, you fucking bitch?" I yelled, yanking the phone cord out of the wall. "The Hells? Or the cops?"

Two kids in their early teens came out of a room.

"Don't start fucking around in front of your kids," I said, a bit out of breath.

I turned to the children. "Don't worry. Wait here. Your mother will be back in a few minutes."

I took the woman by the arm and led her outside.

Bull was also holding the deadbeat by the arm. The guy was in a stoned, dreamy world.

"How'd you find out where I lived?" he asked.

"None of your fucking business," I replied. "I'm asking the questions. Where's my money, you fuck?"

"I don't have it."

"Where's my coke?"

"I don't have it, either."

From his appearance, he had probably used it all.

"You don't give a fuck, do you?"

"What do you think you can do right here?" he said, gesturing with his head, sure he was in no danger.

"What am I going to do?" I repeated. "Nothing."

I nodded at Bull.

In a motion way too fast for his bulk, Bull put the guy in a headlock and stuck his pistol to the guy's head.

"I'll show you what I'm going to do," I then said.

I made another sign to Bull, saying put a bullet in his head. As Bull cocked his pistol, I looked around for the first time.

"Wait," I yelled at Bull. "Look over there."

He turned his head and saw a family watching from a nearby balcony. The deadbeat used that delay to slip out of the headlock and run toward the balcony.

"Call police," he yelled. "Help. Call police."

Bull and I ran to the car, dove in, and sped off.

We headed for the only highway back to Montreal. The souped-up Camaro stood out, so it didn't take long before a cruiser was in my rear-view mirror. I threw Bull my gun.

"Stuff yours and mine above the glove compartment," I told him.

Bull fumbled with the catch but finally tipped our guns into the cavernous space in the dashboard behind the compartment. Our pieces fell near the heater.

We were pulled over and taken away in handcuffs. The next day, both of us were brought in front of a Chicoutimi judge and charged with extortion, death threats, drug trafficking, and use of illegal weapons. He let us loose on bail until our trial some months away.

When I got my Camaro back, I checked under the dashboard and found the pistols. The cops had missed them. Back to Montreal we went.

CHAPTER 9

Soon after Bull and I were released from Chicoutimi jail, we got word the Hells were up to something. They chose Quebec's sovereignist holiday, St. Jean Baptiste Day in June 1995, to put together a warrior unit called the Nomads. Unlike other chapters that are based in certain areas, the Nomads can go anywhere. And their task from day one was to win the war. Their leader was Mom Boucher, the notorious Montreal biker who became a celebrity as the war went on.

A few weeks later, on August 9, Marc Dubé was getting into his decrepit Jeep on an east-end street. He was parked near the Saint-Nom-de-Jesus School on Adam Street, not far from Montreal's Olympic Stadium. The 26-year-old and a friend were on their way somewhere, but Dubé's friend forgot something in a nearby apartment and went back. As Dubé clambered into the Jeep, someone close by hit a remote-control detonator. A bomb under the Jeep exploded, propelling the vehicle high off the pavement. Dubé himself flew ten feet up and landed on the ground, minus his legs.

Pieces of the Jeep rained over a 50-meter area, shattering windows, and hitting two boys playing near the school. Daniel Desrochers fell on the grass after a shard of metal hit his head. His friend was hit in the head, stomach, and back, but his injuries were not life threatening.

Nothing could be done for the driver of the Jeep, but 11-year-old Daniel was rushed to hospital to stop bleeding in his brain. He clung to life for days as Montrealers offered his single mother any help she needed and even a trip to Disney World for the boy when he got better.

He died four days later.

The war had already killed about 20 people, but the public didn't really care since the more gang members dead, the better for society. But with Daniel becoming the first innocent victim, the public looked for someone to blame. At first, the Rock Machine were suspects since Dubé supposedly was a minor dealer for the Hells. The day after Dubé was killed, that impression solidified because a gunman walked into a motorcycle accessory shop owned by the Rock Machine. He fired two guns from the hip "cowboy style" at an employee and a client. The customer died. That left the impression that the Rock Machine killed the Hells dealer, and the Hells retaliated by shooting up the Rock Machine's motorcycle shop.

Renaud immediately contacted the *Journal de Montréal*, telling them the Rock Machine didn't hurt Daniel. "We don't attack, and we certainly don't kill, children."

And for the first time in Quebec history, the Hells put out a press release, saying they weren't involved either.

Despite how it looked, police learned the Hells were behind Daniel's death. It seems their hit team mistook Dubé for a Rock Machine dealer who had an identical Jeep, so they ended up murdering one of their own and unleashing a huge public outcry against all of us.

People were eyeing us with hatred any time we wore our sweaters or were at the clubhouse. I was called an animal and worse. And the government began putting together special anti-gang legislation. We were cursing the Hells for being so stupid and bringing the heat down on us. I felt guilty, knowing the drug war was behind the boy's death. Even if the Rock Machine had no part in it, we were players in the war.

About a month after the Jeep's bombing, Renaud drove me up to Sainte-Agathe in the Laurentians.

"I want you to spend a few days with Thomas," he told me.

"Why?"

"This is not a good time to leave him alone," was all he said.

We rode in silence for a while.

"If you are to know why, it will be Thomas himself who will tell you," he finally said.

I nodded. I knew Thomas (not his real name) a bit because he also did watch at the bunker.

"And if he does tell you," Renaud continued, fixing me with a stern look, "keep it to yourself."

We pulled up to a cottage. Someone was peeking at us from behind the window curtains.

"Look," I told Renaud, "we're being watched."

He turned to me, again very serious.

"Thomas is very jumpy. Watch his back."

Thomas was in a sniffer's heaven as we walked in. He greeted us, and then ran upstairs without a word. I sent a look to Renaud before Thomas bounded down the stairs, handing me a pistol.

"I've already got a gun," I said, showing him my .357.

"Now you have two," Thomas replied, laughing.

I looked again at Renaud, raising an eyebrow.

Renaud walked to the door and said he'll be back in two days to pick me up. The instant Renaud left, Thomas bolted the door, shaking constantly. His eyes were wide, like those of an owl. Two days with this wreck will be a disaster, I thought.

"Do you have any board games or something like that?" I asked.

"In the closet."

I went and looked through all the boxes. Thomas showed some life.

"Do you know how to play Risk?" he asked.

"Sure. I love that game."

Risk imitates a world war. You are the commanding officer of certain countries and attempt to take over whole continents by attacking your opponent. We put our guns next to the game and started rolling the dice.

"War," shouted Thomas, and then went into peals of psychotic laughter. He took a trip to the bathroom and then we started.

His trips to the toilet interrupted the game every ten minutes. I thought it was just nerves until I noticed he had white powder around his nose. He'd use the bathroom walks to check the windows, always with his 9 mm in hand. Finally, he lost interest in Risk, concentrating on looking through the curtains as night set in. Thomas reacted to every noise or creek. At one point, I actually did hear something outside.

"There's someone there," Thomas said, panic in his wild eyes.

"I'm sure it's nothing."

He shook his head.

"Fuck this," I said, getting up, taking my gun just in case. I undid the bolt on the door.

"What are you doing?" Thomas whined.

"I've had enough of this shit. I want to go see for myself."

I stood on the landing. Thomas followed me, still with gun in hand. My flashlight beam caught footprints.

"Look, you fool," I told him with disgust. "They're from an animal."

Thomas stared at them, then at me, then at them.

"Christ, I'm fucked up."

I locked the door and convinced him to smoke an overstuffed joint with me to calm his nerves.

"I'm the one who did it, you know," he said after a long period of quiet.

"Did what?"

"I whacked that prick Emond," he said, looking me in the eyes.

"Shit."

Richard (Crow) Emond was the leader of the Hells chapter in Trois-Rivières and a member of the Filthy Few, a select group of Angels who have killed for the gang. Tony Plescio had spotted Crow shopping at a mall in northeast Montreal. He had called Thomas, who sped over. As Crow and a girlfriend were getting into a car in the parking lot, Thomas shot six times, hitting the

Hells twice in the chest. No one had been arrested except Emond's girlfriend for not cooperating with Montreal homicide detectives.

Crow's assassination was the first big coup for the Rock Machine. Before him, our successful targets were mostly low-level associates. Some Rock Machine associates had tried to kill Boucher with a truck bomb in front of his favorite restaurant, but the vehicle was towed away before it did any harm.

A few days after playing nursemaid to Thomas, I ran into Benoit Grignon, gang prospect. We discussed the war.

"I can't say anything right now," he told me, "but I have something set up. You will surely see it in the papers."

His comments intrigued me, but he refused to say more. "OK," I said. "Come see me on guard duty tomorrow to tell me about it."

"OK."

But he didn't show up the next day at the bunker. The police did, however. I saw their cars roar up on the surveillance cameras, followed by pounding on the front door. I didn't answer. Instead, I called the Rock Machine's lawyer.

"Should I let them in?" I asked Gary Martin.

"Go see if they have a warrant. If they don't have one, tell them to call me."

I went to the door and spoke through the intercom.

"Show me your warrant."

One officer put it up to the window. I was still with Gary on the phone.

"Check the date and signature in the bottom, right-hand corner," the lawyer said. "That'll tell you if it is up to date and which judge signed it."

I read it to him.

"Open the door," he said. "You can't fight that."

I unlocked the steel door. The first cops through grabbed me, pushed me to the floor, and pinned me there. Other cops in bulletproof vests streamed through with dogs. It looked like a police convention. They let me get up and stand at the bar after I was handcuffed.

"Where is it?" one cop asked calmly.

"Where is what?" I had no idea what he wanted.

"Tell us where it is and we won't tear the place apart."

"I don't know what you are talking about."

He kept asking questions.

"Who was there?"

"Who was where?"

He was getting pissed off.

"I don't know what the hell you are talking about," I yelled. "You have your warrant. Do what you gotta do."

I watched with dismay as the cops yanked everything apart, throwing couch cushions on the floor, tossing papers everywhere. I'm going to have to clean it up, I kept thinking.

Police found and carted away a rifle and two pistols from the clubhouse. One of the rottweilers howled as I was taken away for questioning. Gary had called others in the gang, saying I was probably going to be arrested, so they sent over a replacement. My relief waited outside the bunker until the police were finished.

I was taken to a police station and placed in an interrogation room with two plainclothes cops.

"Where's the dynamite?"

"The what?"

"You heard me. Where's the dynamite?"

"I was at the clubhouse when you picked me up. How am I supposed to know what you are talking about?"

"How many were there?" one continued.

Something clicked, and I thought back to my conversation with Benoit. My face must have shown I was starting to clue in.

"Listen," one cop said. "We are not accusing you of anything. But we are sure you know who was involved in a bomb attempt against the Jokers. All we want to know is who was there because right now we cannot identify any of the bodies. They were blown up so bad that the largest piece of flesh we found was the size of a dollar."

I squirmed at that.

"With DNA," the cops continued, "we will eventually know who they were. We are asking you to help us not waste time identifying them so we can tell their families."

I looked at them. First rule of the gang was never help police. The cop looked back sadly.

"You're free to go."

Over the next few days, I got the full story. Four guys in the gang had taken a stolen Dodge Caravan to the Jokers clubhouse in Saint-Luc, a small town about a half-hour south of Montreal. The Jokers were affiliated with the Hells against us. Their clubhouse was on a rural road not far from an auto-recycling yard and bordered by farmers' fields. The gang had recently cleared away trees and fortified their place with fences and lights.

The van was driven into the modified bungalow's driveway. There, three men got out and went for the bunker with packs full of explosives. A sentry saw them and fired a shotgun blast that ignited one pack, setting off the others.

Body pieces were found 100 meters away, and the Dodge was blown clear across the road. The van's driver, named Bret Simmons, was thrown from the truck and crawled into the woods for safety.

Police arrested a dazed man in the Jokers clubhouse and found firearms on a balcony used by sentries. The shooter was never charged because prosecutors ruled he was acting in self-defense. But Bret got eight years.

Dogs brought in to find body parts searched for days, and rumors said they had to be kept from eating pieces of flesh. The Jokers themselves did some scavenging, keeping a few packages of flesh and bones in their freezer. They put a piece of spine on display in a glass jar inside their clubhouse. Police found it a few months later during a raid.

Four days after the incident, Quebec provincial police and Montreal's municipal force combined their anti-biker squads to form the Wolverines, a 60-officer team to fight the Hells and Rock Machine. The RCMP later joined in as well.

One night not long after, I got a call from Toute-Toute asking me to replace him for a couple of hours on watch because he had to do an errand. I agreed and headed to the bunker. I was a few blocks away when I noticed shattered windows on buildings.

The area was filled with police officers and fire trucks. I cut through an alley and saw our clubhouse smoking, and missing its bulletproof window in the front. I parked, ignoring a cop who told me to keep driving. As I went across the police yellow tape, I saw Toute-Toute up on the roof. He seemed fine, except his long straight hair was all frizzy.

A bomb placed against the front of the building had left a large crater. Pieces of the aluminum roof flew far, but the fortified structure suffered little. Officers in the bomb squad told me they would be searching the remains for at least 24 hours. I left and called a full patch, telling him what happened.

A day later, I was ordered to go guard the bricks and materials already delivered to the clubhouse for a quick repair. But city inspectors refused to let me back into the building until it had been deemed safe. So I backed my car right up to the front wall to get a clear view of the street.

Police officers drove up and down the short street to make sure nothing was happening. I watched from my car, with a .357 Magnum in my lap. Nightfall came but I was kept entertained by all the neighbors out to gossip with me. At about 2 a.m., a pretty hooker came toward my car with a bag in her hand. I cocked my revolver even though I knew her face.

"What's in the bag?" I yelled, harshly.

"Don't worry, Honey," she replied. "I thought you would be hungry so I brought you a hot dog and coffee."

Maybe the Hells sent her with poison or something.

"I've just eaten," I lied to spare her feelings. "But you're very kind to think of me."

"Do you mind if I keep you company?" she asked.

"Sure, but not too long."

She got in the passenger door as I uncocked my gun. The sound brought a strange look to her face.

"Sit back," she said, unbuckling my jeans. "This one is on the house."

She raised her head and looked at me. "On one condition."

"What?"

"Please, rub the gun barrel on my ass while I suck you."

"Sure, Honey," I said, chuckling. "Whatever turns you on."

Not long after, a newspaper carrier gave me a paper for free.

"On the house," the old man said.

"What's with all this 'on the house' all of a sudden?" I laughed.

He looked puzzled.

My replacement showed up a few hours later, as did a crowd of gawkers and reporters. Then city inspectors showed up and I followed them through the clubhouse. The barroom on the other side of the bombed wall was in tatters. The only thing that had survived intact was a three-foot-high bottle of corked champagne that decorated one end of the bar.

"I don't believe this," said an engineer inspecting the place. "This place was built for a real war. The foundation didn't even budge an inch."

It passed inspection, and the club repaired it even stronger than before. The blast left Satan deaf, though he kept doing his duties.

One of the Alliance members tried a new tactic. He and another man took rifles and drove a stolen car to an area not far from the Leclerc prison in Laval. When a member of the Nomads went out to the prison courtyard for a walk, he was met with bullets. But the shots missed. The two shooters fled.

The next day, I went to the funeral for Benoit and two other friends—Pierre Patry and Daniel Paul—killed while trying to blow up the Jokers' bunker. Police had secured two blocks around the Verdun church because the event drew a thousand spectators. Police had also taken precautions at the funeral home nearby, checking everyone with metal detectors. They even searched baby strollers for guns and flower arrangements for bombs.

The cops nabbed three guys from the Rowdy Crew, a gang affiliated with the Hells, who were videotaping people going in and out of the funeral home. Our enemies often showed up at funerals to see what we looked like for future hits. To prevent that, we wore bandannas over our faces, though police would grab us, make us uncover our faces, and snap photos for their own intelligence gathering.

At about this time, I, and other lower ranks, spent every weekend visiting bars frequented by Hells dealers. For the first attack, Renaud and Bam-Bam came along to show they weren't afraid to do what they sent their underlings to do. We all waited until the place was packed. Then a few cars screeched up to the bar and everybody piled out. Someone popped the trunk on one car and we grabbed baseball bats from inside. Half a dozen burly guys went in while Renaud stayed outside with me watching for cops. He had a bat in his hands and I had my pistol. We heard screaming from inside before our guys ran out and we peeled off.

During most raids, I jumped the bar counter and yanked out the phone cords so no one could call the police. Another person went to the manager's office and did the same. The back door would be secured, and guys would also guard the front so no one left. All of us wore Rock Machine sweaters.

"Nobody get involved," I would yell to the panicked patrons. Then, whoever knew the territory best would point out the dealers. And the beatings would begin with bats, fists, and boots. At one place, a waitress I knew from childhood recognized my face. She looked at me while others were punching away at a dealer.

"Why are you doing this?" she screamed.

"Don't ask me any questions," I said gruffly. "You should know why, if you let these people in here."

Bam-Bam had us attack a club north of Montreal that his dealers had been thrown out of by the Rowdy Crew. I was astounded to get there and see it was a country and western bar. There was even a place to hitch your horse. We beat out the rival dealers only for the Rowdy Crew to do the same to Bam-Bam's dealers later.

Days later, Renaud ordered me to an urgent meeting in a parking lot, far from police bugs.

"Somebody's backed out on a hit," he said. "You struck me as the guy to take his place."

He told me a three-man team would be sent out to kill a Rowdy Crew member. This was the gang's first demand that I do this kind of work.

I drove north to meet the other two prospects. One was Bull, who had helped me out in Chicoutimi. They told me the original plan had been for a person who knew the target to go into the western bar and get him to come outside into the sights of their guns. But because the guy chickened out, we were now going to stake out the bar in a van. The target was supposed to pick up a girlfriend when she finished waitressing at midnight. When the two of them came out, we were to yank open our van's sliding door and fire away.

Bull gave me a submachine gun. I stared at it.

"How the fuck does it work?" I finally asked.

"Just pull down on the pin and fire away," Bull said, unsure about the quality of the hired help these days.

My mind kept telling me I wasn't cut out for being an assassin. I could never kill someone alone. Maybe if all of us were firing away at the same time, then I could just do like the others.

We parked the van in a dark spot in the parking lot and turned the motor off. Our nerves tensed as we waited. And waited. We restarted the van motor a few times as the interior cooled down in the cold.

We had been told the guy usually showed up 20 minutes in advance to grab a beer, but by 11:50 p.m., he still hadn't arrived. Two of us got out of the van, staying in the shadows, to see if we had missed his car somewhere. We caught a glimpse of his girl staring at our van from the bar's windows. I was sure she saw us get back in the vehicle. Or she had noticed the van's running lights or exhaust smoke when the motor was running.

By midnight, I was tense. We'd been there an hour and no target. This isn't normal, I kept thinking.

"She saw us," I finally said to the other two. "If she did, she probably called her boyfriend. Let's get out of here. If she tipped him off, we'll be the ones caught in an ambush."

"You're right," Bull answered. "Let's go before we get fucked."

We peeled away. I was thankful the guy didn't show up. The next day, I saw Renaud and explained what happened.

"I'm sorry. I didn't want to let you down."

He brushed it off. "That's OK. You did the right thing. What's important is you went down there without questioning me. That's what counts. There will be others."

In December 1995, my brother and I accompanied Johnny Plescio to Montreal's courthouse for protection. Court was particularly dangerous because our rivals knew when we had to make appearances and could be waiting outside. And we couldn't risk being arrested with guns on us. Johnny was to be sentenced in the afternoon for threatening a police officer, so we got there a bit early and went for lunch in the fifth-floor cafeteria. We sat at a table in the back of the room to avoid drawing attention. Nearby tables contained court clerks and a few lawyers.

Within five minutes, we noticed six guys coming toward us. I looked at Robert, who was thinking the same thing.

"Here we go, buddy," I told Johnny.

The insults flew. Then the fists. And finally the chairs. We brawled until courthouse officers pulled us apart. Our assailants turned out to be Jokers.

Police accused us all with disturbing the peace, but couldn't lay assault charges against us or the Jokers because we refused to file charges against each other. Johnny, my brother, and I got $250 fines.

Not long after, we held a party at a steakhouse to promote someone to full-patch member. Following tradition, the identity of the person was kept a surprise until the event. That night, Yvon Roy became a full patch. He never went through the prospect stage, but was promoted to the top because he was respected and making shitloads of cash from drugs.

It was another disappointment for me, since I was hoping to become a prospect. I contented myself with a plate of 16-ounce roast beef and numerous Bloody Caesars. Renaud stood up after the cheering ended for Yvon.

"There's one last promotion," he said.

I went back to my drink, figuring it was anyone but me.

"Peter," Renaud said, walking toward me, "you've been unanimously voted a prospect."

I was dumbfounded as people cheered, realizing the guys had played me good.

"And I'm your godfather," Renaud added before the traditional biker handshake, a grip of the hand and two pats on the back.

He handed me a triple shot of grappa. Tradition ordered that I drink the vile alcoholic concoction from Italy for the rest of the night until I passed out or couldn't stand. All the others at the dinner slapped me on the back and gave me big bear hugs. I thought of all I'd gone through: losing everything in my drugged-out years, living on welfare, and even trying to kill myself twice. This moment was like a rebirth. I'd never felt happier.

Yvon ordered a bottle of Dom Perignon for each of us and we sat together as Renaud kept sending over drinks. He was determined to see me pass out. At one point, I started gagging, and others helped me to the washroom, where I puked up my roast beef. I was there so long that Renaud sent Christian the accountant to get me.

"Hey," I slurred, "these floors are really crooked."

People laughed. "There's nothing wrong with the floors," Christian said.

I went back to drinking.

"OK, everybody," Renaud said at one point. "We're leaving."

"I don't want to," I responded petulantly. Other initiations had ended with most of us partying in clubs and afterwards heading to a hotel, renting an entire floor, and calling prostitutes.

"We're not going home," Renaud assured me. "We're going to a strip club."

"Lead the way," I said, standing drunkenly.

Other hangarounds had been doing security inside and outside, but Renaud grabbed two more and told them to follow me everywhere. One was my brother, Robert.

The 30 of us walked into the Bar Adulte strip club wearing our Rock Machine sweaters. The party continued, but without Mon-Mon because he had parole conditions forbidding him from being in bars. At one point, I attacked the cigarette machine, futilely shaking it to get free smokes. One of the owners came over with a pack and a drink to get me to leave the machine alone. Renaud laughed.

We went to another strip club, the Venus, where I was well known. Our rowdy group was mostly left alone though a few police officers followed me and my bodyguards to the washroom. One cop was a small woman who had a mouth. I laughed in her face. "You guys are too small to do anything," I taunted them. "Call for backup."

When we came out of the washroom, she was still there.

"Hey," I yelled, getting her attention. "Go next door to the Dunkin Donuts for a doughnut and coffee, be a good girl."

I kept drinking as the guys paid for strippers to dance at our table. The alcohol makes it impossible to remember why, but at one point I had one of the dancers in what was supposed to be a friendly headlock. Renaud was in hysterics.

As another girl danced for me, I puked all over her naked body.

Renaud found that even funnier. Then I did it again on another dancer.

My brother and another guy drove me home, pushing and pulling me up the stairs to my second-floor apartment. I'd moved there recently after Sylvie left me. She stormed out of my life after overhearing Mon-Mon asking me about my latest conquest when we were talking once in the basement. I was now living with a drug user named Caroline, who opened the door for my brother.

"Here," Robert said, grinning. "This is yours."

They left me sitting on the floor in the apartment's entrance. I was happy I hadn't passed out. That little victory over Renaud was swirling through my mind as I crawled to bed.

When I finally showed myself at the clubhouse a few days later, everyone remarked about how gallantly I was able to puke. Since the Venus was one of my hangouts, I went back to apologize. As soon as I walked in, the two owners came over and told me there were no hard feelings.

"Are they working, the ones I threw up on?"

Both girls came over, I apologized, and they accepted. I offered to take them to dinner sometime to pay them back. One wanted to go right away.

"Go ask your boss," I said.

One of the owners came over and smiled.

"It's all right. Just have her back by Friday."

"Friday? Today's only Wednesday. Why are you saying Friday?"

"You'll see."

The dancer joined us, and put her arm in mine.

"You know," she said, "throwing up on me is going to cost you more than dinner."

We rented a hotel room and spent the next two days there.

CHAPTER 10

After I bought 100 grams of the best hash I could find, Bull and I cut some of the chewy mass into dice-sized pieces. Each piece went into a condom, which we tied tightly. We enclosed the condom inside a balloon. They looked like oversized grapes.

Bull, in and out of jail his whole life, was telling me drugs made the difference between doing good time and torture. Some of the hash was for our use and the rest could be sold for double what it usually goes for outside the walls.

Bull swallowed about 14 of the grapes. I forced down the other seven with water. That left about half of the hash. Bull made two lengthy cylinders out of what remained, covered them with plastic wrap, and stuffed them up his ass. His years inside made it nothing special for him, but I refused to try it.

We were preparing to head to jail. The high of being named a prospect had been tempered with assault and extortion charges still hanging over me for what happened in Chicoutimi. Gary, our lawyer, made it clear the testimony of the dealer and his neighbors was enough to sink us. I thought about whether it was possible to silence the dealer, but he was too well protected by police. After pocketing the $10,000 I paid to represent us, our lawyer said the most we would do is a year each. We told Gary to plead us "guilty" but make sure we did our time in Montreal, not in Chicoutimi where the Hells ruled everything.

After swallowing the grapes, Bull and I drove to Chicoutimi's courthouse the next day, and were sentenced to seven months each. Off we went to the police station while the local jail tried to figure out what to do with us. We refused to do all our time in protection, which would have meant we'd only be let out of our cells for an hour a day. A sergeant came to see me.

"We have a problem," he said.

"What problem?"

"We got a call from police in Montreal saying you and Corbeil smoke drugs," he said. The guard then pointed to my stomach. "Montreal police believe there is a good chance you are carrying some."

"I don't know what you're talking about."

He eyed me.

"OK," he said. "If you say so."

Bull and I were placed in separate cells that afternoon. By the time dinner rolled around, we were starving, expecting the usual crappy food found in police stations—stale sandwiches. But a cop went to Bull with a hot plate of shepherd's pie.

When my own steaming plate came a bit later, I left it alone and yelled at Bull.

"Don't eat it. It's drugged."

Too late. His 300-pound frame had been begging for food and he had already finished the plate. Twenty minutes later, he was yelling in pain. The hidden laxative had worked.

"Le Gros Anglais, I'm in shit."

I laughed despite knowing I was about to lose 80 grams of good hash.

He ended up shitting everything out, possibly into his own pants since there was no toilet or even a bucket in the cell.

A half-hour later, a guard took me to the sergeant's office.

"Sit down," he said.

He tossed a shit-stained plastic bag containing Bull's grapes and plugs on his desk.

"Look," he said. "Your buddy cooperated with us."

"No, he didn't. He was hungry."

"You're hungry, too. Why didn't you eat your food?"

"Do I look stupid?" I answered, a bit of menace creeping into my voice. "You had just told us you had information that we had drugs in our bodies."

He smiled.

"So what you are saying is you didn't eat because you were afraid of the consequences?"

He smiled. "Since your buddy had drugs, we are convinced you do, too," he added.

"So what? You can't prove any of this."

"Not now," he retorted. "But you will have to shit sooner or later. We are going to throw you in the hole until you do."

"Fine."

"If you want to cooperate, you know what to do."

They took me to a windowless cell in the basement. By the faint light on the ceiling, I could see a bed, a sheet, and a bucket. No toilet. No water. The smell couldn't be described; I didn't want to spend the night. So I sat on the bucket and cooperated with police.

I put my pants back on and then crouched on my knees. My hand went into the bucket, sloshing around until I grabbed four of the seven balloons. There was no water, but there was toilet paper. I used it to remove as much shit as possible from the grapes.

I took one, lifted it over my head, closed my eyes and swallowed it. The smell almost caused it to come back up. Somehow it stayed down. Then another and another and another.

Getting up, I went to the door.

"Guard!"

One came over and I handed him the bucket.

"That's all?" he asked, looking inside.

"Ya. I had just a few in case my buddy and I got separated."

He took me back upstairs and left me with Bull, who was moping.

"I'm sorry," he said. "I was hungry and it didn't cross my mind they would spike our food."

I looked at him with a smile.

"We won't be able to sell anything," I said, "but at least we'll have something to smoke."

"What do you mean? I just saw you come out of the hole."

"I didn't give up all of it."

Bull figured it out and couldn't stop laughing. The next day, we were taken to the local provincial jail and put in protection. We told the guard we refused such treatment. He said it was only for the night, until we went before a judge again on charges of drug possession. It was the same judge who had sentenced us a few days earlier. He lengthened our seven-month sentences by another three. Back at the jail, the guards showed us consent forms saying we refused protection and that we had been advised our decision could lead to injuries or death. We signed.

The guards took us into an eerily empty range where we would stay until arrangements were made to transfer us to Montreal. Not one inmate in sight. We walked to the cell we would share and left our bags. Wandering a bit, we ended up in the TV room where we sat in a corner, our backs to the wall. Before relaxing, we placed chairs in front of us as barricades, making it hard for a crowd to rush us. We sat that way until other inmates appeared, walking slowly, some with eyes locking on ours, mouths saying nothing. I counted about ten of them. Bull and I talked softly, agreeing that only two or three appeared to have the guts to attack us. The others couldn't look us in the eyes. We were outnumbered but no longer shit-scared. I slept well that first night, but Bull couldn't because of my snoring.

At breakfast, we ate with one eye on our plates and the other on our fellow inmates. Before we finished, all except one got up and left. The one who was left was in his early fifties. He came over and sat down.

"My name is Adel," he said in a friendly way.

"What do you want?" I asked. "And what is going on?"

"We all know who you are. I've got to admit, you have a lot of balls coming in here."

"Listen," I said, "we are only going to be here for a week until our transfer to Montreal comes through. The war is on the streets. Not here."

"The war is out there," he agreed, "but two Rock Machine in an area controlled by the Hells is making them look bad. These guys," he said, gesturing to the way the others had left, "are part of Satan's Guards."

Bull stood up.

"If they have something to prove, tell them to make a move. We are not going into protection."

"Why did they all leave?" I asked.

"They're meeting," Adel said. "They asked me to convince you two to walk out of here on your own power, to ask for protection."

"We are not going anywhere," I said. "We are Rock Machine and if they want us out of here, they're going to have to make us leave, if they have the balls."

Adel put his hands on the table to get up.

"I'll try to talk to them, but you guys are out of your minds."

Bull and I sat there, unsure of what would happen next. Ten minutes later, all ten trooped back. We stood up, clenching our fists. They spread out in front of us, saying nothing. But Adel broke away and came next to Bull and I.

"These two guys are here to do their time," he said. "They'll be out of here in a week. The war is on the streets, not in jail."

Adel pointed to the others. "How many of you have gang status to fight for?"

Three said they were supporters, but not full members.

"Then how come you have nothing to smoke from your friends outside the walls? If you are respected by those with patches, where are they now?"

Those without status were nodding their heads, repeating Adel's arguments. It became clear Adel was bringing most of the drugs into the range.

One of those nodding turned to Adel, pointing at us.

"We'll leave them alone if they keep their distance and don't talk to us."

"Fine," I said. "We just want to do our time."

"Well," Adel said, "that leaves you three. If you still feel the same way as before, do what you want."

But now the odds were three against two, and Bull and I were not small. He outweighed two of them put together. Nothing happened for 30 seconds. After a final glare at us, the remaining three walked away.

A few hours later, Adel called us into his cell and lit up a hash joint with us.

"You guys are far from home, and I'm sure you don't know anybody who could bring in anything for you."

"We had some," I said, "but we ended up losing it."

Bull told him the whole embarrassing story. Our conversation and laughter drew the others. They asked Adel if he could spare a joint or two.

"If you want me to give you something, you are going to have to smoke it with us," he said.

They looked at each other. The allure of drugs overrode any war. They shook our hands and introduced themselves.

One night during our stay there, Bull and I were locked in our cell when we heard cars roar up. The noise intensified until the vehicles stopped by the jail. The drivers revved their engines.

"Hey," we heard when the noise lessened, "what the fuck is going on in there?"

"How come they're not dead?" another person yelled.

We were safe at the time because all the inmates were locked in their cells, but we didn't know if that visit would change our new friends back into enemies.

"Holy shit," Bull said to me when the cars left after a bit more yelling. "You know what? Anybody could just throw a bomb at us off the street."

The next night, another car stopped outside and honked its horn. "Kill them," someone yelled. "What are you waiting for?"

Bull and I sat in the dark, our eyes open. We hardly slept until our transfer to Montreal a few days later.

CHAPTER 11

The same turf war between the Hells and Rock Machine outside the walls of Montreal's Bordeaux jail was also going on inside. The Hells were gaining control of B Wing, while all known Rock Machine followers and sympathizers were sent to C Wing. C Wing became known as the Jungle.

Bull and I were led there after being transferred from Chicoutimi. Thirty people huddled around the gate, waiting to welcome us. Bull was a regular in jail, and already knew many of the guys. We were greeted with handshakes and pats on the back.

"We knew you were coming so we prepared your cell," one guy told me. "We washed and painted it. You have the nicest one in the place."

Playing cards at a table nearby was Serge Cyr, known as Merlin in the gang. Merlin had gone in a few weeks before us on a PCP charge. He was with Stéphane Morgan, nicknamed Ti-Cul, which means little guy. I quickly learned those two full patches were among the elite in the wing, though they preferred to stay low. Also in the wing was Michel Bertrand, known as Jumeau, the French word for twin. His twin brother Daniel had been one of the earliest casualties in the war, right after Sylvain Pelletier. Jumeau went on a rampage after his brother's death and he effectively ran the Palmers, an east-end gang that was aligned with the Rock Machine against the Hells.

I was taken to my cell on the first floor. The place had just been painted light blue, and it had a new sink and toilet bowl. The entire wall opposite my cot was covered by the Rock Machine eagle painted in black. Above the door, the artist had stenciled the word "Palmers," in reference to Jumeau's gang. On the wall by the window, I had "Alliance," as well as the initials A.L.V. A.L.M. They stood for *A la vie, à la mort*.

I looked at the eagle for what seemed a long time. It did so much to boost my morale. Such work meant I commanded respect. This was my first real jail sentence, and I'd gone in unsure whether it would be one long battle of fists and kicks. But I was among friends. I walked out of the cell and found Bull.

"I've got the suite," I said, pride escaping my voice.

"Well, I fucking don't."

Bull's cell was on the third floor. When he showed it to me, I recoiled. It was grimy, and the paint job looked like it predated Hitler. He didn't care much, and said he liked the quiet of the top floor.

We went downstairs and got to know our fellow inmates, including a few black members of the Palmers. One rolled up a big "bat," a hash joint, and passed it to us.

The wing housed 190 prisoners over three floors. The top two floors just contained cells, though the main floor I was on also had some tables. Outside the wing was the cafeteria, which we used for each meal. We never met inmates in other wings because they ate at different times. I quickly learned most of the action happened in our wing's basement, nicknamed the submarine. After our cells were unlocked at 7 a.m. each morning, the guards opened the door downstairs to the submarine, and then never descended again until locking up at night. The submarine route began with a circular bank of pay phones for those calling outside. After the phones, we walked down a corridor to the laundry room to the left and the showers and toilets on the right. Just after the showers was the TV room. On the other side, past the laundry room, was the weight room. After that space, we had a recreation area with two pool tables, another for Ping-Pong, a picnic table, and a few benches to lounge on. Then the door to the outside exercise yard.

After a night's rest in my suite, I got down to business. Others were bringing drugs into the wing, but it was mostly for their own use. I saw things bigger. I asked around and found inmates who were getting unescorted weekend passes.

"Hey," I told an older guy, "you got a code this weekend, right?"

"Yeah."

"Go see a friend of mine outside. He'll give you some of my pot to bring back. Whatever you get through, I'll give you a quarter of it. What do you say?"

He'd done it before, so he agreed. I placed a collect call, the only way you can use the prison pay phones, telling Ben that a guy would be coming around. Then I gave the prisoner Ben's address.

When Sunday evening rolled around, I was nervous. I didn't know if the guy would make it past the guards. If they suspected him at all, he'd get thrown into the hole until his body gave up its holdings. But the guy finally showed up, all smiles.

"No problem at all," he said.

He headed to the toilet in the basement, where he shat on a garbage bag. Out came four plugs containing 224 grams of pot, a half pound. He took off the top layer of shit-stained Saran wrap and brought me the plugs. I was amazed. Each was the size of those jumbo BBQ wieners.

"What? Are you gay?" I said half in jest.

"No," he responded, a bit proud. "I've just been doing this a long time."

I gladly gave him his 56 grams. The rest—what I didn't keep for personal use—I sold for $30 a gram, making more than $5,000 selling pot that cost only $1,000 outside. The problem was getting paid because money wasn't allowed behind bars and I wasn't willing to wait until a guy finished his time to collect. So I set up a system with a Verdun girl I knew outside while an inmate took care of the accounting for me. When a guy bought a gram, I'd ask him to pick a random number code, say 8. His debt was $30 and his code was .08, making $30.08. I'd give him the bank-account number of the Verdun girl and tell him to have someone outside deposit $30.08. I used her account because I didn't have one. The girl would go to the bank at the end of the day. The extra pennies would tell her and my accountant which debt to cross off.

I wanted a backup plan in case the guards got too vigilant with guys on weekend passes. I discovered the guy who cuts the grass outside Bordeaux was in C Wing. He agreed to help and told me where he would be cutting the next day, so I called one of my guys outside.

"Prepare one for tomorrow," I said over the phone, being careful not to say too much. "Get someone to throw it onto the grass near the bus shelter. Do it before 10 a.m. and make sure only the guy sees you throw it."

The landscape guy went out on the riding mower, saw the plastic-wrapped plug, and picked it up. While he mowed far from the guard towers, he pretended to scratch his butt by putting his hand down the back of his sweat pants. What he was really doing was ramming the plug up his ass. He never got caught.

My stash of drugs was hidden with trusted inmates who aroused the least suspicion. They used empty toothpaste containers, shampoo bottles, and shaving cream cans. Some carried the drugs up their butts to make sure they wouldn't be stolen because the cells were left open all day.

After a while, a number of people were bringing in plugs after weekend passes, but much less than the amount of my friend who was able to accommodate four hot dogs. Most people could only get in an ounce or two. Mondays were usually reserved for weighing out the parcels into salable sizes. Since there were no scales inside, we improvised using a cigarette-rolling machine. It was turned upside down with a ruler across the top. Plastic cups used to ration pills to sick inmates were put at each end. A cigarette, which weighs a gram, went in one. Pot was put in the other cup until the scale balanced. If someone could afford less than a gram, I would use matches. Each match weighs a point, or one-tenth, of a gram. Five matches would equal half a gram.

I used some of my drugs to pay a guy to clean my cell and do my laundry. I also fronted some inmates money to make their time go easier. Rules allow an inmate's family to deposit $120 a week so he can buy cigarettes, coffee, soda, and junk food from the jail canteen. But those with no family or with girlfriends on welfare could afford little. So I set up canteens in some cells by fronting poorer guys $120 each. They used it to buy as much as possible and stored the goods in their cells. When other inmates ran out of cash, they would go see these guys. If they took a bag of chips, they had to return two. I didn't really do it for profit, since my junk-food needs were being met by money Mon-Mon's wife was depositing in my canteen fund. I would just wander in once in a while and take a bag of chips or soft drink for free. Since the other guys knew I was Rock Machine, it looked good to be treating people with generosity. It was my way of recruiting.

Mon-Mon was taking care of things outside, collecting on our dealers. He also made sure my girlfriend, Caroline, was doing OK.

"Paradis, something is weird with that girl, *tabarnac*," he told me during one of my regular collect calls.

"What's wrong?"

"I went by your fucking place the other day. Your video was missing. Then I went back and the goddamn TV was gone."

"What?" I yelled into the receiver. "What is that coked-up bitch up to?"

"I don't know," he chuckled, "but I think she's turning your place into a furniture store."

"Kick her out," I said, seething. "Take my stuff and put it in storage. Kick the dumb bitch out."

He told me he'd take care of it. And he did. I never saw Caroline again.

In jail, a few guys were brewing moonshine, called baboche. Bull, Ti-Cul, and I found one whose product was sweet, and got him to supply us regularly with ten ounces a week in exchange for hash. I nicknamed him the Cooker. We'd help him by stuffing our pockets with sugar packets from the cafeteria and giving him apples, oranges, and banana peels. He also insisted we steal ketchup packages, saying the stuff was essential for the taste. When the Cooker finished a batch, he'd distribute most of it in water bottles, keeping a bit to start the yeast process in his next mixture. During the day, when guards weren't around, he'd have tubes running from bucket to bucket in his cell. Just before lockup, he'd put the liquid in double-wrapped garbage bags, stuff them in boxes, and hide it all inside metal wall panels.

The panels were also used to hide sharpened spears or bats made by sawing off horizontal bars in the prison bedboards and covering one end with tape to make a handle. Some inmates carried them down a pant leg as protection. The guards finally got wise and removed whatever bars remained in the bedboards before they, too, could be turned into weapons.

Before I went to jail, Renaud had taken me aside.

"Make sure C Wing stays Rock Machine," he said.

I promised him I would. And I became involved in making sure none of our enemies tried to sneak into the wing. Before me, some people made newcomers stomp on pictures of Mom Boucher to prove their allegiances. They faced beatings or being stabbed with homemade knives made from sharpened metal if they refused. But I preferred another method to find Hells sympathizers.

When one suspicious guy was brought in, a dozen of us took him down to the submarine, to a little area off the weight room. We formed a semi-cirle around him. His face was nervous, and his eyes darted to the walls. They were covered in blood—splatters, smears, and dots, all reminders of previous interrogations.

"Look," I started, menacingly. "This is Rock Machine turf. If you are with the Hells, you can walk out of here now if you admit it. We'll let you go, no problem. But if you are and don't admit it, we will find out, and then you will be carried out of here by the guards when we are finished with you. So listen carefully, are you H.A.?"

"No, *tabarnac*, not me," the guy said, glancing at our faces.

The interrogations were done to make sure the Hells didn't sneak in its people and then stage a coup once they were enough in numbers. They'd tried before.

"OK," I answered, motioning to a guy beside me with a notepad. "Then we are going to ask you some questions. Don't lie, because we are going to have our lawyers outside check all this."

That was a bluff, but it worked in making guys feel our power.

"What's your name?" I asked politely.

"Joseph."

"Where you from?"

"Hochelaga-Maisonneuve."

One of the guys near me was from the east end, so he stepped forward and listened closer.

"What's your last name, address, social insurance number?"

He gave them.

"What are you in for?"

"Selling pot."

"Who was your lawyer?"

That would often tell us something since the Hells had lawyers working almost exclusively for them. So did the Rock Machine. The next questions were about whom he bought drugs from, and where he sold. If the bars were known to belong to the H.A., the local guy in our group could tell us. Now guys in the crowd fired off questions, trying to see if his story held together. I looked at our local guy, who shook his head.

"You're a fucking liar," the local guy yelled.

"No, I'm not." His face was sweating.

I was closest, so I swung my fist into his face. When he fell, the others joined in with knuckles and feet. It didn't take long to reduce him to a silent, broken mess. Some of the guys then carried him to the garbage containers and tossed him in. We walked away.

The guards found the guy when they were doing a count of prisoners at the end of the day. He was taken to the infirmary and never brought back. A prison official came to collect his personal effects.

The interrogations were pretty regular when I first transferred in. Some would admit their links to the Hells right after seeing the bloody wall. They would get a few punches and then be allowed to ask for protection from guards. One guy ran as the questioning was getting abusive. He hoped to make it up the stairs to the guard's office, but a few of the guys knocked him off his feet before he got past the laundry room. They carried him into the washroom for his pummeling. He also went into a garbage bin. One of the Palmers got his nickname, Bing-Bang, because he liked being the first to throw a mean punch in those interrogations.

We were on guard for anyone with even the slightest hint of Hells affiliation, even if a guy was just buying a few grams from a Hells dealer. This was war. I felt nothing for the beating victims. Since I had to protect my reputation in the gang, I couldn't look soft. We blamed prison officials for what we did since they must have known these guys would be in danger of being harmed by us. But our jailers kept sticking them with us because the newcomers might not be important enough to figure on police lists as suspected H.A. supporters. Our methods found them out faster than the warden. After a few more beatings, the guards called me in. Snitches had told them I was one of the people responsible.

"What are you guys doing?" a sergeant asked me.

I shrugged. "Hey, it's your fault. Just keep the Hells out of here. We can't guarantee their safety."

"Leave them alone. Just let them do their time."

I looked at the guy.

"Like I said, we can't guarantee their protection."

The prison kept sending us guys, and we kept dunking them in the garbage bins.

After another half dozen, I was again called to an office. On the table were two files with pictures.

"You know those guys?" the sergeant asked.

"No," I said after reading the confidential jail files, and glancing at the photos. "They're from outside Montreal. Can I get some guys in here to look at them?"

The sergeant looked at the other guard.

"OK," he said.

I found two guys from the same region as the men in the files. They looked at the files, saw the details of their crimes, and said the guys were neutral. Nothing to do with the Hells.

"They can come in?" the sergeant asked, looking at me.

"Yeah, no problem."

From then on, they showed us the files of newcomers and stopped fishing inmates out of the garbage bins.

Once in a while, the guards would crack down on my drug couriers. Guards know the drug trade exists in prison even if they don't always see it, but they are more worried about hard drugs like cocaine and heroin than what I was bringing in, which made people mellow out and do their time with little fighting. I didn't appreciate my supply line being interrupted. After one crackdown, I sent out a special order for PCP, which turns docile men into stampeding elephants. When I got the powder, I spiked the communal coffee keg with it.

"Hey," I stopped an inmate, "tell everyone we have special coffee."

Word got around, and many of the poorer inmates took advantage of the free drug. I sold the rest of the PCP at very low prices. About three-quarters of the wing took part on the sole warning that they couldn't fight amongst themselves. Then I waited.

One guy, Patrick, cleaned the whole range while high and even tried to paint everything before we stopped him. He was an exception. The usual reaction was more along the line of Leon, nicknamed The Trigger since he was a holdup specialist. His normal demeanor was volatile; he'd fly off the handle for the least offense. On PCP, he became worse. His kick was sending a steady stream

of insults at guards within earshot. Others would spit on the floor
as the screws walked by. Some would infuriate our keepers by
ignoring everything they said or laughing in their faces and swearing at them. The wing resembled a drunk tank, full of babbling
men looking for any reason to fight. I lay on my bunk, smoking a
hash joint, when a guard came around lunchtime.

"Paradis, the sergeant wants to see you."

I put the joint out in the toilet and flushed it. The guard pretended not to notice.

The sergeant looked worried when we arrived.

"What's happening? This can't continue."

I shrugged my shoulders.

"The guys are upset. Too much tension."

The sergeant said nothing.

"Remove the tension," I continued. "There is only one way to do
that in prison."

"You want us to do nothing about the drugs?"

"No one is pushing cocaine or heroin in our crew," I responded.
"So lay off."

The crackdown ceased for a while. When it resumed, I did the
PCP trick again. When the coffee was spiked, many of the guys
would often do double takes, thinking they saw a woman parading
her sexuality through the range. It was Mimi, a guy who wanted to
be a girl. In jail, we call them he/shes or transtesticles. Mimi, in jail
for being a downtown prostitute, would don lipstick, eyeshadow,
and do her hair when the PCP was free, hoping to convince a
strung-out guy to let her give him a blowjob. She annoyed many,
but I used her as a spy among the other inmates. In exchange, I
gave her two grams of PCP every week. As a joke, I'd sometimes
get her to go pinch a guy's butt. She'd race back on her lady's san-
dals to my cell for protection as an enraged inmate pursued, yelling
obscenities. I'd roll the pissed-off guy a joint to calm him down.

One day, my accountant, a guy named Stretch, came into my cell
asking for PCP. I refused, telling him he was already fucked up

enough on a mixure of the powder and moonshine. He went away angry. Fifteen minutes later, Mimi came in and tossed her hair around.

"Peter," she said in a syrupy voice. "Can you give me a few grams on credit?"

Mimi had already gone through her pay for her snitching duties.

"No way," I said, not bothering to get off my bed.

"Please." Her voice became pathetic. "I'm good for it. Please."

This was the first time she'd persisted.

"What's going on with you tonight?" I asked.

"If I tell you, will you give me two grams?"

"Why do you want that much for? You're not going to do it all by yourself."

"OK, I'll tell you. Stretch asked me to come see you. He wants it."

"Why would you care what he wants?"

She hesitated, and then blurted it out.

"I made a deal with him. If I'm able to get him two grams, he'll let me give him a blowjob."

I shot upright in bed.

"Are you serious?"

She nodded. "He's waiting in my cell right now."

I couldn't stop chuckling while Mimi kept imploring me to help her.

"I promise I'll pay you back, but you got to give me your word you won't tell him what I just told you."

"I won't say anything," I said, "but I got to see this for myself. I'll wait a couple of minutes and then I'll just walk into your cell. That way he won't suspect you told me."

She agreed.

"This is too good," I said. "By the way, this is on the house."

I handed over two grams.

For a moment, I thought about stopping the joke, but then decided Stretch could use a lesson. Though I was smoking about

The fatal bomb under Sylvain Pelletier's Jeep Grand Cherokee on October 28, 1994, is seen as one of the starting points of the violent war between the Hells Angels and the Rock Machine.

ALLÔ POLICE!

ALLÔ POLICE!

(*top*) The split-level fieldstone home that became the Jokers' bunker in Saint-Luc, a town south of Montreal. The building and the car in front show the damage done during the failed attempt by four Rock Machine soldiers to demolish the place on September 21, 1995.

(*bottom*) The remnants of Marc Dubé's Jeep after a planted bomb sent shrapnel for 50 meters, killing 11-year-old Daniel Desrochers on August 9, 1995. It is believed a Hells Angels bomber thought the vehicle belonged to a Rock Machine drug dealer.

Renaud Jomphe, the man who brought Peter
Paradis into the Rock Machine. He often wore
sunglasses, even while indoors.

(*top*) The Rock Machine's Montreal clubhouse was bought for less than $100,000 but the gang spent almost a million dollars on renovations. It was located on a side street in a seedy part of town. The brick-walled courthouse and back alleyway was home to three vicious dogs.

(*bottom*) On October 1, 1995, a bomb planted by the Hells Angels exploded outside the Rock Machine's Montreal Clubouse, smashing in the door and windows, and blowing off the ornamental façade near the roof.

(*top*) The October 1, 1995, explosion caused no structural damage and the bunker was quickly repaired.

(*bottom*) The interior damage done by the bomb.

The flowers and elaborate wreaths show the respect accorded Rock Machine founder Renaud Jomphe after he was assassinated in a Chinese restaurant on October 18, 1996. The large "A" to the right came from the Alliance, a group of drug dealers allied with the Rock Machine. The Palmers were another group working with the gang in the east end. The Rock Machine's eagle head is above the open coffin.

The shattered driver's window of Pierre (Ti-Bum) Beauchamps' Ford Explorer shows how a Hells Angels hit team shot the Rock Machine-friendly independent on a busy commercial street in downtown Montreal on December 20, 1996.

An ambulance attendant looks after Peter Paradis after he is shot at an intersection in Verdun on August 10, 1998. The woman talking to the Montreal police officer is the one who comforted him. A shirtless Daniel (Poutine) Leclerc stands behind Peter. Peter's truck is directly behind him, where it came to rest against the streetlight.

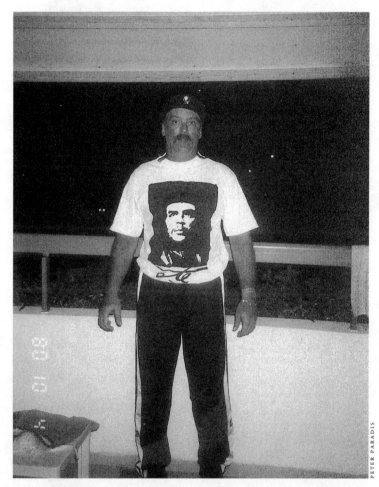

Robert (Toute-Toute) Léger on vacation in Cuba. The Rock Machine member let Peter Paradis recuperate at his chalet in Quebec's Eastern Townships. Léger was later killed at the same place.

(*top*) Johnny Plescio had a rural home north of Montreal, and was known to stash cash in the the nearby woods.

(*bottom*) Richard (Bam-Bam) Lagacé, well known for his explosive temper, wears a Bandidos shirt.

(*top*) Richard (Bam-Bam) Lagacé's coffin is draped with flowers and photos of his loved ones. There is also a picture of him with his motor-cycle. He was shot outside a health club on July 31, 1998.

(*bottom*) For the benefit of a crime-tabloid photographer, Peter Paradis (left) and another biker stand with their backs to the camera in front of the coffin of Richard (Bam-Bam) Lagacé.

(*top*) Johnny Plescio was the first Plescio brother killed in the biker war. He was shot at home on September 8, 1998. The Rock Machine believed his assassins cut his cable TV line and when he got up from his chair his silhouette could be seen out the window, giving the gunman a clear shot. Before the casket was closed, a gang member slipped a *Playboy* magazine into the casket to keep him company.

(*left*) Another floral arrangement at Johnny Plescio's funeral shows how close the Rock Machine and the Bandidos were becoming.

A floral arrangement at Johnny Plescio's funeral used part of the Bandido's slogan—"Bandidos Forever, Forever Bandidos"—along with Johnny's name.

Full-patch Rock Machine member Tony Plescio was killed on October 1, 1999, in front of his wife and child outside a McDonald's restaurant.

ten hash cigarettes a day, I stayed far away from the hard stuff. I left my cell still in stitches.

"What are you laughing for?" one guy asked me.

"You'll see for yourselves soon."

I slid the door to Mimi's second-floor cell open very quietly. Stretch was lying on her bunk and Mimi was hard at work.

"Do me a favor, Mimi," Stretch said, before he saw me. "Try not to look at me so I don't have to see your face."

He was eating a bag of chips at the same time. Then he saw me and his face dropped. I walked out of there laughing out loud, leaving the door wide open. Inmates again asked what's so funny.

"Oh, nothing."

The guys kept their eyes on Mimi's cell. I went back to my own. A sudden roar of laughter erupted. I popped my head out to see Stretch above me, walking out with his eyes glued on his shoes.

The next day he didn't show up for breakfast or lunch. I persuaded him to come out, let everyone get their laughs over with, and it would be forgotten. He came out. That night, before lights out, I sent a guy to leave a note on Stretch's bed signed by Mimi. "I had a great time. Hope we can do it again." With it was a bag of chips.

When the cell doors opened the next morning, I raced to Stretch's cell to make sure he didn't go after Mimi, telling him I was the culprit. He didn't touch the hard stuff again. Others weren't as lucky. Two guys overdosed in their cells from heroin. When that happened, it was lockdown until the guards could figure out what had happened, making sure the guys weren't murdered. No one was allowed out of their cells, and food was brought to us. Some lockdowns lasted for days.

Lockdown brought chaos as the guys were never told why they were cooped up. So they sent up a cacophony of shouts—boots banging on doors, cups rapping against metal, anything to make noise. Many of us tried to keep the drug routes open by tying shoelaces and attaching a gram of hash at the end in a sock. Or sheets would be used. We'd hang the sheets out the outside window and swing the contraption until the guy at the next cell window or two windows down could nab it. He would then use his own sheets to get the hash moving down the line.

During one of the lockdowns, I was sitting on my bed and getting tired of the noise.

"Guard," I yelled. He came over. "Take me to the sergeant."

He got me out.

"Can you do something?" the sergeant asked, gesturing toward the pounding and screaming.

"Dirty pigs. Screws," one guy yelled at just that moment. I smiled and responded.

"Maybe I can, but I want to know how long we are locked up for."

"Just until we finish our investigation. Two or three days."

"Let me go around and talk to people."

They let me wander the empty halls. I went up to the cells of people close to me and handed them hash. I told them I was doing this to keep peace, not because I was helping the screws. To others, I just yelled, "Shut your traps. It won't be long."

It worked. The guards used me like that again, including when one guy was stabbed. During lockdown, a few guys would use their sheets to swing hash past our wing's protection cells on the second floor and on to friendlier cells on the other side. Those protection cells housed about 20 people who couldn't mix with us because they were Hells supporters waiting for room to open up in B Wing, or guys who owed money. They were only let out for an hour a day to use the submarine and yard while the rest of us were locked up. Most of us would yell insults at them through the mesh windows in their cell doors. Others would spit while walking by. Some even urinated in a cup and splashed the piss through the screen. Some of the guys in protection put a sheet up over their door every morning to absorb most of the abuse. Others fought back. Before I got to Bordeaux, one of those protection cells housed a guy who would later become a famous informant against Hells kingpin Maurice (Mom) Boucher. When Stéphane Gagné was in C Wing, he fought back. He marinated his own urine and excrement together for more than a week before putting it in a shampoo bottle with a hollow marker taped to the opening. The marker acted like the barrel of a pistol. When Rock Machine members walked by his cell, he would squirt them with the mixture. He proudly called it "penmarde" in French—shitgun. Even he vomited sometimes when working with it.

Usually, the guys in protection let the hash swing by. But one time, some tried to grab the sheets. When that lockdown ended, a group of us went up there. We yelled that if they tried it again, we'd trick the guards into believing some of our guys needed protection. Then those guys could beat the shit out of the thieves during the precious hour a day all the protection cases got to use the submarine and outside yard together. The attempts stopped.

One day, Bull and I were playing pool in the submarine while some of the black Palmers were talking through a window covered in a mesh grill that connected our basement to part of B Wing's courtyard. They were trying to buy some good Jamaican hash from some independents in the Hells wing.

I spotted one black guy on the other side. I nudged Bull, who had a pool cue in his hand.

"He's a Rocker supporter."

"Eh?"

"Ya, he's the guy supposedly responsible for all the beatings in B Wing."

Bull went up to one of the Palmers.

"Hey," he said, "get that fucker you were talking to to come near the window."

Bull stood next to the grill with his pool stick as the Palmer yelled at the guy, asking if he had any hash. The Rocker supporter put his face close to the mesh.

Bull raised the pool cue and jammed the small end through the mesh, but it couldn't go far enough.

"Dirty fucker," Bull yelled simultaneously.

The other guy jumped back and swore. He looked at me, and said my last name and a few other words I couldn't catch. I was too busy laughing, as were most others on our side of the mesh.

One time, when Bull was high on PCP, I asked him to do one of his regular debt collections for me. I held out a piece of paper with the cell number of a guy who didn't pay me for my drugs. I hadn't finished speaking before he snatched the paper and stalked out of the TV room. The others present were silent, not knowing who the intended victim was.

After half a minute, I started laughing, and the others thought I was a psychopath. Being high on PCP made Bull a bit slow, so it took him 20 minutes to return. I heard him coming, cursing non-stop, his heavy steps accompanied by the clanging of metal. Finally, he stepped into the doorway and yelled.

"I got the fucker!" he said to whoops of laughter.

He held up a mop in one hand and a metal mop wringer in the other. He walked up to me as I gulped for air from laughing so hard. The piece of paper I'd given him had contained the number of the broom closet.

"Very funny," he said to me. "You got a good laugh?"

"Oh, yeah. As much as you laughed in Chicoutimi when I literally ate my own shit. Now we're even."

That made him join in. His eyes showed he was still fucked up on PCP, but he wasn't about to attack me. He looked around at the others enjoying themselves.

"I won't be made a fool for nothing," he said, looking at me. "Give me a fucking unpaid debt. Right now."

The room silenced. I gave him the list of debts. He closed his eyes and put his finger on the paper, finding a name. After walking over to a crowd of guys nearby, he spun one of them around and slugged him, splitting open his face and knocking him to the floor.

"Your money better be there tomorrow," he said. Then he eyed the rest. "And the rest of you better have your money by the end of the week. If not, well, you will get the same treatment."

Everybody paid.

My day of freedom came soon afterward. On September 5, 1996, I walked out of Bordeaux to find Renaud waiting in his car. He honked. Mon-Mon was keeping guard behind him in another vehicle. I went over to Renaud and threw my bag in.

"Salut, my nephew," Renaud said, all smiles.

Mon-Mon walked over.

"*Salut, mon partn.*" We often used the abbreviated English word as if it was French.

They both smiled at me.

"Things are rocking outside," Renaud said.

"Paradis, you'll be kept busy," chimed in Mon-Mon.

Mon-Mon went back to his vehicle and followed us to the Verdun local, a clubhouse Renaud had set up on Lesage Street. During the ride, Renaud told me about an attempt by the Hells to bomb it. They had driven a truck disguised as a Hydro-Québec vehicle up to the place, but the driver got scared and ran off after hitting a traffic sign a bit away. The truck contained 181 kilos of explosives.

Not long after, Mon-Mon handed me $10,000—my share of the business while I was inside. It was a bit skimpy, and I'd noticed he had a lot of new things—furniture, a few skidoos, all-terrain vehicles, a 16-foot fishing boat, and a Harley. I said nothing.

CHAPTER 12

"Put some money away," Renaud said. "What happens if you go back to prison?"

I gave him a cocky smile. I was leaning against the side of his car while he was sitting in the driver's seat. He must have noticed all the fingers on both of my hands were covered in diamond rings worth at least $30,000. One index finger was hidden by a ring in the shape of a dollar sign.

I didn't take him seriously. Sometimes he talked like a parent, taking his godfather role further than usual. I was adding about $1,500 every week to the huge roll of cash I liked to carry in my right pant pocket. It didn't stay there long. A lot was spent on fancy dinners with mistresses, clothes, and gifts to my family. And any time a boy would approach me on the street with chocolate bars to finance a club or hockey team, I'd usually buy the whole box. It was worth it to see the pure joy in his face. Often, I'd give him the cash and let him keep the chocolate as well. In my mind, the good times would never end.

"All I want is a palace, your car," as I said that to Renaud his ears perked up, "and a huge bank account. That's my goal."

"Makes sense," he said. "But why do you want my car?"

It was a stunning new 1996 black Riviera, worth $45,000.

"You're the one who told me not to let nothing stand in my way if I wanted something. I want your car. I'm in love with it and I want it."

He thought about it for a few seconds with an impish grin on his face.

"I'll tell you what," he said. "Give me two weeks and then I'll sell you my car. Just give me the deposit I gave to the dealer and you can finish the payments and the car will be yours."

"I'll do better," I said, whipping out the huge roll of cash. "I'll give you $5,000 right now to make sure you don't change your mind. When it comes time in two weeks, I'll give you the rest."

He smiled and took the cash while fishing his keys out of the ignition. He threw them at me.

"Take it for a spin to see if it handles like you expect."

This car was the only one like it in the area, and I felt powerful and rich to be behind the wheel. I kept seeing heads turn. Reluctantly, I cruised back to the corner were Renaud was standing. He leaned into the window.

"How do you like it?"

"It's a dream."

He got into the passenger side.

"Take me home," he ordered.

I looked at him, completely confused.

"You don't expect me to walk, do you?" He smiled. "It's yours now. Now take me home before I change my mind and make you wait two weeks."

I pulled away.

"Are you happy?"

"What do you think?" I replied.

"What if I told you I could make this a perfect day for you?" Renaud added.

"You already have."

But Renaud kept talking.

"I was supposed to buy this house from Ti-Bum on Dumas Street in Ville Emard. But I already own a house. I can't see what I would do with another. Turn the car around, we'll go see it now."

I felt like someone in a toothpaste commercial because I couldn't stop smiling during that ride. "What's it look like?"

"You'll see when we get there."

Renaud called Ti-Bum and told him to meet us in his driveway.

"Wait in the car," Renaud told me before talking with Ti-Bum.

The outside was huge and I was trying to imagine what it looked like inside. But how was I going to pay for it? The two called me over.

"Let's go inside," Renaud said.

I couldn't believe my eyes. Everything was brand new and it even had an indoor pool. Ti-Bum believed it was worth close to $200,000.

"It was built only a few years ago," he said with pride. "You won't see another house like it. Not around here anyway."

Two floors, a basement, and a garage for my new car. And a huge backyard with a garden and fountains made of stone and ceramics. We went to the indoor swimming pool.

"The only reason I am going to sell you this house is because Renaud is going to back you up and make sure I get my money," Ti-Bum said.

My look to Renaud must have been pretty hangdog because he immediately caught the drift of my thoughts.

"You will give him fifteen percent now and then fifteen hundred dollars a month until it is paid," Renaud said. "And don't worry, there is no interest."

"I can handle that," I said, for the first time thinking this dream could happen. I drove Renaud home.

"Why are you doing this?" I asked him.

"You deserve it," he said. "And I would rather see you putting your money in investments like this than see you blow away your money on nothing and get nothing in return. This is money in the bank. You could always sell the house to get out of a mess and have money to spare. I'm your godfather and it is my responsibility to make sure you make the right decisions. Remember where you were two years ago. I told you I believed in you. Look at you now. You are getting everything you always dreamed of."

"Thanks," I answered. "I would never be able to do this without you."

"Bullshit," he said. "You did all the work to get where you are. You and your partner. Remember how hard you had to work to get here, and don't let anybody take it away."

He got out of the car. "I'm out of town for a week. Don't get sloppy from all this good fortune."

The next day, I drove my new car to a meeting with Bull and Christian on the sidewalk in front of Pierrette Patate, a fry place. Bull and Christian were admiring the car as we talked. I then heard an annoying beep-beep sound. It was a delivery truck backing up, and heading straight for the Riviera.

"Hey!" I said with authority.

The truck kept coming.

"Hey!" My yell this time was much louder. Nothing.

"HEY!" I screamed as the truck's solid metal bumper crunched into the Riviera's engine hood, turning its smooth lines into crumpled tinfoil and shattering the headlights.

I strode toward the driver as he got out of his cab. The short man looked at my black Rock Machine sweater as I bounded at him.

"Oh fuck."

He began backing up slowly.

"Sorry. I'm really sorry."

"What the fuck were you doing?"

"Sorry, I didn't see you."

"You did this," I said, sweeping my hand at the mangled metal, "and you'll pay to fix it."

He looked stricken.

"I don't have insurance."

"What? If you don't pay for this, you have a *problem*."

I got his license number, name, and phone number before giving him the address of Ti-Bum's body shop, telling him the car would be fixed there and he better take care of it.

"Thank you," he said.

When I talked to Renaud next, he laughed.

"You managed to destroy a brand-new car in so short a time?"

We often met at a Chinese restaurant called Kim Hoa because Renaud had a fondness for Asian food. We had used the Lesage Street clubhouse in the past for meetings but Renaud shut it down because of the bombing attempt. Police had had to evacuate one hundred homes after finding the truck, and Renaud didn't want to put lives in danger by keeping the place open in our neck of the woods. The Hells had also staged a public appearance after the attempt, driving their motorcycles by the clubhouse to show their colors. They had a police escort, of course, to quell any trouble.

The purpose of our meetings was to exchange intelligence. Both Renaud and I had ordinary people helping us. A mailman used to tell us if he saw anything unusual on his route. So did numerous street prostitutes we knew. A city employee would call me whenever he saw police cars massing nearby Verdun city hall, readying to do a bust somewhere. When I heard from him, I'd call all my dealers to warn them something was up. There was also someone pretty important in Verdun politics who would do business with us. A waitress I knew would listen in on cops talking as they ate and report back whatever she overheard. And I had a friend at the license bureau who I was hoping to persuade to give me the addresses of various Hells people.

Renaud had words of caution for me one day at Kim Hoa.

"Be careful," he said as I prepared to leave. "Keep your eyes really open. I heard from someone that the H.A. are really on my case now."

In Quebec, lots of police officers called the Hells Angels "Les H.A.," saying it like "Hash Ahh." Renaud pronounced it "Crache Ahh" as an insult. He was saying they were worth spit and nothing more.

"If they are after me," he added, "they are after you."

A few days later, Renaud was again serious.

"We have a meeting next week with my friend," he said. He was talking about Harry (not his real name), a dealer who bought from me but was close to Renaud.

"What about?" I asked.

"He says you won't give him coke because he owes you a bit of money."

"A bit of money?" I said, my anger showing. "He owes me six thousand, and I never said I was going to give him nothing at all. I told him I was going to give him only half the usual amount until he pays his debt. I think that's fair."

Renaud sympathized with me. "I know he's a whiner but he's still my friend. The meeting is next week at 7 p.m."

The best way to describe Renaud's friend is by using the word "weasel." He was a small guy, and arrogant. He owned a tanning salon, and used it freely to be permanently tinted a horrible peach. Though he was in his forties, he dressed like a Florida retiree in a stretch jogging suit and jewelry. Too flashy for my taste. But he had one good point—he was one of my best dealers, pushing half a pound of coke a week. That is if he paid me.

"I don't know what he hopes to accomplish by dragging you into this," I pouted to Renaud, pissed the weasel went over my head.

"I'm not saying I'm siding with him," Renaud said. "But he deserves to be heard. I've always told you that if you make the right decision, I will back you up. No matter what. So let's just give him the benefit of being heard."

"OK." I calmed down.

"Show up for 6:30 p.m. We'll grab a bite to eat before he gets there."

I called Mon-Mon to ask him to come to the meeting. He couldn't stand Harry. The day of the meeting, we arrived a few minutes early while Renaud was finishing up with the gang's accountant and Alain Brunette. They were sitting at a table with Renaud facing the door, making sure to catch sight of anyone coming in. The Rock

Machine's lawyer, Gary Martin, was going to drop by after us to
pick up payment for legal work.

The only other people in the restaurant were a couple having
supper together and a man eating alone with his back to us.

Harry walked in and sat with Mon-Mon and me at a table next
to Renaud. We waited as Renaud kept talking with the others.

"I'm not changing my mind," I told Harry.

"We'll see," he said smugly while getting up to go to the washroom in the back of the eatery. Renaud called me over.

"Go with Alain," he told me. "Take a message to some guy in
Châteauguay." That usually meant put some heavy pressure on
someone.

"But what about the meeting?" I asked.

"I'll finish the meeting with that asshole," Mon-Mon broke in.

"Hey," Renaud barked. "Watch your mouth! He's still my
friend."

"I'm sorry," Mon-Mon said. "I just don't like him and he
doesn't do business straight."

Renaud turned to me. "Hurry up and get out of here. The faster
you leave, the faster you get back. You will have to rough somebody up."

By then, Harry was back from the bathroom. As I walked out the
front door, he was right behind me, telling Renaud he'd be back in
five minutes because he had to make an important phone call.

I left my Riviera parked on the street and got into Alain's truck.
As we headed for the Mercier Bridge, I spent some time telling him
what I thought of Renaud's friend. We were halfway across the
bridge when Alain got a call on his cell phone.

"Ya?"

His face turned serious.

"Oh ya? Check that out. Give me news," he said and hung up.

"What's up?" I asked.

"I don't know, *mon best*. There's been a shooting in Verdun. I
don't know where."

Then my phone rang.

"Is it you?" a voice yelled with panic.

"Who's this?"

"Peter, is that you?" It was my brother.

"What's wrong?"

"There's been a shooting at the Chinese restaurant. I thought it was you. I saw your car in front," my brother kept talking. "Apparently there are two or three dead."

A tear rolled down my face.

"I was just there but I went to do a message with Alain," I told him.

I hung up and looked at Alain. "It was at the Chinese restaurant."

He hit the gas hard and we screeched off the bridge, turned around, and headed back. It felt like forever before we arrived. The eatery was surrounded by cops, yellow tape, and hundreds of onlookers.

We tried to make our way through the crowd, catching sight of ambulances and morgue trucks. Then Mon-Mon was carried out on a stretcher with his head showing. The ambulance attendants were following with oxygen and they appeared to be talking to him. A cop noticed me as I got to the yellow tape. We asked him what happened. He checked his notepad.

"Two dead from multiple gunshots," he said in an official voice.

Tears were in my eyes, but my face was stone. I felt rage.

Ti-Bum arrived, his own eyes watery.

"Is Renaud gone?"

I nodded.

"*Les tabarnacs,*" he said.

My brain was starting to work again.

"There is someone missing here," I told Ti-Bum. My phone rang.

"*Salut,* pass me my friend," Harry's voice was cheerful.

"Your friend is no longer here," I said in a dead voice. "He has gone far, far away. Where are you, you son of a bitch?"

"I'm not around. I'm about twenty minutes from Magog." That town was about 100 kilometers away. Impossible.

"Magog my ass, you son of a bitch," I answered, furious, now certain he had something to do with the shooting. "That was some important phone call you had to make, wasn't it?"

No answer.

"I guess you're disappointed I answered my phone. You fucked up, you asshole. You missed me, you stupid fuck. I'm on to you."

He hung up.

"What was that?" Ti-Bum asked.

"Remember I was telling you who was missing here? It was him on the phone."

"Who?"

"Renaud's friend. I'd bet my life it was him who set this whole thing up. He was the only one who knew we were going to be there. I was supposed to be in there, too, but Renaud sent me off to do a message with Alain."

"How come your car was across the street from the door?" Ti-Bum asked.

"I told you. I left in Alain's vehicle to do a message."

What Ti-Bum said next shook me.

"Maybe our enemies recognized the Riviera and thought Renaud was in there."

Ti-Bum had me thinking this was all my fault for parking in front. Then I shrugged it away. Too coincidental. This was planned, and by Harry.

"My partner's still alive," I said. "He'll tell me what happened."

I went to my car, but police wouldn't let me leave. They checked underneath in case anyone had planted any bombs. Then I unlocked the doors and they searched the interior. When I got to the Montreal General Hospital, I walked straight into Mon-Mon's room. No police officer at the door. Since bikers never tell cops anything about their attackers, police in return refuse to post any guards at hospitals to make sure the killers don't try to finish the job. We do our own security.

Mon-Mon was barely conscious as his tearful wife, Francine, held one of his hands. When he noticed me, he turned his head and let out a small sigh.

"I told you I never trusted that prick," a faint voice said.

Francine turned to me. "The doctors say he will be all right."

"I'll be fine, *tabarnac*," Mon-Mon said, his customary gruffness coming back.

"I'm going to take care of this," I told Mon-Mon as I left.

It took a few days before Mon-Mon was able to tell me everything. Two guys came in from the front door, he said. Two others from the rear door, which was usually locked. But Harry probably hit the panic bar to open it for the killers when he supposedly went to the bathroom.

And the fifth guy was the one eating alone in the middle of the restaurant.

"He was the one who shot Renaud in the head," Mon-Mon said. "There was so much shooting and smoke I couldn't tell who was shooting who. When they charged in, Renaud sat straight up with his two hands on the table. The only thing he said was, 'This is it.'"

Mon-Mon told me a gunman put a pistol point-blank to his face and pulled the trigger, but my partner was able to twist his head fast enough that the bullet went harmlessly past. One projectile did find his shoulder, though.

He had a bandage on his nose, though I wasn't sure if it was because the point-blank bullet had grazed it or from when his face hit the table.

"As the final shots were going off," Mon-Mon continued, "I pretended to be dead, face flat on the table. That's when I saw Christian bleeding from the neck, looking at me. 'Help me,' he said and then stopped breathing. There was nothing I could do."

Later, police told me the guy who had been eating alone had

nothing to do with the hit. The cops said there had been four assassins, all dressed in black. One had fired two pistols, cowboy style. And someone had let two of the killers in through the back door. I was now even more convinced that that someone was Harry.

I was heartbroken, trying to figure out what I was going to do without my mentor. But I also focused on making sure that what he worked for would not die. Renaud's funeral took place three days after the hit. Thousands of people were there, crowding the streets, so the city placed roadblocks everywhere and police were all over. I wore a bandanna up to my eyes to conceal my identity from any Hells spies in the crowd.

In the funeral home, I sat not far from the coffin and hardly moved. I stared at his corpse. I kept thinking of all the wisdom and guidance he had given me over the past two years. The more I sat there, the more my pain and feelings of vulnerability turned to thoughts of revenge and hatred. I got a lot of strength from thinking of how I would pay this back. There was a small service for his family and friends who were not part of the Rock Machine. Then it was our turn. A priest conducted a ten-minute service attended by members from Montreal and Quebec City.

We took turns touching him before the coffin was closed. With tears coming from my eyes, I leaned down, took his hand, and kissed it.

"I won't let you down," I told him. "I know you'll be watching."

Then we all slapped the coffin before it was taken away.

The full patches held a meeting to decide who would have the honor of carrying the coffin to the funeral car outside for the trip to the church.

"I want to be part of this," I said as they went away to talk. "He was my godfather."

"You can't," one responded. "You're not a full patch. Rules are rules."

I was adamant.

When they came back, they told me I would not carry the coffin. But I could lead the pallbearers.

My chest puffed up since the street would see me in such an important position and realize the others respected me. I wanted to fill Renaud's shoes in Verdun. I knew I could do it.

So I put my bandanna over my nose and stepped to the head of the full-patch members, who were also hiding their faces. I remember the local newspaper carried a photo of us as we descended the steps.

Outside, Renaud's wife sat on a Harley-Davidson with a Rock Machine logo on the gas tank. She revved the engine while staying warm in a brown fur coat. Other members rode their two-wheelers. Police gave us an escort. They also arrested a member of the Rowdy Crew who was snapping photos of all of us.

At the church, there was another huge crowd. Only family and friends went in after police told the Rock Machine they had gotten wind of a Hells plot to kill us all by blowing up the place or getting us at the cemetery. They wouldn't do it if only the family was there. So Rock Machine members split up and left.

One thought overpowered all others in my mind as I drove away. I was going to kill Harry.

CHAPTER 13

Renaud's death left me enraged, demoralized, and worried. I couldn't take any time to grieve because Mon-Mon was still recuperating and couldn't help with business. My anger showed itself often to my underlings, who suffered my wrath at the slightest mistakes.

At gang meetings afterwards, Gilles Lambert tried to keep everyone positive. He and Renaud had run the gang since the Cazzettas were jailed, but Gilles himself looked shaken.

"Look," he told us, "it was a big loss. But we've got to go on."

I now had enforcers who doubled as bodyguards. One was Simon Lambert, a small, violent man of few words but with an arctic stare. We called him Cheeky. I'd gotten to know him when he sold pot, but his fascination with guns got my attention. Whenever I mentioned a car might be following us, he would calmly crank his gun, showing no other emotion at all, almost salivating at the idea of violence. I set up Cheeky so he could make money, but all he wanted to do was kill.

Another enforcer was Eric (Beluga) Leclerc, who was in and out of jail constantly for his explosive temper, once even doing time with his father in the same prison. Mon-Mon had met Beluga behind bars once and introduced us. He was impulsive and didn't think ahead. While riding with me one day, he took out his pistol, cocked it, and made for the door when he saw a Rockers member on the street. I grabbed him by the arm, pointing out the cherries on a marked police car parked at the corner. While he was watching my back, Beluga wasn't discreet at all, acting every bit the bodyguard, staring at anyone who got too close to me or even glanced too long my way.

I warned everyone to be careful, especially with Halloween

coming up. It was the perfect time for an assassin to put on a cheap plastic mask and walk up to us. After Renaud's death, everyday things seemed menacing. I wouldn't get a haircut alone, remembering a Mafia assassination in a New York City barber's chair. I only went into car washes if someone got out of the car and waited for me at the exit. My soldiers were told not to go into bars if possible. No sitting next to restaurant windows, either. I didn't get a remote car-starter, but I did check under my vehicle every morning. Whenever I went anywhere, bodyguards always checked out the places first. I wore a bulletproof vest often and bought vests for my bodyguards and my brother. Not one day went by without thinking I could be next to die.

Mon-Mon came out of the hospital and returned to his apartment in LaSalle. By this time, I'd rented a new place just across the street for $800 a month from the construction firm that had erected the building. One night, as I walked in my front door, a subdued Mon-Mon called me on the phone. The bullets seemed to have removed his steam.

"Peter, something fucking fishy is going on. A car slowly followed you down the block as you got home."

The next night, I left my car in the driveway and the lights on in my place while I walked across the street to his place. We sat in the dark and watched three different cars drive by, slowing down as if to find a parking spot. There was plenty of space on the street, but the cars kept driving, returning a few times. I called two guys on the phone, including Richard Parent, who was married common-law to the sister of the Cazzetta brothers. He was a dealer but his big-time coke habit made him unreliable with the gang. Still, he was good help sometimes. I gave him a description of the cars. A while later, I saw one of the suspicious cars zip by, with Richard's car in pursuit. That confirmed it wasn't the police.

The next day, I went to the construction company's offices and spoke to an official there.

"I want to break my lease," I told her.

She lost her friendly air.

"You can't. You have a two-year lease."

"Look, I really don't think it is a good idea I stay. I'm asking you nicely to break it."

I spent five minutes trying to skate around why I had to move. Then I got fed up and removed my thick jacket. Now she saw my gang sweater.

"I'm a Rock Machine, OK," I said bluntly. "You know there are a lot of bombs going off these days. If anything happens to the building or the other tenants, I'm not responsible. You've been warned."

She let me move. I hired a truck and was gone within two weeks, giving the driver an extra $100 to go for a long joyride to lose any tails. I moved into a downtown Montreal place with a Latin-dance teacher named Gabriella. Every Friday and Saturday night, we'd reserve a table at a salsa club. I felt safe knowing my enemies wouldn't think of finding me dancing to Latin music there.

Mon-Mon also moved permanently to his country place north of Montreal. Because he rarely came back to town, I was left frantically taking care of business.

Since Renaud's death, I'd stopped buying from Frankie. I got a few kilos of coke from Ti-Bum, but Mon-Mon really didn't trust him. So I went to see Toute-Toute at his place. He was finally a full patch. Toute-Toute stayed far from the war on the streets, but he gave me great prices on coke. Toute-Toute had no soldiers, so I took care of security on his turf.

When I paid him for the coke, I would often include a few welfare checks among the cash. My dealers accepted the checks for a fee, making it easier for users than going to a bank. The dealers would then hand the checks over to me as partial payment for their stock, often adding on their own checks. I didn't believe in banks, habitually keeping all my cash in a thick roll that I would count and recount as a way of relaxing. If the money got too thick, I would stash it in shoeboxes at home or in a freezer behind big packages of meat. Though Renaud's death hurt me emotionally, it helped financially. Most of his big customers went to Gilles Lambert, his partner, but some of the smaller ones in Verdun saw me at the head of the funeral procession and came over to me. My profits went to about $7,000 a week clear. Even though Mon-Mon was in semi-retirement, I gave him half.

Gabriella had nothing to do with my business or the war. She was one of many respectable women who sometimes gravitate to bikers. Though I was often with strippers or hookers, I also dated dental hygenists, nurses, and waitresses who had no problem with my choice of occupation. Gabriella knew I was a criminal, but didn't ask any questions. She'd often see my bullet-proof vest and pistol. And when we'd go to a restaurant, I'd always ask to sit with my eyes to the door.

Meanwhile, I put together about three teams of soldiers willing to fight the Hells, buying them masks and gloves so they could invade bars looking to break bones if they found anyone from the other side. They also raided numerous homes where Hells dealers sold drugs. My guys went in with baseball bats, stealing the drugs and money and leaving the place and people inside in a shambles. Crooks as well as cops called such a robbery a "burn," knowing no one would ever report it to the police. The Hells did the same to my places.

In December 1996, I drove to Mon-Mon's country retreat to give him his half of our drug profits and pay a holiday visit. While en route, my cell phone rang. It was Bret Simmons calling from Cowansville jail, where he was doing his time for that disastrous raid on the Jokers clubhouse in Saint-Jean.

"Merry Christmas," he said cheerfully.

He passed the phone to other Rock Machine people at the jail, who said the same. Then Bret came back on.

"Giovanni wants to talk to you," he said. It was one of the Cazzetta brothers, the founders of the gang.

"Hello, my brother," Giovanni said. "I know we have never met or talked to each other, but I have heard nothing but good things about you."

"Same here," I responded. We wished each other Merry Christmas.

Calls from jail were commonplace, and the topic of conversation was always the war. Recently, those in jail were chewing out many of us outside for doing little to fight the Hells. They were frustrated at how the gang splintered after Renaud's death, and also by their inability to help out.

"I hear things are pretty rough out there right now," he said.

"You could say so," I said.

"I hear you are pretty much on your own."

"Yes. I am doing everything I can under the circumstances."

"You owe no explanation to me," he answered. "Like I told you, I'm hearing great things about you. We all know what's going on out there and why. Anyway, keep up the good work. Help will be on the way soon. Hang in there."

Without Renaud, I never got around to buying Ti-Bum's house. But I spent more time with him. He was still an independent, but word had gotten around about his connections to our gang. I heard on the street that someone in the Hells organization had put a $25,000 contract out on his head. He told me he had bought it off, meaning he'd paid the killer the same amount not to go through with it. Soon after, there was another contract, this time for double the amount. I thought about his wife and very young child.

When I saw him next, Ti-Bum had big bags under his eyes and little life in his movements. He wasn't in his usual easygoing mood. He said he would pay off that contract as well, and called a meeting with a top leader of the Hells.

"What would you do if you were in my shoes?" he asked, looking plaintively at me, seeking my advice for the first time since I'd known him.

"Do you really want my advice?" I asked.

He nodded, looking me in the eyes.

"If you really want it, then I'm telling you not to trust those people. They kill their own, so what is to stop them from killing you?"

"I'm just going to do business with them. That way, they'll leave me alone."

"Don't do it. You have enough money to retire for life. You don't need this bullshit anymore."

He gave me a dismissive look.

"If you don't want to retire," I continued, "then just tell the Hells you are dropping out of sight, and hand them your business. You can keep financing the Rock Machine with your money, and we'll hand you an envelope every week."

Ti-Bum shook his head.

"Fuck them," he said. "They won't fuck with me."

"What you are doing makes no sense," I told him, frustrated.

"Well," he said with finality. "My decision is made. Don't worry. Everything is going to work out."

The confidence in his voice didn't match his eyes as he got up to say goodbye. We shook hands and he pulled me close for a long hug, patting me on the back. I got a lump in my throat. This was so different from the usual Ti-Bum, who wouldn't let you near his emotions.

A week before Christmas 1996, I went to his place to pick up two kilos of cocaine, one for me and the other for a friend in the Rock Machine. Ti-Bum handed me the coke with a smile. The bags under his eyes were gone.

"Things are going to work out," he said.

"What happened?"

"Well, I agreed to do business with them."

"What?"

"I don't have much choice. What I'll do is sell to them to keep them off my back but I'll keep working with the Rock Machine as well. I've already fronted them forty kilos."

That astounded me. Now Ti-Bum was worth more to the Hells

dead than alive. There was a huge shortage of coke at the time, and the price of a kilo had hit $40,000. Since Ti-Bum had bought his kilos for $28,000, he stood to make a profit of almost half a million from my enemies. He told me the Hells were supposed to pay him for the kilos in the next couple of days.

A day or two later, I was watching the news when they had an item about a guy killed on Ste. Catherine Street inside his Ford Explorer as people did their last-minute holiday shopping. The truck looked familiar. I thought it belonged to Alain Brunette, who liked big 4×4s. I jumped for the phone, calling Alain's cell. He wasn't answering. I kept calling others in the gang to see if they knew where he was. Finally, I found him and went to sleep relieved.

The next morning, I cried when I picked up the paper. There was Ti-Bum's photo with the story about the downtown shooting. Police said one or two shooters pulled up beside his truck and fired away. I now felt completely alone. Renaud was gone, Mon-Mon was recuperating, and now Ti-Bum. My mind kept racing with thoughts that I was next.

I talked to the Rock Machine members about attending Ti-Bum's funeral, but none wanted to go. They didn't know him, dismissing him as a friend of mine and Renaud's with no gang status. I didn't go, finally, because without other Rock Machine members there, I would be a sitting duck. With Ti-Bum's death, the Hells made $1.6 million by not having to pay him for the coke he fronted them. They probably set up that meeting to pay him as an excuse to draw him out in the open. I ended up making $40,000 since I didn't have to pay him back for the kilo I got from him.

Police believed Verdun was now the prime battlefield. Montreal's east end had been conquered by the Hells early on. And now they were moving their troops into my hometown. The only way I knew how to deal with my emotions was to get destructive. I began with plotting Harry's death.

It was pretty easy to see why he'd had Renaud killed even though he was a very close friend. Harry's brother was working the other side, dealing for some of the top Hells Angels. We'd thought nothing of it when Harry was selling for me because the drug war had done that to many families. It was obvious Harry had decided to rejoin his brother.

I knew Harry's routine well since he had been one of my best dealers. Every Thursday at 10 p.m., he'd drop by his tanning salon to pick up the contents of the cash register and spend 15 minutes talking with his employee.

The streets were being lashed by a severe snowstorm when I drove up about 9:45 with two guys. Sebastien had a sawed-off shotgun and Nelson carried a submachine pistol. I had my usual .357.

"At least the weather makes these seem less suspicious," I said while passing out ski masks.

I drove around and around until I saw Harry's car approaching. I then turned the corner and stopped 50 feet from the salon. Nelson looked to me.

"Peter, you shouldn't come with us," he said.

"Fucking right I'm coming," I said, picking up my pistol.

Sebastien chimed in.

"This is our job. You are supposed to take care of business. What happens if you're caught?"

"I don't give a shit."

"That's not too smart," he added. "You are more needed outside than doing life inside. Stay here. Let us do it."

I really wanted to kill Harry myself. I wanted him to see it was me pointing the gun at his head. But the guys were right. I gave in.

"OK," I said. "Go."

They got out, and made their way to the corner, hugging their weapons to their sides. They walked out of sight as I lit a cigarette.

"This one's for you, Renaud," I said softly.

Then I lowered the window to listen for the gunshots over the wind. I wanted to hit the gas the minute the shots were fired so I could pick them up at the corner. But I heard nothing before Nelson and Sebastien ran back toward me. They got in, both breathless.

"The bastard was already driving away by the time we turned the corner," Nelson said.

"What the fuck?" I said, bitter, as we drove away. He must be taking precautions since he knew I blamed him for Renaud's death. He probably got the cash delivered to his car by his employee so he could make a fast getaway.

"Doesn't matter," I told the guys. "This doesn't end here."

I was hearing a lot of rumors about the Hells getting help in my district from people in the Dubois family, a long-established criminal network based in the St. Henri neighborhood next to Verdun. They were supposed to be independent and on good terms with the Rock Machine, but people kept saying some were working with the Rockers. I decided to send a message to all of them.

André Sauvageau, a gang founder nicknamed Curly because he was bald, took me to his parents' home in northern Montreal. We went to their detached garage, where he took out a few salamis. That's what we called thick sticks of dynamite. He taught me to avoid saying the word "explosives" in case police were listening. Better to just put my hand in a fist before opening it quickly while thrusting upwards.

The first target was the Champlain Bar on de l'Eglise Street, well known as a Dubois hangout and popular spot for local dealers to drink away their time. But Mom Boucher had been there a few times for meetings and Rockers had been seen frequenting the place. I sent Jean-Marc Cassey, now my drug and money runner after Gaetan was scared away by the Hells. With Jean-Marc was another guy named Daniel Letourneau. One laid the bomb while the other drove the getaway car. Their work made the news, but the papers got it wrong, putting the blame on the Hells. I was supposedly still on good terms with the Dubois family so I didn't want to correct the error.

Another place was scheduled to disintegrate just a few minutes later. I was mad at Linda Pizza and Pasta on Wellington for letting the Rockers meet there. The owners had told the Rock Machine they were not choosing sides in the war, but their actions spoke louder than words. So Bob Lavigne did that job. But the bomb was a dud. Maybe the severe cold caused the thing to freeze.

Two months later, Toute-Toute asked if I had someone to blow up a bar called the Montecarlo in Lachine, part of his territory. I told Cheeky to do it with his brother, Eric. But neither had a driver's license.

Around this time, I met Anne (not her real name) and we started dating. She had three children from three different men. I liked her because she wasn't after money, just a good time with booze, hash, and PCP. A friend of hers, Mario Filion, had been badgering me to find something for him to do. Since he could drive, he went along with Cheeky and Eric. The explosion rocked the whole street. Anne didn't like Mario taking risks so one night in bed, she implored me to find something safe for him to do.

Two weeks after the Montecarlo bombing, Jean-Marc, my drug runner, had just finished playing floor hockey with friends at a Côte St. Paul recreation center when he was shot twice in the back of the neck. He had wanted to be buried above Renaud's casket if he died. The Rock Machine fulfilled his wish, but didn't tell Renaud's wife first. She flipped when she heard.

With Jean-Marc gone, I found something for Mario to do. The small, quiet guy was given the nickname Hammer after taking over my drug deliveries. Anne wasn't that thrilled.

Two months earlier, I was with François Laporte on Wellington Street, whom we called The Doors for his taste in music, but also because of his last name. He had been a hangaround for a while but chickened out after people in the gang started dying. He pointed out a tall guy on the opposite side of the street. The guy was wearing a Harley-Davidson jacket, jeans, and cowboy boots.

"The guy's name is Polar," The Doors told me. "He sells a bit of hash, not much. But he's told people he doesn't care about selling on Rock Machine territory."

"Who's he working for?" I asked.

"I don't know," was the answer. "But some guys have seen him wearing those 'free' T-shirts."

"Oh, really?"

That gave away his allegiance. The word "free" was used by the Hells as a mantra to explain their rebel lifestyle. The word's meaning came from the time Sorel members of the Hells in 1985 killed five brothers in the Laval chapter who were taking too many drugs. When a number of Montreal and Halifax Hells were arrested and put on trial, supporters sold fundraising shirts calling for authorities to free the jailed members.

"Keep an eye on that guy," I said as we walked on.

Cheeky was with me a few months later as I did my daily rounds of soldiers and dealers. He spotted Polar, saying the guy was going around saying he didn't give a fuck about the Rock Machine. I quickly tried to see his face, worrying he might be planning to come after me sometime with a gun. But I was too late and we kept on with our rounds.

Not long after, Cheeky and I were relaxing in my vehicle while I let Mario drive down Wellington because it was a nice spring day. Cheeky suddenly sat upright in the back seat and tapped me on the shoulder.

"There's the asshole again."

"Which asshole?" I asked.

"Polar."

"Go around the block," I ordered Mario. "I want to get a good look at that guy."

He did as I ordered.

"What's the deal with this guy?" I said thinking about his t-shirt and disparaging comments about my gang. We went around and came back to Wellington. Again, I couldn't get a clear view of his face.

"What do we do?" Cheeky asked me.

"What do you mean?"

Mario steered the car down the next street. I told him to go around again. "Slow down," I added as we got close to the main street.

"What's wrong?" Cheeky asked.

"Nothing. I'm just thinking."

"What do we do?" Cheeky asked again.

"Do what you want."

That gave him the green light. But he hesitated.

"It's up to you," he answered.

"I don't know him, so I don't care. You do what you want. It's your call."

The car was still moving slowly. Cheeky told Mario to stop near the corner.

"Don't worry about it," Cheeky said as if he would take care of the problem.

He had his gun in his hand while pulling a ski mask from a pocket and pointing out his side window, showing where he would run afterwards. He got out.

"He's just trying to show me he has balls," I told Mario. "There are too many fucking people out there. He'll be right back."

Mario moved the car closer to the corner. I caught sight of Polar as a gunshot went off. Polar flew forward and another shot rang out. People screamed while scrambling to get away.

"Fuck," I yelled to a nervous Mario. "He did it. Get the car out of here."

Cheeky lay low for a few days with a hundred dollars I gave him to take care of expenses. We never talked about the killing again. I felt bad knowing I had participated in the destruction of a human being, but consoled myself that he was the enemy. It was the first time I'd seen someone die. For weeks afterwards, my dreams were filled with the sight of Polar pitching forward after the first bullet entered his body. Then those images went away and I forgot about him.

CHAPTER 14

"Oh, shit," I told Cheeky, "It's the *casquettes*."

That was our word in French for cops, referring to their peaked caps. Cheeky looked around, holding his pistol.

We were parked in a blackened side street by the Bain Douche club on St. Laurent Boulevard while another crew in front was about to deposit a bomb at the Hells bar. I had driven my car near the back alley to make sure no one was around to get hurt. Now a cruiser was making its way toward us at a snail's pace.

"Just play along with me," I told Cheeky. He put his gun out of sight.

The cop car kept coming. I honked my horn and made gestures toward the second-floor of a nearby building. I honked again, and again, this time really leaning into the horn. Cheeky pointed and stared at the same place. The car clock read almost 4 a.m.

Hopefully Mario and John (not his real name) were smart enough to hold off on laying the bomb once they heard all my noise.

The cop car came abreast, and the two officers looked at us. They didn't stop, buying the ploy that I was waiting to pick somebody up. Once they were gone, Mario drove around and stopped behind my car. He got out.

"We saw the cops," he said, coming over.

"Where's John?"

"He's putting the bomb in place," he answered, as John ran toward us.

"Good job," I said. "Now get out of here. We'll see you later."

Cheeky and I drove a bit up St. Laurent and looked for a pay phone.

The salamis deposited at the front door of the club had come from Curly, who asked us to do the job to hurt the wallets of some Nomads members. When I'd gone to pick up a black duffel bag of dynamite from him, Curly had played with my mind by telling me to avoid all of Montreal's infamous potholes in case a bump set the dynamite off, and not to put the car's heating too high. That ride was one of the few times I was terrified shitless during the war.

The bomb was twice the size used in the past because Curly really wanted the place turned to dust. All we had to do on the scene was twist two wires together, then set the bomb off by phoning the attached pager.

I pulled over and gave Cheeky the pager number.

"There," I pointed. "There's a phone."

Cheeky got out and turned to me.

"Got a quarter for the phone?"

"Are you serious?" I said to him. He shrugged his shoulders. The guy never could keep a cent in his pockets. I went through mine and found a coin.

Cheeky phoned the number and then came back. We heard nothing.

"Did it work?" he asked.

"I don't fucking know. Call the number again."

"Got another quarter?"

"Oh, for fuck's sake," I said.

He did it again. Again, no boom.

We took off, heading back to Verdun. A cop car screamed by us. Another went by a minute later. Cheeky and I looked at each other and grinned. It worked.

I decided to stop with the bombs for a while because it was causing a lot of heat. Everybody in the Rock Machine was sure the police were working for the Hells. It seemed during this time that only our gang was being hit by raids, never the Hells. We often bitched at cops for that. Two weeks later the cops seemed to confirm this. We were evicted from our clubhouse on Huron Street by the police, as well as from our sister bunker up in Quebec City. The cops also arrested 18 people, including Gilles Lambert. Gilles was charged with living off the proceeds of crime. Renaud's wife was arrested for the same thing. Cars and homes owned by the Cazzetta brothers and their sister Maria, the common-law wife of Richard Parent, were confiscated. The clubhouse seizure left Bandit homeless until Bull agreed to take him.

Then Sasquatch was shot in a drive-by shooting on a highway north of Montreal. The bullet grazed his arm before being stopped by a bulletproof vest.

As a prospect, I didn't know too much about the gang's high-level business at the time, though Mon-Mon often kept me informed. He told me an international biker gang called the Bandidos got in touch with Fred Faucher, a full patch in Quebec City, asking about the war and mentioning our mutual hatred of the Hells. But I quickly learned it was the opposite. Fred e-mailed them, looking to see if we could join forces against our enemy.

The Bandidos were one of the three largest biker gangs in the world, the biggest being the Hells. The Bandidos and the Outlaws competed closely for second place. The Bandidos were a natural choice to be our allies because they had also fought the Hells in a bloody war in Scandinavia, even using anti-tank weapons most likely stolen from a military depot. More than a dozen had been killed before a truce was called and a very public handshake between gang leaders on European TV.

That June, Fred, Toute-Toute, and Johnny went to Sweden for a memorial service for European Bandidos killed in the war there with the Hells. But Quebec police tipped off police there, and the three were tossed out of the country the minute they landed. A month later, Fred, Johnny, and Sasquatch went to Luxembourg for a Bandidos motorcycle run.

One time, so some of the full patches wouldn't be tracked by police leaving the country, my brother used his Mohawk connections and got them smuggled across the U.S. border through the

Akwesasne Indian reserve. From a U.S. airport, they could go where they wanted.

Toute-Toute was doing a lot of the public relations between the Rock Machine and the Bandidos, spending a fortune on airline tickets to visit chapters everywhere. I spent a lot of time with him at his country place in Sainte Catherine-de-Hatley in the picturesque Eastern Townships of Quebec. We'd take a 60-ounce bottle of rum and a bit of coke with us. To forget the war, we'd hop on his boat or jet-skis and terrorize Lake Massawippi.

That summer, the gang also had a huge pig roast for our families up at Mon-Mon's lakeside place north of Montreal. About 40 people were there, and we ended the night with fireworks.

I tried to see my son at my mother's place as much as the war would let me. One time, I took him fishing, putting my gun in the tackle box in case. He saw it but said nothing. On the way back to my mother's, we stopped off for some Kentucky Fried Chicken.

"You know this is seagull, right?" I said, biting into a leg.

He looked at me. "It says chicken."

"Ya, but why do you think the legs are so small?"

He believed me.

Another time, I took him to the McDonald's on Lasalle Boulevard. After leaving the drive-thru, I passed a vehicle and recognized Rockers sitting inside it. I twisted my head to check them out as we drove by. They had recognized my truck. I kept driving, looking back to see if they tried to follow. They didn't but I took a long route back to my mother's house to make sure.

Meanwhile, I got word that Harry was cruising around Verdun in a new red Mercedes convertible. Probably bought with the money he got for setting up Renaud, I thought. One day, I was doing my rounds on Wellington with Cheeky in my vehicle when I spotted the convertible drive by in the opposite direction.

"The bastard," I told Cheeky. "Fucking nerve showing his face."

I thought as I drove. He's a fucking show-off, so he's probably going to parade up and down the street with the top down to make sure everybody sees his new toy.

"Get ready," I said to Cheeky. He got his pistol out. We stopped and waited for Harry to drive back our way. I was driving a Ford Aerostar van, and he wouldn't recognize it.

The convertible drove past. I pulled in behind, but stayed a bit of a distance away.

"He's going to have to take a side street sometime," I told Cheeky. "When he does, we'll wait until he comes to a stop at the next corner. I want you to get out and shoot the son of a bitch."

Cheeky said nothing, just cocked his piece. Harry stopped at the next stop sign. We glided in right behind him. Cheeky went for the door.

"Stop, look at that," I said, pointing to a half-dozen children crossing the street in front of the Mercedes. "I don't want those kids to see this."

I was picturing the terror on their faces at seeing Harry's jerking body spewing blood on his leather seats.

"Peter, let's get him now," Cheeky said in frustration.

"Wait," I said. "We'll get him at the next corner."

Harry started off and we followed.

"Look," I said to Cheeky. "There's a street light on the next corner. We won't miss him there."

The light turned yellow as Harry got close.

"We got him now."

But Harry decided to beat the red light and drove through the intersection.

"I told you we should have killed him when we had the chance," Cheeky said.

Cheeky didn't have children. I did, and I wouldn't want my 11 year old to see such a hit. Two weeks later, we got another try. Harry was doing his parade again. So I told Cheeky to sit on a park bench on 5th Avenue and wait. Harry would have to obey the stop sign there.

"I'm going to get behind him again so when he comes up to you he will be boxed in."

I found Harry and started following him. We turned down 5th Avenue and I could see Cheeky get up from the park bench and cross the street to get close to the driver's side of the convertible. But Harry turned his car into an alley before reaching the stop sign. I picked up Cheeky, but by the time we got moving, Harry was gone. Frustrated, I found Harry's 22-year-old son the next day and gave him a message for his father. Leave or die. He left.

A month later, I got called to do security at an Italian restaurant in northern Montreal. I was on the roof with a submachine gun in my hands and my pistol tucked into my belt, hidden under my Rock Machine sweater. The guest of honor was Mike Kay, the president of the Australian Bandidos. He was in Quebec to check us out. After numerous toasts and photos, he gave a short speech thanking us for our hospitality.

"I'm going back with a report that you guys should belong to the Bandidos," I heard him say when I went down once. "We have the same brotherhood mentality."

That drew cheers from the 20 of us on the restaurant's third floor.

A week later in Quebec City, I did security for Mike Kay during a fancy meal in the revolving restaurant at the Loews hotel. Again, my revolver was hidden under my Rock Machine sweater. All the members also wore their sweaters. The other patrons glanced our way before averting their eyes.

After Mike returned home, a European member named Clark came to spend a few months in Quebec. Clark sold tons of Bandidos shirts while he was here, and he slept over at various members' homes to get to know them well. Most of the time, he was with Johnny at his country place north of Montreal. I went up there one day when Johnny asked me to babysit Clark while he had to do some business. Johnny was getting sick of seeing the guy watching the Playboy channel all day.

Clark always wore his leather vest with the Bandidos's cartoon image of a fat Mexican. We headed for Verdun and drove around.

"This is the war zone," I told him.

A few days later, I asked two of my soldiers to take care of some unfinished business with Harry. Though he had disappeared following my warning, he was still operating his tanning salon on my territory.

"Burn the place," I told one of my guys, who tossed a Molotov cocktail in the window. I didn't want a bomb because people lived upstairs and could be hurt. A bottle filled with fuel would give them enough time to get out. Two days later, I went after a new car wash belonging to the same guys as the Champlain bar. I asked another prospect how much he would charge to do the job. He wanted $500. He then hired a subcontractor to do it.

The Hells had already brought a lot of heat on us by killing Daniel Desrochers, propelling the Canadian government to pass a law in 1997 making it illegal to contribute in an important way to the activities of a gang. It came with a maximum of 14 years in jail. Now we were astounded to see the Hells do something even more stupid than kill the 11-year-old boy. Hitmen first killed a female prison guard as she finished her shift at Bordeaux jail and then they ambushed an empty prison bus a few months later near Rivieres-des-Prairies jail, shooting two guards, killing one. It was part of a Hells plot to murder guards, police officers, judges, and prosecutors in an attempt to destabilize the system. They had another goal as well. They would make all gang newcomers kill someone in the justice system. They believed the newcomer would be trustworthy afterwards because he would never turn informant and risk a first-degree-murder conviction, which brings with it life in prison without possibility of parole for 25 years.

While we in the Rock Machine had no problem killing the Hells, we didn't go after civilians. Not even Michel Auger, a crime reporter at the *Journal de Montréal* who drove us crazy with stories saying we were losing the war and giving away our home addresses in the paper, making it easy for the Hells to find us. The Bandidos suggested we get rid of him, but the Rock Machine wouldn't touch him.

In October 1997, we had a visit from the U.S. national president of the Bandidos, George Wegers. He was also international vice-president and in charge of figuring out what to do with us since the president was doing a long term behind bars. With him came Clark. Mon-Mon had been telling me that European and Australian Bandidos supported our entry into the gang, but the United States was balking because the Hells were telling them we weren't a real motorcycle gang. For once, the Hells were right. Though many of our full patches owned Harleys or used to belong to various biker gangs in their youth, it wasn't mandatory to have a bike in the Rock Machine like it was in the Hells. Wegers told us we should spend a lot of time schmoozing U.S. members to convince them we were worthy.

Before becoming full Bandidos, our club would have to go through an initiation. First, we would be a hangaround club for six months, and then promoted to the prospect level as probationary Bandidos. After a year of that, we could be full Bandidos.

We organized another fancy dinner at the revolving restaurant in Quebec City. I was placed in the hotel garage doing security with a Quebec City hangaround. Upstairs, Wegers, Clark, and 22 Rock Machine members and prospects were eating well.

I was talking to the hangaround, who had little experience in the gang, but who tried to make it up with long hair and the leather biker jacket. My phone rang.

"Get out of the hotel," yelled a voice I couldn't recognize because it was so frazzled. "The place is swarming with cops."

I drove out the garage door and up the ramp, spotting a police car at the top with his roof lights flashing.

"Get down," I told the hangaround. "You look too much like a biker."

The cop let me by, probably figuring all the bikers were in the restaurant. I drove to a Quality Suites hotel and took a room.

"What do we do now?" the nervous guy asked.

"You roll me a joint," I said, tossing him some hash and rolling paper, "and I'll call the lawyer."

The hangaround gave me the number of the local Rock Machine lawyer, who said he'd find out what happened. I then ordered pizza and chicken wings. We waited until 6 a.m., when the lawyer called back, saying everyone would be released in the next hour.

I drove to the clubhouse and waited. Sure enough, the guys showed up, tired but laughing that police couldn't pin anything on them. The whole thing had started from a minor accident outside the hotel involving one of our minivans. When police showed up for the crash, the parked minivan was empty. They looked inside a window and found a bunch of Bandidos sweaters. One of the cops had just taken a biker-identification course so he recognized some of our members doing watch in the lobby. They were arrested at gunpoint, their weapons taken away, and a paper confiscated with the names of everyone else doing watch on it. Police then just went around to all the surveillance spots and nabbed our guards one by one before heading up to the revolving restaurant for the full-patch members.

At the clubhouse, Mon-Mon clapped me on the back and said I was a slippery eel to escape the cops. Others said I had a horseshoe up my ass. Wegers wasn't as lucky. He was tossed out of Canada for lying about his criminal past to get past the border.

Back in Montreal, I was busy trying to keep my drug network together through all the police attention, when Mon-Mon spilled the beans that I was about to be voted in as a full patch. I felt it was a little late in coming, since my territory was the only one fighting the Hells after Renaud's death. The full patches seemed to be staying behind the scenes. I learned the police considered me one of the very few warriors in Montreal actually fighting the Hells with force. But the promotion still thrilled me. I could shed my prospect sweaters, with the silver flames surrounding the gang's name on the arms. I would get new ones, with multicolored flames on the arms depicting me as a top leader.

I thought of all the dirty work I'd done to get such status. I was proud of making it, and the recognition gave me added strength to fight the Hells. The party was in a member's basement north of Montreal. I couldn't let anyone know I already knew or Mon-Mon would get in shit. The guys made me squirm with repeated insults about how I was running my own show in Verdun since the death of Renaud.

"Paradis, you never fucking follow orders," one member said to me.

That brought hoots of agreement and cheers. Others continued for a few minutes and my face was turning red from embarrassment. Finally, Fred Faucher spoke up.

"Give it to him, *tabarnac*," Fred yelled out.

"Since you don't listen to anyone," Gilles finally said, "you might as well be a boss."

CHAPTER 15

I wasted no time showing my dealers and underlings the new diamond Rock Machine ring. My guys were happy because they now had a full-patch boss. When I was only a prospect, any full patch could order them around. Now they only had to listen to me. And they had a better chance of promotion with me behind them.

I was shameless with making them learn to follow orders. One time, I sent Beluga to get me some jeans, socks, and underwear. Since he liked tight white underwear, that's what he bought me. I sent him back for boxers. Mario would be used to get me some hot dogs or return my videos.

Anne seemed to be the most enthralled by my new status. I got word from the street she was lording it over everybody, and they were only tolerating it because she was my girl. Even I had trouble tolerating her sometimes at the nightly dinner table, when I'd usually tune her out as she went on gossiping about minor problems with neighbors or sales clerks.

"Just tell them to go fuck themselves," would be my stock answer.

She'd sometimes listen to me do business and offer her opinion.

"Shut up," I would say, "you don't know what you are talking about."

She'd give me an eyeful at that. Other times, she would annoy me so much I'd page myself an urgent message as an excuse to leave, do some coke, and get a blowjob from a prostitute. If she ever got feisty whenever I had some of my guys over for dinner, they would leave to let us yell it out.

I now attended full-patch masses, held once every two months since the war was taking up everybody's time. To throw off police and the Hells, we'd only pass on the location in person a few days before each mass, or send a message to Quebec City by prospect, never over the phone.

Mon-Mon almost never attended since he had lost his resolve. I was still splitting my profits, giving him anywhere from $6,000 to $10,000 every two weeks, depending on how many wholesale kilos I sold in addition to the usual business. At one of the first meetings, the subject of Mon-Mon came up.

"Peter, you've got to do something about Mon-Mon," Johnny said, looking at me. "Get him off his ass and doing something."

I said nothing. I'd been hearing grumblings for a while that the other full patches didn't like Mon-Mon spending more than a year recuperating after he was shot.

"Are you still giving him half?" Johnny asked.

"Yes."

The room was filled with swear words.

"Are you fucking Santa Claus?" one of the guys yelled.

"What do you think you are, a good Samaritan?" went another.

"Christ, can I be your partner, too?" Johnny asked with a heap of sarcasm.

"You are now a full patch," Curly cut in. "Do something about Mon-Mon."

"If he's too scared to come into the city, make him retire," Johnny added.

The comments didn't let up. I felt bad, since Mon-Mon had taught me about brotherhood. I couldn't push him away.

"Put your foot down and fucking settle this," Johnny was continuing, working himself into a lather.

"Hey," I finally got space to say, "this is my problem. I'll deal with it."

"Stop being a Boy Scout," Johnny said with something approaching contempt. "Get him off his ass or cut him off."

"I have too much respect for him. I'm not going to let him fall."

That made Johnny freak.

"Where are you going to draw the line?" he said, throwing his hands in the air. "Are you going to let him sit at home for the rest of his fucking life?"

"I said I'll deal with it."

That ended it, but the guys' looks revealed their disgust with me. Business went back to the usual subject. We needed to kill a full-patch Hells to boost morale among our troops and make a splash in the media, which had written us off as close to death. One newspaper even suggested we should change our name from Rock Machine to the Scattered Remains. Some suggestions for targets were thrown out, and everyone promised to do their best. Then the dues. We designated one member to take our $1,000 monthly payments for the lawyers, as well as an extra couple of hundred to pay prison canteens and a few hundred more for the latest funeral. Some of the guys, like Stéphane Morgan, couldn't give anything because their territory had been wiped out by the Hells. Ti-Cul made promises to pay up, but we knew it was just to avoid embarrassment. Only guys such as Toute-Toute and me in the southwest areas we still controlled were making decent money. So was Johnny, who was operating in north-end St. Léonard.

I'd often drop by my mother's and hand her a thousand dollars to pay off debts or treat herself. Or even though I despise seafood, I'd head to the Atwater Market and pick up five pounds of jumbo shrimp and some lobsters as presents. She never asked where the cash was coming from. She was anxious for me, but happy I was doing better than when I was coked up.

John, who had helped bomb the Bain Douche bar, approached me in 1997. He usually sold out of an arcade on Wellington Street.

"Peter, my business is real low. I'm sure that asshole has some-thing to do with it."

After a body-piercing place opened up next door to the arcade, John's business had dwindled. I'd been keeping my eye on the place since spotting $60,000 Harleys parked in front many times. But when I'd confronted the owner of the store, called the Rage Underground, he vowed he wasn't selling drugs. I'd tested him by sending people into his store asking if he knew where to get anything to smoke. He'd always said no. But John was still adamant.

"Pete, I sent in one of my customers to see the guy. She said he had no hash to sell but would smoke a joint with her in the back."

That was enough for me. I barged back into the shop the next day. I stopped so close to the owner his eyes started to cross.

"Remember me?" I said with a chill in my voice. "I thought you said you had nothing to do with drugs."

"OK, OK," he answered, trying to mollify me. "I sell a joint or two to friends."

I took that as an understatement. He had to be related to the Hells, because if he was working for one of the groups that was on good terms with the Rock Machine, he would have said so. He couldn't have missed my gang sweater.

"OK," I answered. "Don't say I didn't warn you."

I turned and walked out.

My first plan was to burn down the place. He'd get the message and leave.

At one point, I happened to pick up three new pistols I had ordered a while back from Tony for $1,000. A month or so later, I took them out of my closet and showed them to John and Cheeky while we were smoking some hash and downing a few beers.

"What are you going to do with them?" Cheeky asked. He picked up the .357 Magnum, checking out its sightline.

"They're for our protection," I answered.

He really wanted the .357 but I took it from him and left him with the .38 Special, not as impressive a weapon.

"This will do," he said, polishing his new toy.

John had the .45 Magnum in his hands, admiring the extra long barrel, spinning the cylinder.

"It's yours," I told him. Then I warned them, "I'm telling you both right now not to wave them around for nothing."

We talked for a while about the war, and John came back to the Rage Underground's owner.

"What are we going to do about that asshole?" he asked.

"I'm not sure," I said. "I'm just thinking about having his fucking place burned down. If he's only selling to people he knows, he can set up elsewhere and they will follow him there. Montreal's a big city."

"Why don't you let me take care of this?" John said in a low voice, still playing with his pistol.

I looked at him. Then I turned to Cheeky. He winked at me and nodded his head.

"I don't know right now," I said. And we left it at that.

A few months later, I met John on the street to talk about the Rage again.

"He's my problem," John said. "Let me take care of the situation."

I wasn't sure if he meant to kill the guy or burn down his place.

"OK," I said. "But wait until after the holidays are over."

Christmas Eve was a few days away. When it came, I told Anne there was something hidden in our tree at home. She searched for an hour as her friends shouted encouragement. She checked every ornament until she found a pair of diamond earrings. Her children, used to a life on welfare, were astounded by all the presents under the tree.

We then went to my mother's place for our traditional dinner. John and another enforcer came along as bodyguards, eating dinner with us, and then leaving afterwards. They were armed. I had stashed my gun in my coat as I had walked in. Too much hugging and patting to leave the piece tucked into my belt in the small of my back.

When everybody collapsed in the living room after the meal, I got down on one knee in front of Anne and gave her a $5,000 engagement ring. She squealed and said yes. I felt I loved her, and hoped this would provide some stability in my life. Most of the other gang members were in long-term relationships.

John called me a few days later for a meeting.

"What's the matter?" I asked him.

"I'm going to do him tomorrow."

I knew he meant he was going to kill the guy.

"Hold on a minute," I said. "Let me think."

My mind raced through the possibilities. I was sure the cops would pull me in as a suspect right away. I wanted to be far away with an alibi when it happened. Then I remembered the show at the Molson Centre I was supposed to see with Anne and her kids.

"Look," I finally said. "If you are going to whack him, do it while I'm at the ice show. It starts at one and finishes at three. I need an alibi."

John agreed.

"When you finish," I said, "beep me on my pager with all identical numbers to confirm it is over and done with."

"OK," he said. "Have a good time at the show."

I played the family man and went to the *Beauty and the Beast* ice show just three days into the new year of 1998. My beeper went off constantly. Every time, I checked the pager, but it wasn't a message from John. Anne noticed my preoccupation.

"Don't worry," I told her. "I won't answer any calls until the show is over."

My insides were a mess as I waited for somebody to die. I felt I knew something I shouldn't, and that I had a power only reserved for God. I couldn't tell John to back off. He wanted to prove himself to me and the Rock Machine. I would look weak if I showed mercy. The guilt was overwhelming me, and the guy wasn't even dead yet.

My beeper rang. I stared at the message.

4444.

My face went dead. Anne looked over with concern.

"Are you all right?"

"Yes," I said, pretending it was a routine call.

The rest of the day, she kept looking at me, trying to gauge my mood. The news that night included a piece about a murder in Verdun. Anne's head almost snapped as she turned to face me on the couch, her eyes boring into mine. She said nothing although I could see her suspicions.

The news said the shop owner, Eric Perfechino, was shot twice by a man who hid his face behind a scarf while walking in. An employee witnessed the killing but couldn't recognize the shooter. John was in the clear.

Not long after, I headed to the apartment on de l'Eglise I had rented for some of my guys, including John and Cheeky. I stored explosives, submachine pistols, and some drugs there. While checking out the drug cache, I became livid when I discovered about a pound of pot and 1,000 hits of acid missing.

"Fucking ingrates," I said under my breath. "I take care of those bastards and this is how they pay me back."

It couldn't be Cheeky: he was in jail. I'd been paying his canteen of $100 a week so he could buy stuff inside. Finally, I got a guy to smuggle a quarter pound of pot to him so he could sell it inside. His profits from that were now paying for all he needed. The list of suspects narrowed to Réjean, a friend of Cheeky's who was staying at the place. I told Beluga.

"Let me whack him," he said. "You can't trust that fucker anymore. Think about what he'll do after this."

That was the logical answer, I thought. It would send a message to the others. I sent Beluga to find Réjean (not his real name) and bring him to my apartment.

When they walked in, I told a frightened Réjean to stay in the kitchen and I took Beluga to another room.

"Punch him in the face every time I give you a signal," I told him.

We went back in. Beluga crossed his arms and stood behind Réjean, who was sitting in a straight-backed chair. I stood before him.

"Why did you take my dope?" I asked.

"What dope?"

I nodded to Beluga.

He slapped Réjean in the face with the back of his hand, the blow knocking him off the chair. Beluga grabbed him under the arms and hoisted him back in the seat.

"Don't play stupid," I continued. "I know you took it."

"I didn't, I swear."

Another signal to Beluga. Réjean managed to stay in the chair despite the second blow.

"Look, you asshole. I'm missing a pound of dope and a shitload of acid. You are the only guy who could have taken it."

"No, Peter, that's not true."

Beluga slapped Réjean in the face without waiting for my nod. Réjean's nose was bleeding non-stop and he was close to cracking.

"Get him something for his nose," I told Beluga. We walked a bit away from our victim. "Listen, when he confesses, pull your piece out. Don't kill him, just pretend you will. After all, he is Cheeky's friend."

Réjean confessed soon after. His eyes widened when Beluga pulled out his gun and made a motion to put it to his head. Réjean began crying and pleading. I waited a minute to let him suffer.

"OK, asshole, listen to me good. Get the fuck out of here. Get your shit out of my place and don't come back."

I dismissed him, but Beluga stayed behind.

"Let me whack him on the way," he asked.

"No. He's scared enough. I'll let Cheeky deal with him."

Cheeky, feeling responsible for his friend, made arrangements for Réjean to pay me back. I got one payment before he disappeared.

That spring, the Rock Machine was invited to attend the funerals for two Outlaws who were gunned down in the parking lot of a London, Ontario, strip club. I drove down with two friends in the Irish mob to pay my respects. The Outlaws shared our hatred for the Hells.

We followed a long column of motorcycles to the cemetery after the service. When the two caskets were lowered into the ground, the father of one of the dead bikers took a shovel and tossed in the first load of dirt. He passed it to the next biker, who did the same. It came around to me, but I passed it on without tossing in anything. It wasn't my place. Many Outlaws I met had no trouble telling me what they thought of the Hells, whom they had called maggots for the past 25 years. Despite the gray drizzle that day, my spirits were high knowing others shared our fight against the Hells.

The Rock Machine kept good contacts with the Outlaws. We sometimes bought guns from them and in exchange passed them dynamite. The Outlaws still had a bunker in Montreal's St. Henri neighborhood, a leftover of its lost war in the 1980s with the Hells. The Plescio brothers, Mon-Mon, and I went to visit the place on Casgrain Street after the Outlaws offered to sell it to us to replace the Huron Street place seized by the cops. The Outlaws wanted $125,000, though they were willing to take a down payment and accept monthly payments after that. We sat down at the bunker's bar to discuss the war.

One of the Outlaws pointed to the wall, where two dozen memorial plaques hung, testimony to fallen gang members.

"We took a bad beating," he said of their past war with the Hells. "You guys seem to be going through the same thing. We'll help you any way we can."

His eyes were sad, and his thoughts were obviously lost in the past.

"You have lost a lot of men, and there is going to be a lot more killed," he told us.

The building interested us, though we didn't like its location near an elevated highway. A killer could have stopped his car on the highway and fired gunshots or even a bazooka at us. The place burned down before we could buy it.

While making my drug rounds one day, I drove by Bob Lavigne's place. I saw two cops get out of an unmarked car and head for Bob. I pulled over and confronted them in the middle of the street.

"We just want to have a word with Bob," one said.

"Not alone, you're not," I responded.

The cop's name was Clement Rose. He was a detective sergeant in the anti-gang squad. Neither one of us remembered it, but we'd met six years before. He was the morality-squad cop who grappled with my brother when I was arrested in the after-hours club for the second time.

Bob watched as a full-patch Rock Machine and two cops came at him. He had joined me in the early Rock Machine days, becoming a hangaround and one of my best dealers.

Rose introduced himself.

"It is my job to tell you your life is in danger," he told a startled Bob. "We got word that the Rockers plan to do something."

The cops left. Bob looked really worried.

"Don't worry about it," I told him. "They are just trying to rattle you."

"Yeah, yeah," he said and walked inside his home on 3rd Avenue.

A few days later, I went to see him again. I had just enough time to say hi before Bob reached for his Alliance ring and took it off, pushing it at me.

"I can't do this," he said, embarrassed, "I have a family. And now I have a contract on my head."

I was dumbfounded as I played with his Alliance ring.

"I hope you don't mind if I pull out. All I want to do is grow some weed, and I'll sell it all to you."

Ironically, I'd been planning to promote him to prospect in a little while. But I understood his reasons and I let him go. I transferred his business to a guy already working for him.

I headed soon after to St. Joseph's Oratory, a sacred site in Montreal where my grandmother used to climb up the many steps on her knees to show her faith and piety. I walked up and bought a few candles at the gift shop. After lighting one in the church, I kept the others for intimate nights with Anne. I also gave $10 bills to the elderly ladies collecting money for various diseases.

In the church, I said a quick "Our Father" and then sat in a pew, falling into a stare. After a few minutes of peace, I got up and went to the cafeteria for something to eat. Mario, my runner, walked in and saw me. He came over.

"Go get something to eat so you don't look suspicious," I told him. He went off and came back.

"Why the hell did you pick this place to meet?" he asked.

"We're safe here. No Hells."

I was armed anyway. So was Mario. I gave him shit every time I caught him without a pistol.

The war continued. I had my crews busting into other shooting galleries all the time. I also gave a neighboring crew the address of a dealer named Ping-Pong who used to sell for me. One day, he came to see me and said he was getting out of the business. I asked him to reconsider. But I heard nothing from him until a junkie told me the guy was back in business, but this time for the Rockers. A few days later, a Rock Machine crew broke into his place with baseball bats. But Ping-Pong was in great shape, and he ran out the back door, losing everyone. Another day, I got a call to a meeting from Serge, a good friend in the Dubois family. We had sold hash together on the Verdun boardwalk so long ago.

"One of my guys got burned," he said, getting serious. "Could it be you guys who did it?"

"I don't know. Let me check it out and I'll get back to you."

I found out it was Beluga, but he'd already sold the drugs and spent the cash he stole. It was a common problem, hitting a Dubois dealer instead of a Hells. My guys weren't asking any questions before they waded in. I didn't hold it against them anyway. If it was a Dubois dealer, we just handed back the drugs and money with a lame apology. Since Beluga was my guy and I was responsible for him, I personally gave Serge back about $500 in cash and another $500 in coke.

Beluga continued to get a bad rap with the Dubois clan. He was at a campground where many criminals went to get away from the city, at the same time as Alain Dubois, who was bad-mouthing me in front of everyone. Beluga lost his short fuse and stuffed a 9 mm in Alain's face, threatening to pull the trigger if the guy didn't shut up. Members of the Dubois gang screamed for Beluga's head when they saw me next, but I did nothing. I should have given him a medal.

Such episodes were convincing me that Alain Dubois was getting close to the Hells. I was on good terms with everyone else in the Dubois crew, but couldn't understand what he was doing. He seemed to be letting the Hells and their puppet club, the Rockers, take over his territory. He denied ties to the Hells, but I was getting word from others in his crime family that he was lying. In the end, he became a Rocker, got arrested with his new friends, and then gave back his patches.

During another meeting with the Dubois clan, Beluga tapped me on the shoulder. We were at the Coin d'Or bar.

"There's an old bum staring at you," he said.

I looked up and saw a scruffy man in his fifties at the other end of the room. I didn't feel threatened and went back to my conversation. When the meeting was over, I got up and headed for the door.

"Pete," Beluga yelled. "You forgot to pay."

I pulled out my roll of cash, paid for everything and gave the waitress a $25 tip. I was putting my wad of cash in order as I went to the door when the scruffy man got up from his table and stood in front of me. Beluga went to push him out of the way, but I stopped him.

"Do you have some extra money?" the man asked.

It was my father.

For a brief moment, I felt sorry for him. But it didn't last as memories of childhood came back. My brother had run into our father once, and chewed him out for being a deadbeat, but I wasn't interested in going over old history. I turned to the waitress and gave her some cash.

"Bring him a beer." Then I turned back to my father. "Here. Have one on me."

"Thanks," he said. "But do you have some extra bucks so I can eat?"

"No." I put my roll of cash in my pocket. "See ya."

I walked out the door. Beluga trotted behind.

"Who was that?"

My brain was flashing back to childhood, to all the hurt and misery.

"That bum was my biological father."

Nobody said anything.

Summer hit and I planned a show of force on Wellington Street. When police closed off the commercial street to traffic for a side-walk sale, I invited about 30 full patches and prospects to take over the picnic tables in front of a Greek restaurant owned by an acquaintance named Spiros. A few armed hangarounds were doing security, making sure we weren't bothered.

I sat unarmed but wearing a bulletproof vest at a table with others as we ate and drank beer all afternoon in our Rock Machine sweaters. People who didn't know us gawked and rushed away while some of my friends came over to say hello.

We drew cops, and one of the uniformed officers came up to me.

"We don't want any problems here," he said.

"There is not going to be any trouble," I answered.

Officers then went up to people at random and asked for identification. Jimmy Larivée was grabbed for unpaid tickets. They put the handcuffs on him and were about to lead him away when I stood up.

"No, no, no," I said, taking out my roll of cash. "You're not taking him anywhere. How much?"

Jimmy wasn't my guy, but his boss had no money on him. The cops got a receipt book and I handed over $350 to free Jimmy. Then I paid for two other guys.

A meeting of full patches was scheduled soon after. To avoid police snooping in, such masses were held in rented cabins in the woods, private reception halls, hotels, homes, the basement of a dollar store and even, my favorite, the rented hall of a convent in the western suburbs of Montreal. For the convent, we pretended to be an association of ski-doo riders and left the biker clothes at home. The two nuns who led us to the meeting hall had no clue.

When it was Bam-Bam's turn to choose a meeting place, he began drawing a map for us. I let Toute-Toute oversee the directions since I was hopeless outside my area. As Bam-Bam drew, Toute-Toute and I looked at each other. Another barn.

"Trust me, *tabarnac*," Bam-Bam said, knowing how all the city members would bitch. "It is not as bad as you think."

We drove to the farm on the meeting day. Once out of Toute-Toute's truck, an unbelievable stench hit us. It was much worse than the usual cow manure and horse shit.

As we walked to the barn, I gagged and almost vomited, seeking refuge behind a lit cigarette to change the odor.

"Hey," Bam-Bam yelled upon seeing us. "No fucking smoking. You want to set all the goddamn hay on fire?"

I ignored him and lit a new cigarette off the dying embers of the last.

The meeting was to take place in one part of the barn. From the other half came a constant chirping. I walked over, and the stench worsened. I looked into a pen and saw hundreds of yellow furballs. The place was a chick hatchery.

I walked back and Bam-Bam came over with a smile.

"I told you it wouldn't be too bad," he said.

"Are you fucking with me?" I responded.

"Don't tell me this smells like shit," he countered with injured pride.

He was right. It didn't smell like shit. I would have been happy if it had.

The meeting began, and as we spoke, the chicks began competing with us for noise level. Everyone was fed up because we kept having to yell and repeat ourselves. Then I ran out of cigarettes.

Mon-Mon and I sat next to each other, me on a crate, him on a log. He was a country boy so the smell didn't affect him. Johnny wasted no time in reaming out Mon-Mon for missing meetings and leaving me alone with the business. He pointed at me.

"He's a fucking idiot to give you half his money. We can't believe he's so fucking stupid. And you," pointing to Mon-Mon, "are useless."

Mon-Mon's face turned red and he exploded.

"You motherfucker," Mon-Mon said.

"Get off your ass, you lazy fuck," Johnny continued.

The inevitable happened. I saw Mon-Mon reach for his gun.

His pistol was usually in his belt and his hand moved that way. Then he remembered leaving the weapon in his truck.

Now Johnny and Mon-Mon were on their feet, inches apart, cursing and threatening each other. Curly got between them.

"Enough!"

"I don't need or deserve this crap," Mon-Mon said. He looked at me and then stormed out to his truck.

I felt like shit. Everyone was looking at me to see what I'd do. I got up and went to Curly.

"This can't end like this. Not like this."

Curly and I went outside. Mon-Mon was standing by his truck, his gun in his jeans. He looked at me.

"Tell me what you want me to do," he said, obviously hurt.

"Just make your presence known in Verdun and we'll work something out."

Curly talked quietly. "Let's all calm down. Come back to the meeting, Mon-Mon."

"Johnny better not start on me again," he said, "because I'm not going to fuck around."

Most of us raced to finish the meeting with Johnny and Mon-Mon, this time armed, glaring at each other, ready to pounce at the slightest hint of insult. It was Bam-Bam's last meeting in a barn. On July 30, 1998, he was shot in the back of the head as he came out of a health club in Saint-Lin, a farming town north of Montreal. He broke his own rules by having a routine—he worked out at regular intervals. He was killed the same day as Yvon Roy, who became a full patch the same night I was made a prospect. Yvon was assassinated while mowing his lawn.

Yvon's family didn't want a funeral but we held a large affair for Bam-Bam at Saint-Lin town hall and a nearby church. We invited a photographer from the crime tabloid *Allo-Police* to snap a shot of me in my Rock Machine sweater in front of Bam-Bam's coffin. It was too much for Bam-Bam's brother. He lunged to push me out of the way.

"Tabarnac," he said, crying. "This is not a circus."

A few of his family members pulled him away. I felt sorry for him but still posed for the photo.

CHAPTER 16

One hot August afternoon in 1998, I took my weekly trip to Viandal's butcher shop to buy steaks, roasts, and veal. I was staying away from cocaine, but getting fat on food as the drug profits were rolling in. With me was Poutine, a club prospect who came along for the ride as bodyguard. His real name is Daniel Leclerc, but the nickname stuck because he kept having meetings in greasy spoons despite hating their main product, a fat-filled Quebec delicacy of fries, cheese curds, and brown gravy.

"Why do you want all that meat?" Poutine asked me in the shop. I had about three hundred dollars' worth.

"Saves trips. Less danger," I told him as I paid. The owner gave me a discount because I bought so much.

"Check things outside," I told Poutine as I collected the meat from the counter.

Poutine headed out, looking around the busy commercial street for enemies. He saw nothing. From the beginning of the war, I'd been told to be careful, not establish any habits. I'd listened, and always took different routes, but my butcher-shop routine was safe, I thought, because it was so close to home. Besides, I was wearing a bulletproof vest despite the humid Montreal heat. Poutine checked for any fast movement as I walked out of the shop to my GMC Jimmy. I got in, but he stayed alert by my truck's front bumper while I started the engine and eased its nose out of the parking space. Then Poutine got in. We drove down Hickson Avenue toward my home to drop off the steaks before making the rounds of my dealers. Since I was so close to home, I shrugged off my vest and threw it in the back seat.

For safety reasons, I always kept a gun in my truck. I had paid an electrician $500 to rig up a secret compartment under the armrest between the front seats. Though I'd been stopped many times by police, they never found it. To open the hiding place, you had to twist the heater controls, turn on the fan, put the vehicle in neutral, and then hit the brakes. That day, I had taken the gun out and put it in the glove compartment for easy access. During the drive, I kept looking in my rear-view mirror to see if someone was following us. I wasn't worried about cops.

I noticed a black Toyota Corolla with heavily tinted windows slowly coming up behind us. The street was narrow, with parked cars on each side of a single lane for traffic. As we approached a red light, I told Poutine to get my .357 Magnum out of the glove compartment. The light changed and I drove on.

"What's wrong?" he asked, looking at me. He put the pistol under his thigh.

"I'm not sure," I answered. I was still watching the slow car.

The light in front of me turned yellow. I slowed. Then a car parked at the corner darted through the light just as it turned red, leaving an empty spot next to my Jimmy. Women started pushing their baby strollers across the intersection, tugging along older children who didn't walk fast enough.

As I watched the Corolla, the front passenger window rolled down as it approached my truck. Something was wrong. The black car swerved into the just-vacated spot next to me. I caught a flash of metal.

A gun. The guy pointing it was wearing a baseball cap backwards. His long hair was loose, brushing at his goatee. He was almost lying down with his back resting on the driver so he could aim the gun up at me in the truck. I looked into his eyes and thought I recognized him. He was a full patch in the Death Riders, a puppet club that did the bidding of the Hells.

My window shattered from the first bullet and I felt something in my chest.

"Fuck," I yelled as Poutine sat dumbfounded on my gun. Both of us frantically tried to unbuckle our seatbelts to get out, but our hands kept fumbling with the catches.

I leaned down near the steering wheel to hide my head from sight, my seatbelt straining at its limit. No more bullets.

After a few seconds, I put my head up to see what was happening. That brought on more shots.

I felt around for my gun while using one arm to protect myself from my worst nightmare—a shot to the head. Our useless wrestling in the truck cab must have seemed comic to anyone watching us. Over and over again, I pushed Poutine toward his door. So he couldn't reach back to unbuckle himself. We remained belted in.

More bullets thudded into the truck and me. With each impact, I grunted involuntarily. They felt like stabs from a hot metal rod.

"What the fuck are you doing?" I yelled at Poutine. "Give me my gun."

But I couldn't budge his meaty leg over the pistol. He sat almost paralyzed, moving in slow motion, saying nothing. I yelled furiously.

"I'm hit again. Get the fuck out of the truck."

Outside, mothers and children screamed and ran. Despite my wounds and panic, I kept my foot on the brake pedal. One way to escape the shots would have been to plow through all the people in the crosswalk. I couldn't do that.

I finally freed Poutine's belt and he jumped out his door. Though he had time to shoot at the car with my pistol, he just ran. By this time, I had four bullets in me. (Police later found two additional slugs from the assassin's gun imbedded in my truck and a nearby building.)

I finally got my seatbelt undone. The road in front of me was clear so I let go of the brake pedal and crawled over to the passenger's seat. As I stumbled out of the truck, the Corolla's driver gunned the engine and the car screamed away.

My truck, still in drive, slowly rolled into a street light. I felt weak and dizzy as I hobbled after the truck and leaned against a corner-store wall. Poutine ran over.

"Those fuckers," he said furiously. "No way does this finish like this."

He looked at my wounds.

"Someone called 911. Are you going to be OK?" he asked, his voice trembling and his eyes wide.

"I don't know."

"What should I do? The police are on the way."

Great help he was. I was bleeding to death, and he couldn't think for himself.

"Get rid of my gun," I told him, grimacing as my adrenaline high wore off and the pain hit.

He ran to a nearby alley and tossed the pistol in a dumpster. I lay down on the sidewalk as an ambulance siren grew louder. A lady in her forties came over to where I lay, soon joined by a man half her age.

"Hang on," the lady told me. Her help was comforting. "Concentrate on your breathing."

Poutine came back.

"Jesus Christ," he said, eyeing me. "Are you going to make it?"

Then he became enraged, maybe to make up for his uselessness just minutes before.

"Those sons of bitches are going to pay for this. I promise. They are going to pay."

I was rushed to the Montreal General Hospital. In the ambulance, my rage came out as I ripped off my oxygen mask to swear while attendants kept fighting to put it back on.

"Bastards. I'm going to get them," I yelled. "Fuckers, they'll see what we can do."

At the hospital, I remember bright lights on an operating table and somebody staring down at me with sympathetic eyes.

"Am I going to make it?"

"We don't know right now," the man said, taking hold of my

hand. I never saw him again but I think he was a priest. Just before I passed out, my thoughts went to all the people I loved.

Later that night, when I woke up, my strict Catholic upbringing came back to me. I believed God saved me, giving me a second chance. I was sure I would live, though I got scared when my family showed up. The more they cried, the more convinced I became the doctors had told them something I didn't know. My grandmother came with my mother, but Granna stayed on the other side of my bed's privacy curtain.

"I can't look at him like this," she said, crying. "I can't."

"Please tell her I want to see her," I told my mother in a faint voice.

Granna peeked her head around the curtain, but the pitch of her crying increased on seeing all the bandages and tubes.

"Oh, Peter. I'm praying for you. You are not going to die."

Anne and my brother showed up as well. The two of them fought in front of me over who got to take care of the $800 that had been in my pockets.

That first night, I had unexpected guests—two Montreal police officers. One was Benoit Roberge, the analyst on biker gangs.

"How are you feeling?" one asked.

"What do you think?" I replied.

I wasn't friendly. Cops weren't my favorite people.

"What do you want?"

"Did you see who shot you?"

I said nothing. One tried again.

"Just tell us his name. We won't tell anyone you gave us the information."

Still no answer from me.

"People will think it was an eyewitness at the scene of the crime who told us."

They got nowhere.

"Read the papers," I told them.

"Huh?"

"You'll find out who did this by reading about the next killing."

They got the picture. The Rock Machine would find my assassins and take care of them privately. No police. My brother walked by, spotted them, and stormed into the room.

"Get out," Robert yelled at the cops. "You've no right to harass him in his state. Get the fuck out."

"Relax," Roberge said. "We were just leaving."

The next morning, I got a private room. Within ten minutes, gang members joined me to make sure the Hells didn't finish what they had started.

I had been feeling an uncomfortable weight between my legs but I couldn't get up to check it out. Since I'd been shot so close to the groin, I figured the nurses had put an icepack down there. I reached down under the sheets with both hands, feeling something about the size of a cantalope. I started to lift it up, but panic struck me.

"Come here," I told Beluga. "Tell me what you see. I can't stretch enough to get a look."

He stood by the hospital bed and lifted the sheet so only he could see.

"Oh fuck!"

He backed away from the bed with a strange look of concern on his face.

"What's the matter?" I was yelling. "Is everything there?"

He was trying not to laugh.

"What the fuck is it?" I roared.

"You should get a camera and take a picture of this," Beluga finally said. "It would be good proof to show a chick that you are equipped."

"What do you mean?" I answered, almost crazy with fear.

He started to laugh, using his two hands to show me how swollen my balls had become. Then he took delight in describing how black and blue they appeared. I panicked, and called for a nurse or doctor. I was sure sex was a thing of the past for me. The doctor walked in, calming me down by saying everything would return to normal.

That day's newspaper had a story about my shooting and my territory. "Police expect the worst," read the headline. Unnamed police sources told the reporter that people should expect a resurgence of violence in my area, calling it a real powder keg. The story continued that southwest Montreal had been strongly Rock Machine for years, and I was now in charge after Renaud's death. Even though the Hells originally thought they could conquer it easily, they found themselves in another Vietnam, a police officer said.

To avoid another attempt on my life, armed bodyguards patrolled outside the hospital and the corridor by my room. That stressed out the staff, who became worried about being caught in a shootout. One of the doctors came to see me.

"Why are all these people here?" he asked.

"Listen, I am a full-patch member of the Rock Machine organization. If these people aren't here, there is a very good chance you will come into the room sometime and find me dead."

He was confused, and I was becoming short-tempered from my wounds.

"How do you think I got here in the first place?"

He finally understood and left after I told him to keep my room number secret. I tried to make it easier for the hospital staff by getting my bodyguards to lose the biker clothes, and come dressed in Bermuda shorts or preppy clothes. To blend in, Jimmy Larivée ended up putting on a hospital robe that shows your ass in the back. And those funny hospital slippers. But he still carried his pistol in his shorts.

The pain was hell, and the needles and IVs made me feel like a voodoo doll. One night, I woke up my whole floor by yelling for a larger dose of morphine. As I got better, I kept asking my gang when they would retaliate. All of them had been full of boasts to kill and beat up enemies. But nothing happened. I also began running my drug operation from my hospital bed. No drugs passed hands, but my underlings were constantly coming and going.

Anne came to see me two or three hours a day, and she was exasperated by all the business I was conducting. She'd constantly fidget, pulling and tugging on all the tubes going into me, wanting to know what they were for.

"You're hurting me," I kept telling her.

But she'd start again.

"Just don't touch me or anything else. Am I speaking in a foreign language or are you just natually brain dead?"

She calmed down. But then she spotted something new.

"Oh, I didn't see this tube," she said, giving it a yank.

I roared with pain. She had found the catheter in my penis.

She just sat there with a blank look on her face.

"When am I going to get some attention?" she asked in a huff a day later when Mon-Mon was visiting.

I had been neglecting her, I suppose. But her pouting while I was recovering in hospital struck me as childish. She had everything she wanted—money, clothes, and diamonds.

"What part of this don't you understand?" I asked her sarcastically.

"I don't care about your business. I want your attention."

"Hey," Mon-Mon said to get Anne's attention. "Why don't you give it a rest? Don't you think he is going through enough?"

She turned around and gave him a look deadlier than the bullets in me. She got up.

"Are you going to let him talk to me like that?" she spat out after getting up.

"Like what? He's right."

"You heartless son of a bitch," she yelled at me. "All you care about is money and your friends."

"Money didn't seem to bother you before." The sarcasm in my voice couldn't be missed. I kept going.

"I don't know what your problem is. You were living in a dump and your kids couldn't get three meals a day until I came around. Eating noodles in tomato juice four times a week is not well fed in my opinion. You have everything you want. If you don't appreciate anything I am doing for you and your kids, you know what to do."

"You're right," she replied sadly, a tear rolling off her cheek. "I know exactly what I am supposed to do. I've had enough of this bullshit."

She took off her diamond rings and threw all three in my face, including the engagement ring. Then she walked out.

I was very hurt, but eventually realized it was for the better if our relationship blew up over such a minor thing. Her timing stunk, though. A day later, the phone rang in my hospital room for the first time.

"Peter, it's Brigitte."

"How did you get through to this number?" I asked, my mind racing wildly. I didn't care who it was, I wanted to know how somebody could find me in the hospital. If she could, so could the Hells. When she spoke next, her voice made it clear she was hurt by my reaction. She said she asked the hospital switchboard to patch her through to my room.

"I have to see you," she said.

"Not right now." I wanted to get off the phone and scream at the hospital staff.

"Promise me you'll call me."

I promised and hung up. Then I yelled for the doctor. When he came, I told him they were idiots to even tell people I was at the hospital.

"If anyone calls, I'm not here."

A few days later, Poutine came by. His face was serious as he leaned over my bed. Jimmy was with him.

"I got something lined up," Poutine whispered. "Revenge."

That got me interested.

"Make sure it is somebody well known and in my territory," I whispered back. "I want them to know my territory is still mine and that not killing me was a mistake. Got that?"

I wanted a clear message I was still in control of southwest Montreal. Poutine said something about a saint, but I couldn't understand him.

By then, the hospital staff was sick of my gang. I was discharged after only eight days, while some of my wounds were still bleeding. When they handed me my personal effects, I grabbed my wallet and opened it to see if everything was there.

"Fuck," I said to Beluga, "look at that."

There was a bullet imbedded inside. It explained why I had a big bruise on my ass.

I left the Montreal General surrounded by eight armed bodyguards, three with me in one car, and five following in a Ford Aerostar containing a submachine gun. I wanted to make a stop before going to Toute-Toute's cottage in the Eastern Townships. He'd offered to let me recuperate there.

"Take me to Verdun," I told Mario. "There's something I have to do."

"What the hell do you want in Verdun?" he asked. "You just got shot there last week."

"That's my point. That's exactly why I want to go back there. As a matter of fact, take me to exactly where I got shot."

"Are you sure?" Mario asked nervously.

"Does it look like I'm fucking around?"

We got out at the corner.

"Follow me on foot," I told everyone in my car, while those in the van kept watch by inching along the road. I walked across the street to a sports store, where a young man in his twenties worked behind the counter. I approached with my hand held out in a handshake. The man stood there with his mouth open.

"Do you know who I am?" I asked.

"How could I forget?" He was one of the bystanders who had

comforted me while I was lying on the sidewalk. "How are you doing?"

"Better." Then I explained why I was there. "I just wanted to thank you personally for what you did for me last week. I don't know how to thank you but if I could ever do anything for you, just ask. I'm not a hard person to find."

"You're welcome."

He told me the lady with him that day worked in a jeans store two buildings over. That was my next stop.

A woman came straight over to me as I walked in. She asked how I felt. It wasn't the one who had consoled me but she had seen the shooting. We shook hands.

"It wasn't your time," she said.

I never got the chance to thank the right woman, who supposedly worked in a nearby eatery.

"Where are you going now?" Beluga asked as I sauntered down the sidewalk, enjoying the sunny day.

"Keep your eyes open and just follow."

It was time for a public show. I walked slowly down Wellington, making sure everyone saw me. It took time because I was still weak. The van followed, eliciting honks from other drivers who wanted to go faster. The guys in the van responded with the finger. I saw a lot of people I knew. Some came over to encourage me to get better. Others looked like they had seen a ghost.

I was so weak I almost passed out before sitting down on a bench.

"Are you satisfied?" Beluga asked.

"Yes. I'm sure my message to this town is very clear. Fuck the Hells. They should have killed me because now I'm going to take them to hell."

I wanted revenge. But I also wanted a long rest. The shooting had hurt me mentally as well as physically.

"I'm tired," I told my bodyguards. "Let's go."

CHAPTER 17

The bullet whizzed by my ear as I ran. I ducked down an alley, and my pursuer followed, his gun never running out of bullets. I turned a corner and stopped. I'd lost him, I thought. But he reappeared in front of me, shooting his pistol almost point-blank. I spun around and ran, my lungs wanting to give out and my face full of sweat. The bullets approached in slow motion.

I opened my eyes and felt Simba licking my sweaty face. I pushed the German shepherd away with a grunt and sat up. My bed was soaked in perspiration. Another nightmare. I got up and tossed my scrunched-up pillow back up to the head of the bed, covering my 9 mm.

Beluga's snores kept going at a steady rhythm. As a night guard, he was useless. But it didn't matter since Simba was always alert. I'd bought him for $2,000 just a week before I was shot. Now he was my constant companion at the lakeside chalet.

I smoked a joint to calm my nerves and went back to bed, though I had trouble closing my eyes and taking a chance nothing would happen to me while I slept. Dreams of people breaking into the chalet and finishing me off were common. So I lay there while all the tortured memories of my shooting came back. Beluga's monstrous snoring kept me company.

After I did my walkabout in Verdun, a gang member had driven me down to the cabin and I passed out right after removing my shoes. I got up the next day, changed my bandages, took my medication, and passed out again. After two days, I finally felt better so I roamed down to Lake Massawippi, just 50 feet from the cabin, and stared at the calm water for half an hour. It was so peaceful.

For the first time in my life, I noticed trees swaying and flowers blooming.

My hideout was pretty primitive, its inside walls made of fake wood paneling. The kitchen where Beluga did the cooking, always with a pistol at his side, was small. The outside lot included a swimming pool and scattered on the grass nearby were toys abandoned by Toute-Toute's daughter.

Beluga came up to me as I held a wildflower, studying it intently.

"You all right?" he asked.

"Yeah, I guess."

"Don't worry," he added. "You'll be back to your old self in a couple of weeks."

"I hope so," I laughed.

My routine became simple. Every morning, I strolled down to the lakefront to feed the wild ducks some bread. I'd sit on the dock for hours, stroking Simba's mane.

Fuck this war, I suddenly thought out there one day, my 9 mm on the rotting planks beside me. I want out of this life. Just walk away. I could do that. But would the Hells believe I had retired? Or would they see me without any protection and finish the job?

I then thought about all the people close to me who had died in the past four years, all the funerals, and all my soldiers and dealers who depended on me in this war. I had repeated again and again about how they had to be committed to the Rock Machine. How could I then turn around and quit? I played with my Rock Machine ring constantly, thinking about the gang and all we'd been through.

I heard a noise. I grabbed the gun and put my finger on the trigger. Before I could turn around, something pressed against my neck. Simba's tongue. After a nervous laugh, I let him lie down to be pampered.

My mind went back to the priest who had been standing over me on the operating table. He looked real but not real at the same time. He'd never returned to see me while I was recuperating.

Would they allow priests into the sterile operating room, anyway?

Beluga then called me, saying Poutine was on the phone.

"Do you remember I told you I had this thing set up?" he said right away.

"Sure, I remember," I said with a smile. "Get your ass down here. We can talk about it then. I'm getting bored. I can use the company."

"Don't you have Beluga?"

"I'm getting a little tired of seeing that face all the time."

He laughed and agreed I was being tortured.

"I'll leave in an hour or so," he added.

"By the way, bring something to smoke."

"I understand," he replied.

That night, we smoked the hash he brought and made our plans. A bomb was to be planted under a truck belonging to Jean-Claude Saint-Pierre, a dealer for the Rockers. That was the "saint" he had been referring to in the hospital.

"Consider him dead," he said. "Just give me forty-eight hours."

"He has a wife and kids," I said. "Make sure they aren't in the truck when you do this."

Two days later, the news carried an item about two men with Rockers connections who were badly injured when their Ford truck exploded in Côte St. Paul. But they lived. Poutine came down to see me the same night.

"I'm sorry," he said. "I'm really pissed they didn't die."

"Don't worry," I answered. "It's not your fault. What are the odds of someone surviving a bomb in their vehicle?"

"Rare," he said. "One in a million."

The two men inside were saved because of their choice of vehicle. The Ford F150 was one of the few trucks to come with a metal plate underneath that deflected most of the blast, though Saint-Pierre won't be able to shit without difficulty for the rest of his life.

"Look on the bright side," I told Poutine. "Everyone knows who those guys are and where that bomb came from. It will give them something to fucking think about. And I don't think we have to worry about those two for a while."

Poutine wasn't mollified.

"I'm still disappointed I let you down. But I've got someone else in mind."

"Go ahead. But after that, lay low for a bit. You know how the cops like bombs. I don't need any more of them with a microscope up my ass."

We learned later that the anti-gang squad reacted to the Ford's explosion by starting a special operation called Project Amorce. Montreal police wanted to put an end to all the bombings, so they put two cops who had been keeping an eye on Verdun in charge—Det. Sgt. Clement Rose and his partner, Claude Lambert.

A few days later, the news carried another bombing item, this one on Ropery Street. People felt the ground shake as far as two blocks away when the bomb in a Grand Prix car blew out the windows in adjacent buildings, sending glass shards into homes. But the driver was able to get out of his car on his own legs, suffering injury to just one arm. That explosion strengthened the resolve of Montreal police, and they started preparing warrants for wiretaps and raids. Rose quickly got word from an informant on the street that Poutine and Jimmy Larivée were behind it.

More bad news came the same day as the Ropery Street explosion. For the past 24 hours, police had been looking for some sort of gang crime up in Laval because they'd found a getaway car torched with two machine pistols in the back, the sure sign of a biker hit. Then Tony Plescio went to his brother's home in Laval and found Johnny riddled with bullets. I soon heard that Johnny had probably been watching TV when the hit team cut his cable wire. When Johnny got up and went to his TV, it made him a perfect silhouette in the window. Police estimated that more than 20 bullets were fired at him.

I went back to the city for the funeral. When we arrived wearing bandannas to escape the TV cameras, police pulled us to the side and made us lower our masks to take the usual pictures for their files. I had sent a wreath with Mon-Mon, who came despite his recent fights with Johnny. Flowers were sent by Rock Machine members incarcerated at Cowansville prison and by the local Italian mafia as well as Bandidos chapters around the world. Many of the wreaths were in the traditional Bandidos colors of red and yellow. One was signed "The Cable Guy" in huge letters. I always wondered if Johnny's killer sent that as a joke since he had chopped the cable feed to lure him into his sights.

Johnny's body wore a Bandidos sweater and someone had lain a red rose across his chest. After the brief ceremony, I was beside Johnny's mother and we ended up hugging.

"You'se are going to do something, right?" she told me through constant tears. "You are going to avenge him?"

I nodded.

Johnny's death was a big blow. He was a money man, and without cash, fighting the Hells would get harder. When visiting his place north of Montreal, I'd seen him walk or drive an all-terrain vehicle into a nearby forest to go pick up some cash he'd hidden somewhere. I hoped he'd told his family where the loot was because Ti-Bum had used similar precautions. When Ti-Bum had died, his family had torn apart the most logical places in his home and businesses, but hadn't been able to find his fortune.

Curly came up to me at Johnny's funeral.

"We're going to buy two bazookas and really get those bastards," he said.

"Fucking good idea," I answered.

"Can you chip in?"

I took out my roll and handed him $3,000.

"I want to be there to use them," I told him.

I dreamed of having a Hells killed, and then seeing 30 or 40 of his fellow bikers at a wake in one of their clubhouses. We'd set up the bazookas nearby and just blast the building into little pieces, not caring if women or children were inside. Only full patches were to know of the bazookas for the moment. But my guys needed a morale boost so, the next day, I told my brother, Mario and Beluga.

After that, I went back to Toute-Toute's cabin with Beluga. Brigitte came down a few days later and she told me how she'd heard about my shooting. A friend had called her and said the radio was talking about a Pierre Paradis shot in Verdun. Brigitte figured it was probably me even though the name was a bit off.

"Motherfucker better not be dead," she said that day to herself as she phoned my mother. My mother had no idea and immediately hung up to call the hospital. Brigitte started crying, and our 12-year-old son walked in on her. She told him nothing since he had no idea what I did. Brigitte had decided when our son was 4 to get him out of the inner city, so she moved to the suburb of Laval, very much a middle-class city. She shielded our son from my criminal activities, saying I was often unable to see him because of business trips. When I was shot, Brigitte sent him off to the country so he wouldn't hear anything on the news. But he found out anyway and she had to tell him about the Rock Machine and drug dealing.

"That's why he had all that money," was his first reaction. He'd always seen me with huge rolls of cash. But he never thought to ask, like a typical child who assumes his parents have typically boring jobs.

During that visit, Brigitte and I decided to try living together after 11 years apart. We'd seen each other at various intervals, sometimes sleeping together even though we were dating others. She had flown into a rage when our son told her I was going to marry Anne. She told me she had always loved me.

While Brigitte was at the cottage, I got a visit from Stéphane Morgan, the full patch we called Ti-Cul. He and Beluga raided my Emprecet, the painkiller the doctors had prescribed. I wasn't using it, preferring pot to dull the pain. Beluga wasn't impressed with the free pills.

"They're not so strong," he boasted, popping them like mints.

We were sitting around the coffee table in the living room, our pistols in front of us. We had the crime tabloid *Allo Police* on the table open to the story and photo of my shooting, as well as my pills, hash, pot, and PCP.

Beluga and Ti-Cul mixed the Emprecet with sleeping pills Brigitte had brought down. And they added the PCP. During one of these pill-and-booze binges, Stéphane broke down and cried. That scared me, because he was one of the toughest guys in the gang.

"What's wrong?" I asked.

"I'm fed up. I've been fucking abandoned by my brothers in the Rock Machine."

He sobbed uncontrollably.

"This is not supposed to fucking happen. I'm a full patch, for Christ's sake. I'm not supposed to be left out after remaining loyal for so long. Now, I don't know when the fuck my next meal is going to come."

I knew all this. Ti-Cul had been dropping by in the past couple of years, asking for money for food and to buy gas so he could get around to salvage his decimated business. I'd hand over a few hundred dollars, not expecting it back. He always paid me with a big hug, and I could tell his pride was hurt just having to ask. He would say I was the only one who helped.

Ti-Cul stopped crying and pulled his gun out, waving it around in a rage.

"I'm a fucking killer. Who wouldn't want me on their team?"

I nodded and he looked at me, the gun at his side. He told me about a hit he did one night in 1996 at a crowded afterhours bar in Montreal called the Sunrise. He spotted a guy with the Hells, followed him to the washroom, and killed him right there.

"Let me work with you," he said. "I don't want half your profits like Mon-Mon, who's sitting on his ass doing nothing. Just give me a fair share. I'll show you what I'm capable of."

"You got it," I said, giving him a hug. "Just give me some time while I sort things out with Mon-Mon."

I knew Mon-Mon wouldn't last much longer, so I needed Ti-Cul. Both Brigitte and Stéphane returned to Montreal. I kept doing my morning trips to the ducks, but my pager and cell phone were back in operation, pulling me almost involuntarily to Verdun and my drug business. Mon-Mon had had my bullet-riddled truck fixed and then repainted from black to gray so it wouldn't be recognized. Beluga and I would use it to go back into the city, maybe stay a day, and then return to the chalet. I never felt safe in the city, often stopping my truck to put on my bulletproof vest when the downtown high-rises came into sight. During one of the trips, we went to Brigitte's apartment in Laval to get her and my son to come down and spend some time at the chalet. We had just picked them up when a Laval police cruiser came up behind us, its lights flashing.

"What the fuck do they want?" I cursed.

Beluga was sitting behind me. He took a pistol from his belt and tossed it at me. I stuffed his gun with mine in my armrest hiding place and pushed it closed. It wouldn't click shut.

"Is the gun hidden?" Beluga asked. My son sat mutely beside him.

"The fucking thing won't work," I replied, giving the armrest another push.

I saw two cops get out of the cruiser. One came toward me, while the other stayed behind, close to the cop car's front lights.

"Is it hidden?" Beluga asked again.

"No."

The cop was at my back bumper. This time, I slammed the armrest down and, thankfully, heard a click.

The police officer tapped at Beluga's window.

"Get out of the vehicle," he said, specifying only Beluga, who complied.

"Turn around and lean against the car," the cop added.

Beluga assumed the position.

"What's your name?" the officer asked while frisking him.

I stifled a snort when Beluga gave a false name. The cop smiled.

"Stop screwing around, Eric. We know who you are."

I couldn't help laughing. They had him on an outstanding warrant. The cops took him away without even asking for my identification.

What I didn't know was that Detective Sergeant Rose had asked Laval police to stop me. He told them Beluga and I were probably carrying guns, but to give me enough time to hide mine. Rose didn't want me put away in jail for a simple gun-possession charge and to lose his chance to get me for more serious accusations. But Montreal police couldn't ignore the outstanding warrant against Beluga, so they told Laval police to grab just him.

Beluga was led to the cruiser behind us, and the cops took away his bulletproof vest. He talked with detectives afterwards, boasting that he hated the Hells so much that he would continue to fight them even if he ended up in a wheelchair. Cheeky was already inside on a weapons charge, so that deprived me of two of my best enforcers. I decided to lie low until they were let out.

Police began their wiretaps the next day, targeting myself, Poutine, Jimmy, John, and several others. Four days later, Brigitte and I stopped in at one of my drug houses on Bannantyne Street. She waited outside on the balcony as I conducted business while my brother was there. She came in after a few minutes and went up to the woman who lived there.

"Jill, a car drove by three times. And I saw a head on top of the church across the street."

We paid no attention. Ten minutes later, the door burst in.

"It's the police," someone yelled.

Robert and I scrambled out the back door with Brigitte on our heels.

"Police," yelled uniformed officers waiting for us, pointing sub-machine guns. "Get down. Lie down."

We fell on our stomachs, but Robert kept fidgeting.

"Stop moving," a cop yelled out, getting nervous.

Robert stopped, but moved again.

"Knock it off," I told him. "They are really jumpy."

He squirmed again and the heavily armed cop again barked out a command.

"I'm not going to stick my face in shit for them," Robert told me. "Look."

Right next to his head was a clump of dog droppings. I laughed.

The cops caught Robert carrying a pen gun, a small tube made for a .22-calibre bullet. All you had to do was pull back the end and let it go. A cheap firing pin would hit the bullet and send it on its way. They were popular in Verdun as easy-to-hide weapons. At the police station, a female cop asked me questions for their forms.

"Occupation?"

"I don't work. I'm a Rock Machine."

They laid no charges against me, but the cops didn't want to let Brigitte go because she had unpaid tickets. I gave them $500 from my pocket to save her a night at the women's prison. While she was in the cell, a detective walked up to her.

"So, your Paradis's new cunt, eh?"

Brigitte went ballistic. Our son saw me on the news being hand-cuffed alongside his Uncle Robert.

The next day, the cops arrested Mario on an outstanding warrant and got papers from him that showed I had rented a storage garage in Laval. He had helped move my belongings there after Anne and I broke up. Thinking the storage unit contained pot, police got a warrant, went in, and found nothing illegal. But they did discover an envelope of photos I had cut from the local newspaper to identify enemies in the Hells camp.

Business was being affected by my absence, the arrests, and a heightened police presence following Poutine's explosions. I was now making a few thousand a week and spending a lot of time commuting back and forth to fix things. One weekend, I took Brigitte to a hotel and we had a good talk about our future. The next day, one of Toute-Toute's relatives called to say the chalet had been ransacked by police. They had left a yellow happy face in a window, with "Have a nice day" written below it. But a second message was more ominous. It was the ace of spades from a deck of cards. Brigitte told me that meant death.

I called the cops. They admitted to the smiley face, but not the ace. I blew up anyway, saying they were threatening me and playing dirty. I also asked the cops to return Toute-Toute's shotgun and two bulletproof vests that had been seized. Rose said there was no problem with the vests, but the shotgun would be tested first to see if it had been used in a crime. I told Rose I didn't trust the cops down in the Eastern Townships because they were probably corrupt and in the pay of the Hells, who had a chapter in the large town of Sherbrooke, not far away.

"Peter, your place might not be safe," Rose said. "That area is full of H.A. and our raid didn't help you."

"Ya, people will get suspicious about who was here after you guys came through," I said.

"If I was in your place, I'd say your location is burned," Rose responded.

Rose picked up on my fear, realizing I was paranoid about my safety. But he had an ulterior motive for agreeing with me. A surveillance team was regularly keeping tabs on me, with some officers even borrowing boats and pretending to be fishing near Toute-Toute's cabin. Their overtime for driving an hour and a half every morning to Sainte-Catherine-de-Hatley and the same distance back at night threatened to bankrupt the operation. Rose was thrilled when I moved to Brigitte's place in Laval soon after.

The gang had another family event similar to the pig roast two summers before. Brigitte, my son, and I joined others at a ski resort in the Laurentian hills north of Montreal to descend down the mountain on inner tubes. With our ranks so low, only about 15 people showed up.

In October, a judge allowed police to bug my truck. A specialized squad called General Motors, giving them my truck's serial number. GM told police the codes to make five keys, one of which would probably fit in the ignition. So police waited until the lights were out in Brigitte's apartment on Dagenais Street before creeping up to the truck and trying the door. One of the keys worked. An officer got in and put the key in the ignition. Nothing. The other four keys were also useless. They reasoned my truck was probably a mixture of scrapped or stolen car parts that had been put together to make a full vehicle; the ignition scavenged from a different vehicle than the doors. They were right.

That night, a locksmith had brought along 200 keys just in case. Police tried all. None fit. The cops needed to start the car and drive it away to a secure spot because installing a bug takes a few hours and having a bunch of men fiddling with a vehicle outside my place at night was too suspicious. Investigators were stumped until a few days later, when they followed me to a club where I left my truck and its keys for a few hours. They had been tipped off, so a van with a locksmith inside was right behind me. They got ahold of my keys for a few minutes, made a quick copy in their van, and roared off before I came back.

One night soon after, I was asleep at Brigitte's place when cops videotaped how I had parked my truck in the lot, making sure to catch the angle of the front wheels. One officer got in with his newly made keys and drove off. Another parked a car in my spot to make sure it wasn't taken in the hours needed to install the bug.

I slept peacefully as the cops brought my truck back two hours later and parked exactly as I had left it with the help of their videotape.

CHAPTER 18

Early one morning, my pager woke me. All identical numbers. I knew what that meant so I dressed quickly, strode to my truck, and raced from Laval to the southern tip of Montreal, where I took a small bridge to Ile Notre Dame, one of the islands built for Expo 67. At the old French Pavilion, a valet opened my car door.

"Hello, Mr. Paradis," he said before getting into the driver's seat and parking my Jimmy.

I walked into the building, now the Montreal Casino. At the entrance to the high-rollers area, the attendants recognized me so I didn't have to show my VIP card. Denis was there.

"Hey, Peter," he said, pointing to a particular Flaming Seven machine. "That's why I beeped you. That's the machine you want."

Denis was what people at the casino called a scavenger. He rummaged around for coins left in trays or forgotten credits on machines. He also kept his eyes open.

"A fish just maxed out after sinking twenty grand into the machine," Denis laughed. "He ran out of credit cards."

I plopped myself in front of the machine with a bucket of $5 tokens. Denis and I worked on the principle that a machine will pay out at least some money after taking in so much. So he called me when some suckers had just lost a fortune. I would show up and reap the spoils. After plugging the machine with a few hundred dollars in tokens, it lit up, handing me $9,000. I gave Denis $100 and treated him to drinks at the bar.

The casino had become my safe playground. I was trying to insulate myself from the war by staying away from Verdun. Business could be done by my soldiers, and they could reach me when they wanted by cell. The casino was full of police officers doing security, and if anyone did try anything, they would be quickly arrested since there were only two ways on and off the island.

Denis wasn't my only help with the machines. One of the casino employees would also steer me to the machines with a lot of cash in them. With his first tip, I got an $8,000 jackpot almost right away with three flaming sevens. He ended up being the one who reset the machine and paid me the money in cash.

"You know, that tip is definitely worth ten percent," I said in a low voice.

"We're not allowed to accept money or gamble," he answered.

"I understand."

He then pointed me to another machine. As I was playing, I heard a voice behind me.

"Were you serious about that ten percent?"

"Fucking right. Call me," I said, giving him my number. We met at a Verdun pizzeria, where I handed over an envelope with $800 in it.

I sometimes left $15,000 lighter, but the odds were in my favor with all the help I was getting. That money was helping me finance the war since drug sales were stagnant. Brigitte often went with me even though she didn't like to gamble. Since I was spending so much in the high-rollers section, I was getting free tickets to shows at the casino theater as well as meals worth hundreds of dollars. That kept her busy and happy for a while. I also treated my mother and bodyguards with all the freebies I was getting.

One time, Brigitte and I left our Laval place for the casino when I realized I'd forgotten my pistol under a sweater on the living-room sofa. I had put it there after grabbing it from a side table where I usually hid it at home. A day later, my son went up to Brigitte and told her he'd sat on the gun by mistake. He asked her to tell me to be more careful. My son was too intimidated to tell me directly. We never talked about what I did, and he never complained about not going out much as a family. But he told Brigitte he was constantly worried, thinking he'd arrive home one day from school and his parents would be dead.

We were living in Brigitte's first-floor apartment while looking for something larger. I was enjoying the family life, though Brigitte and my son were a bit put off by my habits. I didn't like being on the ground floor since anyone could just walk up to a window and start firing. I would periodically scan the area near the apartment's outside wall for footprints in the dirt or snow, sometimes mistaking my own from a previous search as that of an enemy spy. I kept the blinds drawn and the windows closed at all times. If I heard talking in the hallway through our front door, I'd reach for my gun until Brigitte recognized the neighbors' voices. I would also pile the garbage bags in front of the patio door so any intruder would trip over them. My son didn't dare ask me to go play outside with him.

Our son got the apartment's one room and Brigitte and I slept on a sofa bed in the living room. I remember a dream where I was hovering in the air above our bed, watching myself and Brigitte sleep. I was shaking my head in despair and sadness. What frightened me was the room was exactly as I'd seen it before going to sleep that night, including an empty bottle of beer I'd just finished on the nightstand. I never talked about the dreams because my soldiers would think I was going nuts. I had lots of trouble sleeping, often lying for hours thinking about the priest in the operating room, and the resulting fatigue made me irritable. Smoking joints was the only thing that helped.

Back at the casino, Brigitte and I hit four jackpots one night, making almost $40,000. People were going nuts, rubbing their $5 tokens on my arm for good luck. I gave my mother a few thousand for her bills and asked her to hide another $17,000 for me. I left with $20,000 in thousand-dollar bills, picked up some coke from my drug cache and headed home with Brigitte. The next night, I was watching the hockey game when Brigitte came back from washing our clothes at the public laundry room in the building.

"Sweetheart, I think I screwed up," she said.

"What are you talking about?"

"I accidentally washed your wallet."

I bolted straight up, my face white as a ghost.

"What's the big deal? All you keep in there is your ID and driver's license."

"This is the big deal." I cracked open the wallet to show her the thousand-dollar bills, all 20 of them.

"Oh my God," she said. "And the wallet was just lying there in bottom of the dryer for anyone to take."

I spread the wet bills out on our kitchen counter and used a blow dryer to revive them. That was Brigitte's only attempt at money-laundering.

That fall of 1998, Mon-Mon came to see me at Toute-Toute's home. He ended our partnership and we parted after a hug. That meant things were clear to call up Ti-Cul, who still wanted to be my partner. I just needed some time to clear up the matter with the other full patches first. But Ti-Cul didn't survive long enough. He was gunned down with another man as they sat in a car. I felt he wouldn't have died if the Rock Machine had taken care of him.

His mother wanted an open casket, and she got it despite objections from the Rock Machine, who weren't happy with the corpse's appearance. Even though the embalmers tried their best to cover up the bullet holes, they were still visible. I heard Serge Cyr speaking to some guys at the funeral.

"Why didn't he use his gun?" he said.

One of the other guys nodded.

"He should have been more careful."

I was shocked, and gave them a long stare. It was unheard of to criticize someone who died for the Rock Machine. This was the second time I had heard such talk. Bam-Bam also got blamed for going to his health club on a regular basis. Both Bam-Bam and

Stéphane deserved respect, I thought. How would the full patches have talked about me if my shooting had been fatal?

Brigitte was very nervous after that, constantly making sure bodyguards were around. And she was sick of only going to the casino. To help her forget it all, I would give her hundreds of dollars at a time to go shopping. But she used the money to help out friends and family instead. One day, she was particularly unhappy.

"Here," I said, tossing her $1,000, "why don't you go shopping?"

She hurled it back.

"I don't want to go shopping anymore. It bores me."

I'd never heard a woman say that.

"I'm getting tired of this life," she said. "We can't go anywhere or do anything together."

"What more do you want from me?" I asked impatiently. "I can't give you more than what I'm doing."

"I'm not saying you are doing nothing. I just feel like I'm living in a gold cage."

She began crying. I couldn't understand. When we were younger, we were poor and wasted on coke. Now we had money, which I thought would solve everything.

We didn't talk much for the next few weeks as I kept busy in Verdun. I finally got fed up and asked her to take a drive with me for a change of pace to Toute-Toute's place in Lachine. As we took the scenic route, I kept looking in the rear-view mirror at a car following us. Brigitte noticed.

"What's wrong?" she asked, looking behind us.

I turned onto a street to see if the car followed. It did. Those aren't cops, I thought.

"Put your seat down flat and stay low," I told Brigitte.

Her frightened eyes looked at me as she did what I had ordered. I floored the accelerator and drove the wrong way up a one-way street. The car sped up and followed. I pulled my gun out of its hiding place in the armrest.

"Don't worry," I told a terrified Brigitte. "When I go around the next corner, I want you to get out and hide behind a parked car."

I turned, braked quickly, and she jumped out. I floored the truck again, drove down a bit farther and slammed on the brakes. I threw open the door, ran out, and hid motionless behind a tree. My gun was cocked.

The pursuing car braked at the corner upon seeing my truck idling in the road with nobody in it. I stared, trying to see how many people sat inside. The seconds went by like a snail. Then the car started up, driving away from us. Brigitte was white as we got back in the truck.

"This is crazy," she said.

Later that month, we learned Mon-Mon's son had killed himself. Brigitte and I had just been to their home. His death, coming so soon after Stéphane's, shocked Brigitte. It was the second person she had just met who was now dead. She was worried that her son would end up like Mon-Mon's after living a while with me. She took my son and went to visit her family in the country to get a break.

Not long after, I was driving down Wellington Street when I saw Harry walk out of the Pause Soleil tanning salon. I'd heard he was planning to open a new place after I set fire to his old salon. To me, this was proof he was back. I asked one of my guys to set it alight.

A few days after it burned, I got a call saying the salon's owner wanted to talk to me. We set up a meeting at a pawnshop. In walked an old friend of mine.

"Why did you have my place burned down?" he asked after we greeted each other.

"Oh shit," I said with an embarrassed laugh. "I'm really sorry. I thought you had something to do with Harry."

He didn't.

CHAPTER 19

"I don't know who to trust," Chris (not his real name) told me as we drove.

"If you want my opinion," I said, taking him to a dark parking lot, "don't trust anybody in this world, my boy."

We talked about pot as we drove. I stayed away from the real reason for the meeting. He owed me a $6,000 drug debt from way back, and I was sick of waiting for it. He went on, saying it'd been a while since he'd seen Cheeky, who had just recently got out of jail.

"You'll see him," I said. "He's right behind us."

Chris turned around to check out the car following us. "That's him?"

"Yup, that's him. Hammer's driving and Poutine is sitting behind."

"All right," Chris said, laughing.

Before picking up Chris, I'd had a talk with Cheeky about the old debt.

"I'm sick of this fucker's games," I told him. "He's owed me this cash for years."

"Let me take this prick out," Cheeky responded.

The unpaid debt was making me look weak, but Chris had his good points. He was a friend since childhood. Best of all, his mother was screwing a member of the Dubois crew, and Chris was feeding me some useful information through her. Was that info worth waiting for my money?

"I'll tell you what," I told an impatient Cheeky. "You'll follow me in another car acting as security. If I give you a hand signal, that will mean get out and whack him."

That night, sitting in my truck at the parking lot, Chris didn't seem to give a damn about his debt.

"You owed me this for years," I told him. "I haven't even been charging you interest. I know you're still sniffing and partying. But you better get it straight, *mon tabarnac*, you are definitely going to pay me."

Nothing sunk in. So I asked Chris to step out of the truck. I didn't want any of his blood to splatter inside the cab.

"This is a pretty dark place," he said, squinting at the security car, not realizing it held a trigger-happy Cheeky.

I was about to signal my gunman when Chris said he would pay back his debt by selling for me. I was undecided for a long time, until my business sense won out. If I had him killed, I would lose both my information on the Dubois crew as well as my debt. I let him live.

He never knew how close he came to death.

Neither did Mario, my drug runner. I was getting pissed off with his whining and complaining all the time.

"I don't know who he thinks he is, that little fucking poodle," I told Cheeky. "He keeps disappearing, and not making his pickups."

When Cheeky heard me say I wanted to fire him, he jumped in.

"Let me whack him," he said.

Cheeky had his reasons, too. He didn't like the fact that Mario had seen him kill Polar.

"I'm not going to have him whacked for that," I told Cheeky.

"But if you fire him, what makes you so sure he won't talk to the cops? This is a witness I don't need, and I really don't trust."

"Let me think about it. Don't do nothing until I tell you."

I knew he was right, but I immediately rejected the idea, thinking there were other ways to deal with Hammer. I ordered him to my place.

"I'm sick of your bitching," I said with all seriousness. "If you keep it up, I'm taking away your car and I'll make fucking sure you won't be able to show your face in Verdun. Got that? The only thing you'll be able to do is sell fucking pencils on a street corner."

He got the message, and I took away his hangaround ring to teach him a lesson. To me, that was the ultimate humiliation, losing stature in the gang. I told Cheeky that Hammer was young and had to be taught.

"Don't tell me you haven't made any mistakes since I've met you," I said. He squirmed.

This was in January 1999, and I had sprung a surprise on Brigitte to make up for the harrowing car ride before Christmas. I told her we would be going to Cuba just as soon as we got our passports and tickets. She was thrilled. We decided to go with Alain Brunette and his wife, Ginette, as well as Toute-Toute and his wife, Suzanne.

When I was talking to Curly about trying to protect Brigitte from the gang's business, he flew into a rage.

"I'm going to give you some advice. Alain's wife has a big fucking mouth. Me, I've told my wife that if she ever meets that woman, to not say one fucking word."

Curly said he would raise the issue of Ginette's gossiping, and that of other wives, at the next full-patch meeting.

"The Rock Machine are not women. What's in the family should stay in the family," he said, meaning the men should tell their wives nothing.

"Christ, at Ti-Cul's funeral, Ginette told Tony's woman that we had SS members, and Tony's woman asked him what an SS is."

SS meant assassins. Curly's own girlfriend asked him after that whether he was a killer. He got even more outraged that Ginette had told the other wives they should make sure they had some money in hand at all times because their men would likely be killed in the war.

Not least, Curly was also pissed off because Alain had inadvertently bought coke that had originated with the Hells, thus putting profit in the enemy's pockets. But he had the most problems with Ginette wearing the pants in her relationship and telling Alain off sometimes in front of the other guys.

"If my woman had called me a fat asshole like that, I'll tell you one thing. I'd have slapped her in the face."

Then he got back to helping me deal with Ginette on the trip to Cuba.

"In your place, I'd tell her to shut her trap," he said in his usual volcanic voice. "I'd tell her she doesn't have balls between her legs. She has a cunt. And she shouldn't meddle in business that has nothing to do with her. The wife of a Rock Machine is not a Rock Machine."

Biker gangs are not the most enlightened when it comes to women's rights. The Bandidos, the gang we were trying to join, had leather vests for the wives, with a patch on the back that called the wearer "Property of the Bandidos."

I was on the phone to Curly a few weeks later, but this time I was the one on a rant.

"Those stupid fuckers!" I yelled. "How many fucking times do I have to tell them not to go to bars? They are trouble."

Cheeky, Beluga, and Poutine had been arrested at an Old Montreal bar for threats and possession of weapons. They told me they were there to do security for a full patch, but the full patch wasn't even at the bar. I couldn't do anything about Poutine since he wasn't part of my gang, but the other two would feel my wrath. Beluga and Cheeky had been promoted to prospect just a month before.

"I'm going to take away their rings," I told Curly, "and give them back just before I leave for the airport, just to make them think. There will be no more of this, no fucking way, man."

It was the ultimate discipline for anyone who wanted to go up in the gang.

"You have to discipline them," he agreed. "Take it to the table."

He meant to a meeting of full patches.

We were talking about an event on January 30, 1999, at the Queue Leu-Leu bar. Cheeky spotted someone he knew and went up to him with Beluga in tow.

"We recognize you," Cheeky told the guy. "We're going to whack you tonight."

He continued.

"We're Rock Machine. As soon as you walk out of here, you're dead. If you call the police or anyone else, we'll kill you tomorrow."

"Why are you doing this?" the man asked.

"Because you fucking annoy us," Cheeky added. "You are part of another gang."

He took out his pistol and pointed it at the guy.

"You're going to croak."

Beluga also got in a few words.

"You got a real fucking problem tonight," he said, glowering. "A real fucking problem."

They left the guy to ponder his demise and went to the bar. He promptly called the cops. Cheeky and Beluga were arrested, and the cops took away their bulletproof vests. They also grabbed Poutine, but found no guns until one fell out of a woman's pocket. Poutine had given it to her to hide.

Earlier, a patrol car had noticed my guys drive up in a Ford Aerostar. They passed that on to the officers in the bar, who found the truck and searched it for arms. At first, they found nothing. Then they started playing with the buttons. Hours later, after hitting the rear defrost, the center console between the front seats made a sound and popped a bit off the floor. Inside was a .357 Magnum. Police also found cellphones in the van, but decided not to confiscate them since surveillance crews were already listening in on us. I was pissed my crew had burned the Aerostar so fast. Curly had just loaned it to me so my guys could patrol the streets of Verdun.

"Here they go getting themselves arrested just before I really need them for the first of the month," I told Curly, bemoaning how their absence would affect all the extra business on welfare day. "They just keep fucking up, and I'm about to head off to Cuba. What a time to do something stupid. Fuck, I'm running a daycare centre."

The news got even worse. Beluga had spilled the beans to Gilles Lambert in jail that he knew about the bazookas. That got me in shit since it was supposed to be a secret among full patches. In the end, I didn't take away their prospect rings, thinking it would be too much for them. But I made them feel real small for weeks. They also did their duties properly for once, since they knew I had a temper. Nonetheless, they were happy to get their names in the paper for that stupid stunt.

Curly also kept me up to date on news of our talks with the Bandidos, which had been dragging on. He said some Rock Machine members in Quebec City didn't want to become a motorcycle gang because the police would harass us even more once we had leather vests and patches. There was also divided feeling over whether the Rock Machine should declare itself a motorcycle club and get our own patches as the first step toward joining the Bandidos. Some members were worried such a move would delay our entry into the Bandidos as full members. We wouldn't be full members right away, more like prospects.

The plan was to create leather Rock Machine vests with our logo but using the Bandidos traditional red and yellow colors. The vests would have a patch in the front saying "Support your local Bandidos" to show we were affiliated with the much larger gang. Then when the Bandidos were satisfied with us, they would give us full status and we would change our colors to theirs. The Rock Machine's name would die off.

February 7 came and went. That was when I was supposed to die. Police had called me and told me the Death Riders of Laval had increased the price on my head by $7,000, and they were supposed to fulfill the contract that day. Instead, I took off to Cuba for two weeks. Every night I sang karaoke, getting compliments from tourists for my repertoire of Elvis Presley and Frank Sinatra. Toute-Toute and Alain didn't let me live it down. Alain and I also made fools of ourselves trying to fit our bulk into a two-person kayak while tourists on the beach laughed and filmed us with camcorders. After a week in Cuba, I called Mario from my hotel room. We chatted about the clear ocean and hot weather in Cuba before he told me in code that cocaine was very scarce in Montreal.

"Go see Le Gros Fou," I said, "and tell him what's happening. Go see him fucking fast because he's the one who will lose the most by being too generous. Tell him to boost it. Boost it."

"OK," Mario replied.

I asked him if he wanted a souvenir T-shirt or a key chain. He chose a T-shirt. Hammer got off the phone and called Phil Côté, a guy who started with me at the beginning and who now was my best seller. His nickname in English meant The Crazy One. He looked crazy after having his teeth knocked out with a bat when a Hells raiding team busted into his place.

Phil was a bit groggy from being woken up when Mario called at noon.

"You know your tools?" Mario started. "Well, boost the total price a bit, actually by quite a bit. It is dry everywhere."

"I don't understand," Phil replied. "You'll have to come see me."

"I'm pretty far away," Mario replied. He tried again.

"The amount of your business, boost it for everyone. It's dry."

Phil still didn't understand the code, and Mario gave up.

"OK, I'll go see you a bit later."

While they were discussing business, I went for a swim with dolphins, one of my dreams. For 45 minutes, I played like a child. One swam right up to me and kissed my cheek while another let me hold its dorsal fin for a fast ride. I dreaded going back home.

"Back to the war and the bullshit," I said to Brigitte as we got on the plane.

Her face fell.

When we landed in Montreal, one of my bodyguards met us, telling me to call my brother right away. I knew it was about my grandmother. She had been hospitalized before I left for Cuba, but she appeared fine, even asking me to bring her something. The woman had been a rock in our family, helping my mother after our father left us, and even getting very close to my son. Cancer had struck, and it was diagnosed as terminal. When I got to the hospital, my mother was there, crying as she held Granna's hand.

"Look, Mummy," she said. "Peter is here."

I put my hand over my mother's. Then I left, tears running down my face as I walked by my bodyguards. They didn't dare look me in the face. I was supposed to be the strong warrior.

The doctor told us to go home and get some sleep. The next day, Robert's wife called.

"The priest is giving her last rites," she said.

I rushed back. Everyone was in tears as I again took my grandmother's hand.

"She's still fighting for breath," my aunt said.

"Let go," my uncle said to the tiny figure on the bed. "Go to sleep."

"Please don't die, Mummy," my mother cried. "Don't leave me."

My grandmother gave a final breath. I held my mother, who had lost all control of her legs. My uncle went outside for some air. He had a heart attack, and was rushed back inside, to emergency.

I attended my grandmother's funeral with two cars full of bodyguards following the funeral procession to the cemetery. They wouldn't let anybody get close to the limo I was in with my mother. At the gravesite, they stood a bit away, but made their presence known. My extended family of cousins and uncles got, for the first time, an idea of my life. On the one hand, it showed my power. But on the other I was embarrassed in front of those law-abiding people.

The nightmares had gone away in Cuba. Now they came back.

I'd see members of my family crying in a funeral home, but the angle wouldn't let me see who was in the coffin. It wasn't my grandmother, because she was there in the room. I'd ask someone to tell me who was dead, but they would just look at me in fright, and cry even harder.

Back I went to dealing with my gang's mistakes, trying to keep them out of jail. Unbeknown to me, Poutine had roped two of my guys into doing a burn south of Montreal. He was tipped off to where the Jokers would be storing 100 pounds of pot en route to the United States. Since the criminal world is a small one, he learned of it through his father-in-law, Gaetan Michelin, who was acting as a courier for the Jokers.

Gaetan delivered the 100 pounds in four hockey bags to a truck garage near Saint-Jean-sur-Richelieu. The pot was worth $260,000 in Canada, but $400,000 once over the U.S. border. He left the pot with a trucker. Poutine was waiting outside with Hammer, The Doors, and another guy.

As soon as Gaetan drove away, Poutine kept watch outside while the other three burst in, pointing pistols at the trucker.

"Shut your mouth and don't talk," one gunman said to him. Then, one gunman saw a bag was missing.

"There's only three bags. Where's the other one?"

The trucker pointed to where he'd moved it to a corner. His hands and mouth were taped, and the robbers left.

When he got loose, the trucker called Gaetan, who put him on the line with his boss. The trucker explained the gunmen knew to look for four bags. Those words made Gaetan an immediate suspect in the burn since he was one of the very few to know how the pot was packaged. The next day, his bullet-ridden body was found north of Montreal.

Poutine took his father-in-law's death pretty well.

"They found him with three bullets to the head at the edge of a field," he told Beluga the same day.

"Well, that's not good."

"It's not good for him, in any case," Poutine said and chuckled.

I met up with Beluga, who had just come off a heavy coke binge, neglecting the minor drug network I'd helped him set up. He had also spent $5,000 of my money on a good time with his girlfriend and others. Neither Beluga nor Cheeky liked the business side, often saying they just wanted to do hits for the gang. I kept hammering into their brains they needed a business to get ahead in the Rock Machine.

"There is only one way to make goddamn money," I told Beluga that day, "over the long term."

He sort of nodded.

"Like I explained to the other guy," I continued, referring to Cheeky, "what's going to happen if there is peace sometime, even if it is not this year or the next? What will you do? Who will you shoot?"

"I know, Pete."

"If things are straightened out like that, what does that leave you?"

"Fuck all."

"If there is peace, you're screwed."

"Anyway, listen, I'm not fucked up in the head, you know."

"But you have to take the business more seriously, Beluga. What you're doing makes no sense."

I was referring to his drug binge while I was in Cuba.

"But you went away for two weeks," he said.

"So what?"

"You are my guiding light, big guy. If you're not there, I'm fucked."

"Yeah, well, Christ. You have to learn. What will happen if I go inside?"

"That wouldn't be good. That wouldn't be good at all."

"That means?"

"It shows when you are not around. Things keep working but,

my screwups . . . well, you're not there to tell me, 'What did you do, you fucker?'"

"Beluga," I said, exasperated he hadn't been able to fend for himself, "you're now a prospect, goddammit."

"I know."

"You should be capable."

"I'm able, but, Christ, I still need you."

I told him I was pissed at Mario for fucking off on me and helping Poutine in the pot burn. I wasn't happy with Poutine, either, thinking the burn would bring too much heat down on us.

It didn't take long. A week later, police arrested Beluga and Cheeky. Again, the pair were happy the papers gave space to their arrests. Police found a submachine gun hidden in the back of Cheeky's TV because Beluga had bragged about it on a wiretapped phone. They also retrieved masks, gloves, shotgun shells, and bullets under his sofa cushions. A silencer was found in a chest of drawers. Police got snapshots of the ceremony before Christmas where Bull became a full patch, Cheeky was made prospect and Mario became a hangaround. I'm in many of the shots, giving the camera the finger. I got a kick out of the photo of little Mario in a Rambo stance with a submachine gun. Beluga was also made a prospect, but he missed the party because he was in jail.

Those March 1999 arrests left me with no bodyguards. I hoped to do one final drug deal and take off, losing myself for a while with Brigitte to salvage our relationship, which was deteriorating fast. She asked a friend for help the day after the arrests.

"Come get me and I'll take the kid with me. I don't want to sleep here tonight. I'll tell Peter to come get his things. Oh boy, he was panicking yesterday. He was enraged. I'm going to call him on his cell and tell him to forget me, to get out of my life, and the kid wants nothing to do with his father."

But she couldn't leave me, not then.

Four days later, police raided the rest of my drug network, put-

213

ting more than a dozen behind bars. Among others, the cops got Phil Côté and Mario. They left me free to hear my reaction on the wiretaps. Maybe I would incriminate myself. I was at the casino when my brother called to tell me. He'd gotten a good view when the cops busted Larry Korejwo and Lori-Lise Prevost, a couple with four kids who lived down the street from him. Larry was a childhood friend who stashed my drugs in exchange for lower prices on coke to sell or use. When the cops went in to Larry's, they found 20 pounds of pot in the basement, some cocaine, and 700 PCP pills. The cops, to their shock, also found traces of coke and a pound of pot next to the youngest child's crib. In their reports, police complained about the disgusting state of the apartment, mentioning the whole place stank of urine.

Brigitte called me soon after.

"How's it going?" she asked.

"Could be better. They just went into Larry's place."

"With the children and everything?" was her first response.

"I don't know where to go," I said.

I was worried the police would follow me home and raid our place, too.

"You can't come home," Brigitte said. "I'm freaking out."

"I know, plus, goddammit, I have no more money in my pockets." I'd lost a few thousand that night at the casino.

She suggested I hide out down south, treating this as a good time to take a vacation.

"Fuck and shit," I said. "I'm knocked out. They don't give up at all."

I called up Michel Bertrand the next day. He commiserated with me.

"They don't stop hitting you," he said.

"Not only that, but that scumbag Bédard was driving around while it was all going on," I said, referring to a Rocker named Kenny Bédard. "Someone saw him. He was in his car and he was laughing. He was going up and down the streets."

I then called Lori-Lise at my brother's home. She said Clement Rose had told her to talk or else her new baby wouldn't recognize her by the time she got out of prison.

"They mentioned you," she said. "I said I don't know who you are talking about."

"So what did Rose say of me?"

"He said he knows that because of how much they found, that I'm holding it for somebody and it was obviously for a biker like Peter Paradis. I said I don't even know what you are talking about."

"These people are nuts," I said.

I called Toute-Toute a day later.

"It's a nightmare. I'm out on the street."

I blamed it on Poutine for the pot burn.

"He's the one who brought the heat," Toute-Toute added, "and you're paying for his screwup."

I told him I was embarrassed to ask, but would he lend me $1,000 for bail to get at least one guy out. He said OK.

After staying away from Brigitte's place for a while, I went home. Four days after my drug cache was nabbed, I was watching the second period of a hockey game while Brigitte was fixing us snacks in the kitchen. The front door vibrated as a loud bang startled me. I reached for my gun, hidden in the night table.

Then another bang, and the front door jumped off the hinges. Men in helmets, bulletproof vests, and combat boots stormed in.

"Don't move! Police!" one yelled.

I saw a gun barrel pointing straight at me despite the flashlight attached to the top that was blinding my eyes.

"Don't move!"

"Settle down," I said sarcastically, putting my hands in the air. "I'm not moving."

"Get on your stomach!"

I lay on the floor and stared at their boots. I turned my head and saw Brigitte in a similar position, getting handcuffed.

"You're hurting me," she kept saying.

"You fuckers better not touch her," I yelled. "She has nothing to do with anything."

She was scared. "Are you OK?" I asked.

"We got it," a cop said excitedly.

"You got what, a bud of pot? Is that what this big show is about?"

"Do you think we are here for that?" a detective told me. They'd found my pistol. "You are under arrest."

"Yeah, yeah. Why is it you keep busting us? The only thing you guys are missing are your H.A. colors. Where's your warrant?"

He slid it under my nose on the floor.

They marched me in front of the TV lights. I snarled at the cameraman to stop shooting. He didn't. At the police station, Rose and Lambert were waiting, telling me they planned the raid when my son was away at a friend's to spare him from seeing his parents in handcuffs. They also told me my phone had been wired for some time and I was going down.

"So be it," I said. "I got beat. But I'll come out even stronger when I get out."

I got bail the next day and returned home. The front door was propped up against the frame and Brigitte, pale and in tears, was at the kitchen table.

"Don't worry," I said. "We'll just move away like we intended to."

A few days later, I came home to find a note on the phone. It said she loved me, but couldn't live through the stress and fear of being near me. She and my son were gone.

CHAPTER 20

With my gang decimated, I moved into my brother's place in Verdun with his wife and two kids. I was alarmed to see that Robert never used the bulletproof vest I'd bought him.

"Don't be stupid," I said. "Look what happened to me. One day, you're going to get pegged."

The only good news I got in the next few weeks was that a high-ranking Hells named "Biff" Hamel had been killed in a parking lot after leaving a pediatrician's office with his young child.

My business slowed to almost nothing, but I began using more coke myself to forget Brigitte's departure. After a night at the casino, I got home and went into the guest bedroom to give a quarter pound of coke to a new runner who hadn't been arrested in the police sweep two months ago. Robert was with his wife Suzanne in the living room when he got paged by a customer who wanted to meet at the corner to pay a few hundred dollars she owed me for drugs. Robert left to pick up the cash.

I heard a loud gunshot and then jumping and running sounds.

"Peter!" Suzanne yelled. "Oh my God."

A hit team in the house, I thought, getting up, looking for my gun. Shit, I'd left it in the truck, thinking all the police surveillance would keep me safe. I ran barefoot out the back door, hoping to circle the block and get to my vehicle out front. I ran up the alley, but stopped when I saw a white van waiting, the motor running, and two men inside. It looked like a getaway vehicle. I turned around, and headed back, banging on a neighbor's back door. He let me in and I called 911 for an ambulance. Then I raced through his home to the front.

I saw Robert lying on the ground and felt a pain I couldn't describe. I was the one who had gotten him involved in the Rock Machine. He'd always followed me, and now there he was, on the street with a bullet in his back.

"I can't move," he said through the pain.

"Keep breathing," I said. "Hang on. Help is on the way."

Then my mother arrived after Suzanne's sister called her. She got out of her husband's car before it came to a stop and went under the police tape.

"You can't go there," a cop yelled at her.

"No one's stopping me. That's my son."

She stooped over him.

"Hang in, Robert. Hang in there."

I went over.

"Mommy, go back over there," I said, pointing behind the tape. "They are filming you."

I went over to the cameraman and told him very seriously not to use any images of my mother. Then I looked at all the bystanders on their balconies and the street, my rage bursting through because there must have been some Hells supporters among them.

"We'll see about this, you bunch of fucking hypocrites," I yelled. "Fucking Hells supporters. We'll see."

My mother followed the ambulance to the hospital, where she went up to Robert's bed.

"Hang in there," she said. "Granna's with you."

I thought of all my dead friends, the fear of being shot again, the arrests, the police harassment, the loss of Brigitte and my son. The nightmares, my body creaking all the time from stress. Now my only brother. Is all this worth it?

I went to Robert, taking his blood-stained hand in mine. Tubes and wires ran from machines to everywhere, just like when I was shot.

"How are you doing?"

He was too weak to answer, so he grunted.

"Don't worry," I continued, my voice stronger than I felt. "You'll pull through."

I couldn't stop my curiosity.

"Did you see who shot you?"

"He was black," Suzanne answered for him.

"Was he bald?"

"Yes," she said, surprised.

My brother grunted again, getting our attention. He pointed to his ear.

"He had an earring," I said. I knew who it was. The same guy was suspected of killing Renaud, Christian, and Ti-Bum.

I looked at my brother, and he opened his mouth. He did that to get me to laugh because he looked ridiculous without his false teeth. That's when I realized he would be all right.

Father Cameron, the priest I'd known since childhood, was there. He asked if I wanted to be blessed. Even though my two bodyguards were with me, I accepted. Before I left, I stationed a guard at Robert's door.

Two days later, my brother was transferred to another room, and was in good enough shape to explain what happened. As Robert went to the corner, he noticed a man crossing the street in front of him. The guy looked to the ground as they got close. My brother found that suspicious so he turned around a few seconds later and saw the guy pulling out a gun. Robert ran but the gunman managed to get him in the lower back with a .22-calibre bullet, the favorite tool of hitmen. The tiny projectile bounced around like a pinball inside of him, cracking three ribs before coming to rest near his neck. The shot tossed Robert to the ground, where he lay on his stomach. The gunman came over and pointed the gun at the back of Robert's head. He pulled the trigger, but the gun jammed. In frustration, he ran away.

While I was at the hospital, Merlin showed up.

"Why don't you move away?" he asked me. "Are you waiting to get killed?"

"What, are you asking or telling me?" I retorted. "Are you telling me to give up?"

"It's not worth it," he answered.

Since Merlin was there, I took the opportunity to pay him for 50 Percodans I wanted delivered to help me mellow out from the war. I gave one of my soldiers a brand new gun to do watch and also told him someone would come by to give him the Percodans. After I left, police raided the hospital room. They knew they'd often find guns on those doing watch. They also found my Percodans.

After two weeks, Robert came home, but I didn't feel we were safe staying in Verdun. Since my business was in tatters, and I had to stay away from my gang because I was sure the cops were still watching us, I moved to Ottawa and got my brother and his family to follow two weeks later. We took two apartments in the same building. I used John Parker as my name.

Sasquatch was already in Ottawa, having fled there when the Rockers took over his downtown territory. He did some selling while trying to expand the Rock Machine into Ontario. We saw each other almost every day.

When I was there, I missed out on the Rock Machine going from calling itself a drug gang to taking on the title of official motorcycle gang, a necessary stage to becoming Bandidos. The opposition of some Quebec City members was overcome and we replaced our sweaters with leather vests that had the letters MC, for motorcycle club, on them. During a trip back to Montreal, I saw Toute-Toute with our new Rock Machine vests, and got one for myself. On the back, we had our trademark eagle head. In front were various patches, including one that said Support your Local Bandidos, which labeled us as their hangaround club. Another was No. 13. While unlucky for many, bikers consider that number to be good fortune. A small patch had 1% on it. That came from the birth of outlaw motorcycle gangs after World War II. The 1% was adopted as a patch by the Hells and others after the president of the American Motorcycle Association responded to bad publicity by saying 99 percent of bikers are law-abiding, while only 1 percent are outlaws.

Back in Ottawa, I noticed my neighbor had a lot of people going in and out so I went over to borrow a cup of sugar. After he got to know me, I asked if I could buy some coke or pot. He had it delivered. That told me he was pretty low in the totem pole of the drug world. His product was of terrible quality so I called up one of my guys in Montreal and asked him to bring me 28 grams of uncut coke.

Soon after, I was at my neighbor's place again. Over a beer, I asked him why so many prostitutes kept coming back if he had such awful coke.

"I have an empty room," he explained. "I let them smoke their crack back there. It also prevents their pimps from finding them and taking away their money."

We kept drinking.

"Would the girls take coke as payment?" I asked.

"Sure," he said, going for the telephone. "I'll call my friend right away. What do you need?"

"I don't need anything," I said, pulling out my 28-gram rock of coke.

"Holy shit. I haven't seen rock cocaine in years. Where'd you get that?"

"That's not important." I made two lines. "Try this. Let me know what you think."

He was impressed. "You got a gold mine here. Are you going to sell any of it?"

"No, but I can work something out for you so that you make money. If you make money, I make money. But first," I said, winking, "nature calls."

He knew what I meant so he went to the back room and brought a blonde back.

"Here," he said, "what do you think of this one?"

She came over to my chair, sat on my lap, and started rubbing my crotch.

"This will do fine," I said with a smile. "I'm going next door. Be back in an hour."

A few days later, I met a good-looking hooker there and took her to my place. She began stripping until I stopped her.

"Put your clothes back on. I want to talk to you about something."

"Is there something wrong with me?" she asked.

"No, I'd like to fuck your lights out, but there's something I want to talk to you about first."

She sat down. I could tell she was new to prostitution because her face hadn't become hard yet.

"Why are you in the hooker business?"

"I got hooked on coke. Selling my body is the only way I can pay for it."

"What if I told you I could give you coke without having to work for it?"

"What do you mean?"

"I'll make a deal with you. You go out on the streets. Not as a hooker, but to promote my coke to the girls working the streets."

"That's it?"

"No, of course not. I don't know any women here and let's just say I want you to stay here with me and keep my bed warm at night. Do we have a deal?"

"Yes," she said with a smile.

"Now I'm going to fuck your lights out."

She started sending even more hookers to my neighbor, who was having lots of fun with my quality coke. I was staying at arm's length, taking in almost $100 a day just from supplying him. It wasn't like before, but it kept Robert and me from starving. I kept little contact with Montreal, though I learned that Merlin, the same guy who told me to move away, was now shooting off his mouth that I fled the war in fear.

There was a dry spell in Ottawa for coke at the time, and I was making even more cash after finding a big dealer happy to get pure Montreal blow. Then, in September 1999, I got a call one morning from a lawyer in Montreal.

"Get anything illegal out of your place," he told me.

I took my gun downstairs to Robert's first-floor apartment.

The lawyer called back soon after.

"Are you sure nobody knows where you are?"

"I'm sure," was my cocky answer.

"I don't know where you are," he said, "but the police seem to because your building is surrounded."

Police often call our lawyers before arrests to convince us it isn't worth any gunplay. With the lawyer on the phone, I went to the wall-to-wall windows in the living room. I saw the SWAT team pointing guns up at me. I backed away.

"Fuck."

"You better show yourself," the lawyer said. "And put your hands in the air."

I hung up and did as he said. Through the window, I heard the cops yelling.

"Keep your hands where we can see them. Don't move. We're coming to get you."

"I'm not going anywhere," I yelled back.

The door burst open and I was handcuffed. So was my hooker companion. As they took us out the back way, I saw my neighbor being handcuffed on his belly.

The cops took me back to provincial police headquarters in Montreal. I was put in an interrogation room with an RCMP officer named Tom O'Neill, part of the Wolverine anti-biker squad. He offered me a cigarette.

"Do you work for a living?" he asked.

"Obviously not," I said, sarcastically. "I'm a full-patch Rock Machine. You know that, and that's all I have to say."

"I understand," he said. "Aren't you tired of this life?"

"What do you want me to say?" I sneered back.

"Well, Peter, it's your choice. But I'm going to ask you something anyway."

"What?"

"Why don't you come work with us?"

"Are you serious?" I spit out, astounded he had the balls to suggest I turn stool.

"Sure, why don't you join us on Team Canada?"

"You know I can't. I might as well sign my death certificate right away. I'd be a dead man."

"Well," he said, "it's my job to ask you."

I got a shock after going through court. Police hadn't nabbed me for my drug sales in Ottawa. A prosecutor had been studying all 33,000 wiretap conversations caught by police against my gang. Jean-Claude Boyer had also seen all the guns and drugs the raids had picked up. So he called back the investigators.

"I see gang in this," he told them.

This is where the death of Daniel Desrochers came back to haunt me. When the 11 year old was killed by shrapnel, the federal government had passed a law making it illegal to contribute to the activities of a criminal gang. The law was immediately controversial, and few prosecutors used it because defense lawyers kept promising to fight all the way to the top courts, saying it contravened the right to free association. Now Boyer wanted to try the law against my gang. That meant I faced up to 14 years in jail.

My Ottawa arrest was to bring me back to Montreal to face the new gangsterism charge. Beluga, Cheeky, Hammer, Poutine, and a few others also got nabbed for it. Our lawyers were telling us the charge would never stick, and they would fight it up to the Supreme Court.

My brother was pissed at me when I got back to Ottawa after getting bail again.

"You're a fucker," he told me for bringing my gun down to his apartment before the cops showed up. "I could have got caught."

I couldn't stop laughing because he'd been at his window directly underneath mine when the cops yelled at me to put up my hands and not move. He stood there in his undershorts and followed their instructions, thinking the cops were yelling at him.

Since the Ottawa papers wrote about my arrest, blowing my cover, I moved back to the Montreal area, living with a cousin in suburban Montreal. I wanted to stay away from Verdun. I'd already ditched my truck, thinking it was too well known.

The Hells hit us again. This time it was Tony's turn. A year after his brother Johnny was slain, Tony was killed outside of a McDonald's restaurant while with his wife and daughter. His wife was shot in the foot. I didn't go to the funeral because of my bail conditions.

Other full patches made it clear they didn't want me to phone or even page them because of all the police on my tail. I used Robert as a middleman. I was running out of cash, so I asked a few if they wanted to buy my $15,000 Bandidos gold bracelet studded with three-karat diamonds. No one wanted it, saying they had no money. I also had a diamond-studded gold cross worth thousands. I didn't want to sell it, but I offered to give it to another gang member as collateral on a loan. My brother kept telling me no one wanted to help. I didn't ask Mon-Mon because he was living off welfare by now, having sold many of his belongings to pay bills.

So, to get by, I sold the beaten-up Oldsmobile Calais I'd bought for a few thousand. And my big screen TV. Then I started stealing steaks.

I carried no gun because of my bail conditions. During one of my numerous trips with my dealers to the Montreal courthouse to appear in front of a judge in the gangsterism case, my brother and a few others acted as protectors. We were waiting in the corridor by the washrooms when I spotted a few Rockers. All of a sudden, the few Rockers turned into 20, then 30. They had been waiting for us, easily tipped off because all court appearances are public knowledge. I noticed one guy taking Polaroid photos of us, and another with a videocamera. There were about 10 of us, but most of my group were not warriors, just dealers.

"Stand your ground," I told them.

My brother wanted to rush the Rockers.

"At least we'll nail two or three off the bat," he said.

I spotted Danny Kane among my enemies. Rumor had it he was gay, and the lover of Aimé Simard, a Rocker who became police informant and spilled the beans on their relationship in court. Kane kept putting his arm around Rocker Pierre Provencher.

"Hey, little faggot," I yelled to get his attention.

Kane looked at me, looked away, and kept talking to the others. But he put his hand up and made a hand signal at me like a duck quacking. That referred to their favorite nickname for the Rock Machine—ducks. As in hunting season is always open on sitting ducks in the Rock Machine since so many of us had been killed by their hit teams.

I responded by imitating someone giving a blowjob.

"Dick-licking faggot!"

By this time, police and courthouse constables were converging on us. Tom O'Neill came over.

"Not here, Peter," the RCMP officer said.

"What do you mean, not here?" I responded. "If anything happens, it is self-defense. Do the math."

Some of the Wolverine officers called their office for backup to keep things cool.

One of my guys called Merlin for backup. He balked at coming so I took the phone.

"We need help," I said. "We're not enough here."

"Aren't you surrounded by cops and security?" he asked.

"Yes we are, genius," I responded. "But we are going to have to leave the building at some point. I'm really disappointed in you."

He got the point and promised to find reinforcements. After that, my group stared down the Rockers for what seemed like hours until the courthouse constables cleared a path to our courtroom.

When the court proceedings were over, police led us down a private fire escape to the exterior of the courthouse so we wouldn't have to run the gauntlet. By that time, Rock Machine reinforcements arrived and drove us away to safety.

During one of those court appearances, my lawyer, Marion Burelle, told me the Crown was offering six years in jail if I pleaded guilty. If I took it, I could get out in two or three. But Marion dismissed the plea bargain, saying I would probably be offered even less by the time we got to trial.

Just after Christmas 1999, I got news Bob Lavigne killed himself during the holidays. Everything was bleak at the time. My body was reacting to the stress with strange cracking in all my joints. And I kept thinking of a story I'd heard about a fisherman out in a small boat when the sea got rough. A tourist approached and offered to take him back to shore. He refused, wanting to keep fishing so he could feed his family. Then a big fishing boat came by and told the old man to abandon his sinking boat. No. Then the coast guard. Again no. The stubborn man eventually drowned. When he got up to heaven, he told God he had a score to settle with Him. Why'd you stand by and let me drown? the man asked. I didn't, God said, I sent you the tourists, the fishing boat, and the coast guard. You just didn't see them for what they were.

My preliminary hearing was approaching in the new year. I was sick of being scared so I told my lawyer to tell the judge on the first day that I had no fixed address. That automatically would see my bail revoked. At least I'd be safe inside. Poutine decided to do the same thing. The Sunday night before we had to go to court, I went to my brother's place for supper. I gave him a list of about $150,000 in drug debts, asking him to collect what he could while I was inside.

The doorbell rang.

"Are you expecting anybody?" I asked.

"No," he said, picking up his gun.

Before we opened the door, I recognized the voices. It was Jimmy Larivée and his boss, Poutine, who was now a full patch.

We gave each other the usual biker handshake and they came in.

"Are you ready for court?" I asked Poutine.

"Sure, he said, pulling out a couple of plugs of hash he was going to stuff up his butt for jail. Poutine took some out and started rolling a cigar-sized joint.

"Hey," Jimmy said, "I've got something to show you."

He dug into a plastic bag. "It's a trophy."

"A trophy?" I asked.

"Yes, I went and took care of some business."

He laughed while taking out a Rockers sweater. We all joined him because the only way he got that was by beating its owner. Jimmy was a little guy, but he made up for his stature with sheer violence.

"What are you guys doing?" Poutine asked me.

"Nothing much. Just going through my front list so my brother can collect some money while I'm in jail."

I told my brother about Gilles Nolet, a friend and jewel thief who was just getting out of jail. Nolet owed me $15,000, but would need some time to get back in business. He could probably pay a few thousand here and there. I asked Poutine if Jimmy could drive my brother since Robert didn't have a car.

"What do you want me to do with him?" Jimmy asked. His tone of voice suggested he wouldn't mind killing the guy.

"Don't hurt him whatsoever," I said. "He owes me fifteen grand and the last thing I want is this guy dead."

"When is he supposed to pay you?"

"Don't go to see him expecting to collect all the money at once. You'll be getting so much every time he does a job. If he makes four or five thousand, leave him half of his profit. He'll most likely use it to buy coke. That way, I get paid and we still make sales. He's happy and we're happy."

"What if he tells me to fuck off and refuses to pay? What do I do?"

"Don't worry, he'll pay."

Jimmy persisted. I finally told him all he would have to do is threaten the guy, nothing more.

"What if nothing works and he tells me to fuck off?"

"Do what you want," I said, exasperated. "I'll wash my hands of all this and just put his debt in the loss column."

"I can kill him?"

"I just told you. If he doesn't understand or doesn't care, why should I? Do what you want, but I'm telling you that he'll pay up."

In the end, my brother didn't go with him. Instead, Jimmy took along another gang associate named Pascal Conway.

In court the next day, Poutine and I had our bail revoked and were taken to Rivieres-des-Prairies jail. As we were in the bullpen, being taken to join Cheeky and Beluga, Poutine recognized a guy in a nearby cell. The guy recognized me.

"Shit, you fat fuck," he said to me. "It's because of you I got my bottom patches."

He meant he got his prospect patch on his Death Rider vest. I clued in fast.

"You're the shithead who was the driver, eh?" I retorted.

"Yes, *tabarnac*, you're a big clown, aren't you? You let your truck hit the fucking post."

We exchanged jeers.

"You're full of holes," he continued.

"Yeah, well, when I get your boss, I won't miss him."

I now knew both guys who had done the hit on me. I'd never revealed the first guy's name to anyone in the Rock Machine because I wanted the revenge for myself. I didn't want them taking care of it.

Two days later, I was watching the news on the jail TV to see if they would mention our gangsterism case. They did. Then the announcer talked about a double homicide at the Adulte strip club near Verdun. Poutine and I looked at each other.

"It better not be what I think it is," I told Poutine with menace.

"It must be the little guy," he answered, meaning Jimmy.

"It better not be. I just told him three days ago that killing would be a last resort."

The TV had no names that night. But the next day, the news showed my friend Nolet's photo along with another man's.

Every morning, we were bused under heavy security to the court-house and then bused back. We weren't sure if the guards thought we'd try to escape or the Hells would try to ambush us. I had no money for the canteen so I asked my brother to contact some other full patches and see if they would help me out. I'd given thousands of dollars in the past for people's canteens in prison, making sure they always felt part of the Rock Machine family. The only thing I'd gotten during five weeks inside was a can of tobacco from Pou-tine and the $40 my mother had deposited at the prison for me.

Robert called one guy. He said he didn't know what to do or who to call. They always knew who to call before, I thought when hearing his response. I dismissed him as a fucking prick.

Then my brother said he tried another.

"Tell him to do his time," was that one's response.

Robert passed that on.

"What?" I said, astounded. "Are you for fucking real?"

"Yes," Robert answered.

"I don't believe those fuckers."

I hung up the prison pay phone.

Why are they abandoning me? I kept asking myself.

CHAPTER 21

I sat in prison steaming, trying not to let the others see my rage at my brothers in the Rock Machine. In a way, they made my decision easier. Since my shooting, I'd thought often about retiring. My biggest worry wasn't the Rock Machine, but the Hells. I didn't think they would accept my retirement. Also, what would I do? Get a real job? My last one was 15 years ago, as a stripper. In my hefty state, that line of work was out of the question.

The only thing keeping me back was knowing I would have to leave my family behind, including my son. I hadn't been the best father, but I still wanted to be part of his life.

All the pain of the past year and a half rushed through my mind. I decided to contact the cops. But it would be impossible to do it from prison. I had to get out. Five weeks into the preliminary hearing, I gave a new address to the judge and was let go. The rest happened quickly. I contacted Rose and Lambert, they took me to a hotel, and I pleaded guilty.

Next came loneliness. I was locked up in a room at a police station 24 hours a day, and not allowed to call anyone. Even if I could use a phone, the only ones I would want to call would be my family. I wasn't even sure about Robert, considering he was still with the Rock Machine.

The police spent days interrogating me. I told them the Rock Machine in Montreal had been planning to start its own Nomad chapter like the Hells to be made up of all the fiercest fighters. But it never came to anything because the person who tried to start it was too heavily into heroin.

"Why did you plead guilty?" Claude Lambert asked me during one of the interrogations.

"I had no life. I had fuck all. I was fed up."

He listened quietly.

"I was not raised this way. I had so many options I should have taken. I have the right to another chance at life. I got four bullets in my body but I'm still here."

I told him I was first blinded by money and then caught up in the war.

"Do you have lots of cash or belongings?" he asked.

I laughed. "I have my shorts."

Being cooped up in a dry, windowless cell was causing me nosebleeds. I said nothing until it became constant, then I threw a blood-soaked tissue on a table as I sat with some cops. They took me out for a trip the next week.

I had to pass a polygraph test before they would sign an informant's contract with me. Such tests are not admissible in court, but police use them to see if witnesses or suspects can be trusted. They were particularly interested in the deaths of jewel thief Gilles Nolet and the other man in the strip club, Normand Barolet. I went into the procedure very nervous. Even though police had promised me I couldn't be accused of any crime I admitted to unless they had outside corroborating evidence, I still didn't trust them. I was worried they would spring a first-degree-murder charge on me for some of the killings I was involved in. The fear of a life sentence made me soft-pedal my implication in all the deaths. I did tell most of the truth—I never gave a direct order to kill anyone. I omitted the fact that my words, even though not direct, left the impression that my gang members had the green light to kill. Without such tacit approval, they would never have done anything. In the death of Gilles Nolet, I told them I didn't want him dead but the killers went ahead and did it anyway. I omitted that I told Jimmy I didn't care what he did to Gilles if he refused to pay. I never expected Gilles to be a problem.

I slept badly the night before the polygraph. And I was scared after the technician played a game with me when I was wired up. He asked me to choose a card from a deck. The technician then told me to say no to all the guesses he would make to find the right card. We did the exercise and then he checked the machine, writing down something on a piece of paper and then turning it over on the table.

"So what was the number?" he asked me.

"Eight."

He lifted the paper. There was an eight. Then the questions started.

"Do you intend to answer everything honestly?"

"Yes."

"Independently from this case, did you lie about anything else?"

"No."

"Did you ask anyone to kill Gilles?"

"No."

"Did you order Gilles's death?"

"No."

"Did you pay anybody to kill Gilles?"

"No."

We did it again to double-check my answers. He then left as I lit a cigarette and waited. The technician walked back in with Michel Tremblay, a homicide detective. They told me I didn't pass.

Tremblay was convinced I had ordered the killing, and that I couldn't have become a full patch without being personally involved in serious crimes like murder.

"Why would I kill someone who was a friend?" I answered, getting mad. "It is not smart business to lose $15,000."

This went on for a while until I was taken back to my cell. They came to see me 15 minutes later.

"It's not too late to make things right by telling the truth," Tremblay said.

"I am telling the truth."

"We are sure that if you take a polygraph on the other homicides, you will fail."

I got angrier, and that session ended badly. But they kept their word. They didn't charge me in the killings because they had no evidence against me but my word. And they had promised what I said could not be used against me.

Prosecutor Jean-Claude Boyer became a fixture in my life. If I hadn't walked into police hands, he believed, I would have been dead within weeks because the Hells were closing in on me. Jean-Claude and I started negotiating what sentence I would get. I had no lawyer, believing I could trust Jean-Claude. He wanted me to do 12 years—5 for drug trafficking and 7 for gangsterism. I figured I was getting screwed, considering he had offered 6 years before I became informant.

Jean-Claude said the gangsterism law was new, and by giving me a whopping 7 years, it would set a precedent and help society. Other judges would be able to point to my sentence and give similar time to other criminals. I was told I wouldn't actually do the full time and I would become eligible for parole after just 2 years. Once out, I would get my new identity and be relocated. I agreed, possibly because I was in a honeymoon period of wanting to help the justice system.

I was transferred from police cells to a jail, where I got a surprise. I was kept away from regular prisoners but allowed to frequent another informant, this time from the Hells organization. It made a pretty postcard to see the two of us playing cribbage to pass the time. We had no choice. It was either each other or no one. I could finally call my family and I was allowed into the sunshine one hour a day. I was soon transferred to a second jail, where I had access to the yard all day but was alone.

Despite getting a federal sentence, I was kept in provincial jails because of my informant status. But that didn't mean I was treated better. The guards, fed up with some of the crazy informants they'd housed before I arrived, hardly talked to me. I was allowed to have a TV in my cell, but it took two weeks to convince the guards to actually give it to me. It took another two weeks of asking before I got the extension cord necessary to plug it in. All this isolation was taking its toll on my mental health. I was sullen and feeling like a neglected dog. The jail offered me anti-depressants. I was convinced it was a ploy to weaken me just before I had to negotiate my informant's contract. I refused.

I got a roommate, though, a good friend of the Rockers. That perked me up because we had a common interest—the war. We played chess while watching the news of various hits on the outside, trying to guess who was the latest victim before the media announced a name. I got very good.

My only contact with the outside world was my mother. She told me one day that Brigitte had called and wanted to speak to me. I was undecided what to do. She had hurt me when she left with our son just after my arrest and the loss of my business. It was a low moment for me and she had made it worse. What did she want now?

When I called her a week later, the conversation was uncomfortable at first, each of us not knowing where the other stood.

"It's the best thing you could have done," Brigitte finally blurted out.

I was relieved. The ice was broken. We talked and joked a bit; our emotions stayed hidden. She learned of my becoming an informant when our son woke her one morning and threw the paper at her. It was around his birthday, and only one year since my grandmother had died. He had been close to her. The story talked about how I would get a new identity and be relocated.

"Just great," my son told a startled Brigitte. "Last year, I lost Granna on my birthday. Now I'm losing my father."

Brigitte couldn't believe the paper that day. Then it sunk in. Her next thought was why didn't I change sides while she was still in my life. I didn't know any of this when we talked on the phone that day in May 2000.

"Take me with you," Brigitte suddenly said, surprising even herself. She hadn't planned to say anything so impetuous. It was from the gut.

I listened as she spilled out what had happened to her since she left with my son.

"I didn't leave you to hurt you," she told me. "That decision almost killed me."

She said she was worried about our son's safety and that a hit team would have another try at me while the boy was with me.

"You chose that life," she said, "but I didn't and I couldn't live it anymore."

She then told me she went on a huge coke binge in the four or five months after leaving me. It was our son who got her to stop. "My father is no longer here," he told her. "But I am." She went into rehab for a month and a half.

It was a lot for me to digest. For once, I listened and said nothing. We talked often after that, and her return to my life probably kept me from going crazy dealing with the bureaucracy of the justice system.

The next month, negotiations began for my informant's contract and I soon realized I was at a disadvantage. I'd already pleaded guilty, and my becoming a stool was well known. What leverage did I have now? I couldn't go back.

In a conference room, I told the government officials what I wanted. New identity, relocation, a small allowance for my son while I was in prison, tattoo removal. They agreed readily to that. I also wanted three years where I could get back on my feet. To do that, I needed to be paid the standard $400-a-week allowance during that time. They refused, and the meeting was immediately over.

I was taken back to the jail, and thought they would dump me right away. For three weeks, I waited. Then I picked up the phone and called my controller in the witness-protection program.

"What the hell's going on?" I asked him. "I've had enough of these psychological mind games. I'm a human being, not a lab monkey."

"You are asking for too much," he said flatly.

"How am I to survive when I get released from prison?"

The conversation was going nowhere. I tried another tack. I said I'd accept a two-year allowance at $400 a week if the government would pay for courses at a private school so I could learn a trade.

"You guys are the ones who offered to help me get my life started over again. If you pay for my education, it will give me a chance to survive."

The government agreed, adding a condition that if I failed the courses, I would have to reimburse the money from my allowance. I had no problem with that, and they budgeted $5,000 for my schooling. After that, I was transferred to a third jail to spend the bulk of my time. Once again, my wing mates were informants who used to be in the Hells organization. One told me the Hells would never have believed me if I had just retired. They would still have tried to kill me.

As I waited to testify, news kept coming of the war outside. The Rock Machine had started three chapters in Ontario. Frankie Bourget, my old drug supplier, was killed at a Granby campsite by a hit team. The Hells pulled off a publicity coup by inviting well-known singers Ginette Reno and Jean-Pierre Ferland to perform at the wedding of a member. Then the Hells stupidly shot crime reporter Michel Auger five times in the back as he arrived for work at the *Journal de Montréal*. He lived, but the outcry was so strong that the federal government decided to strengthen the anti-gang law.

Throughout all this, I was still rooting for the Rock Machine. Old habits die hard, and my hatred of the Hells didn't dissipate. Auger's shooting proved they were out of control. Then I got the surprise of my life. Fred Faucher actually held a meeting with Mom Boucher in a cubicle at the Quebec City courthouse. That was soon followed by a dinner between Rock Machine members like Sasquatch and various Hells and Nomads at a ritzy downtown restaurant. Pictures showed Sas giving Mom a hug. I couldn't believe my eyes, or the news that there was a truce on, possibly to alleviate the heat brought on by shooting the reporter. I thought the Hells were pulling some sort of double-cross.

While sitting in prison, I read through all the evidence the police had amassed against me and my gang to prepare my testimony against my old gang. To my shock, I realized police had at least three people close to and in the Rock Machine who were giving them regular updates on the gang's actions. One was well placed enough to tell them my exact address in Ottawa, and the others had snitched on Mario and Beluga.

Then came November 23, 2000, the day I was to testify. The trial was getting a lot of publicity because it was the first time in Canada that a gang had defended itself against the new gangster-ism charges, and Rock Machine lawyers were planning to file a constitutional challenge once the trial was near its end. Security was tight as I ran the gauntlet of TV cameras to the courtroom, keeping my game face on, showing no emotion. My son was watching on TV.

"Boy, he looks pissed off," he told Brigitte.

As I walked to the witness box, I stopped close to Poutine, who was sitting in the spectator seats. I stared at him with menace. I despised him, having had enough time to see how the disastrous pot burn and other screwups on his part were partly responsible for my demise. He looked away.

Cheeky and Beluga were in the prisoner's box wearing confident scowls. Phil Côté was beside them with the usual ridiculous look that comes from having no teeth. After I was sworn in, I was asked when I held my last job.

"Good God," I answered. "It's been . . . I think I was eighteen or nineteen. That means it was close to sixteen years ago. I danced in clubs, go-go clubs."

I kept looking at the judge, not wanting to be psyched out by the stares of the defense lawyers or their clients. But as the hours passed, it got much easier. Over seven days, I told the court about the killings, the bazookas, the gang structure, even all the code words we used on phones to talk about drugs.

Out of the 33,000 conversations police recorded while following my gang, not once did they hear the words cocaine, pot, hash, or PCP. They kept hearing me say, "Get me a small beer," or "Prepare a big case of beer."

The judge was especially intrigued by the code. I explained that a small beer was a quarter gram of coke and a big beer was a full gram. Whenever I said a small case, I wanted seven grams of coke. A big case was twenty-eight grams.

"Why do you use codes?" asked prosecutor Hélène Morin, who was working the case with Jean-Claude.

"Often it is when I am around people. That's where I think I picked up the habit. You are around people who are not in the business and your pager goes off. You are on the cellular. For example, at a Christmas party with family, you won't say in front of everyone, 'Send me two grams of hash and four grams of coke,' you know."

But the main reason, I told her, was to confuse the police if they were listening in on wiretaps.

Poutine had his own code—circle meant cocaine, triangle denoted pot, and square was for hash.

Then the defense's turn came to cross-examine me. The Crown was telling me the cross could take weeks. I was apprehensive when Jacques Bouchard stood up, but his questions did little. Just 20 minutes into his second day, he sat down, surprising everyone.

Most of the surprises came outside the courthouse that month. The Rock Machine became probationary members of the Bandidos, taking them just one step away from becoming full members of an international biker organization.

The truce was still on in Quebec in mid-December when Beluga joined a few others in jail and asked for a transfer to the Hells wing. They had defected, as did Poutine and a few full-patch Rock Machine members outside. Sasquatch was one of them. Curly followed a while later, as did Bull Corbeil. During the truce, the Hells had given the Rock Machine an ultimatum: join or be killed when the hostilities resumed in the new year. The Hells even accepted a Rock Machine who had killed one of their top leaders.

I got a kick when the Rock Machine told a reporter they hated defectors more than informants.

Then the Hells, in one swoop, patched over about 170 members of several Ontario motorcycle gangs, pushing their expansion into Canada's richest province to thwart the more modest moves by the Rock Machine. A police wiretap caught Mom Boucher, in jail on multiple murder charges, boasting that the Ontario expansion was his proudest moment.

When the trial resumed in the new year, Beluga and Poutine, as new Hells, were segregated from other members of my former gang to make sure there was no violence. Bouchard tried what he could to fight the gangsterism charges, including asking Beluga to stand up in court one day.

"Take a good look at this individual, your honor," Bouchard told Quebec Court Judge Robert Sansfaçon.

"He's big and fat," the lawyer continued, startling the court. "He looks a bit stupid. He has a mean air to him. That's the only role he played in Peter Paradis's gang."

Bouchard had decided not to bother fighting the constitutionality of the new law, grudgingly admitting to reporters that it didn't violate any fundamental rights. Instead, he was trying to show that I was the real gangster, and my underlings were too minor to be found guilty of the new law. It didn't work. When the judge gave his 150-page verdict, he found Beluga, Mario, Phil, and Cheeky guilty of gangsterism. But Poutine was spared, only going to jail for drug trafficking. The rest of those on trial also got drug sentences.

For me, the judge's verdict was vindicating. He said I was credible and my testimony was corroborated by other evidence. He also mentioned I got a severe sentence for my crimes and my contract wasn't that generous.

"He wasn't contradicted on any subject," Sansfaçon wrote. "In all of his numerous and exhaustive statements made to police, only the fact that he kept quiet at the beginning of his implication in three murders could be used against him. However, he explained he was fearful of his relationship with investigators when he began to collaborate because he has always lived the criminal life. Anyway, he admitted to them afterwards and testified without any reticence about them in this trial."

My big surprise was when the members of my former gang all got lighter sentences than me.

When I finished testifying, I was finally allowed my first code to see Brigitte and my son outside of jail. Police took me in a van to her place, bringing me in through the back entrance. She opened her apartment door and laughed as I hugged her. My smiling son stood behind her. I grabbed his hand for a shake, using my grip to pull him into a hug as he giggled.

My protectors stayed in the living room while I went alone into my son's room with him and closed the door.

"Son, I have to talk to you."

"What about?"

All my guilt rushed out.

"I'm so sorry for what I did to you."

"Sorry about what?"

That gave me a lump in the throat. I felt close to tears.

"I'm sorry for being such a bad father to you." I took a deep breath and continued. "Do you know what your father did for a living?"

"Now I do."

I looked into his eyes.

"When I was just a few years older than yourself, I started taking drugs and lost total control. I became addicted. I did not want you to see me in such a state."

"Is that why I didn't see you much?"

"Yes."

"I guess you were in that kind of state a lot," he said so innocently.

"Yes."

"Do you really understand what I am saying?"

"Yes."

I thought that was too blunt, so I continued.

"Son, let me put it like this. You have every reason to be mad at me for not being there for you. I always loved you, but I was in my own fucked-up world of drugs. Even though your mother and I were separated, that shouldn't have stopped me from being a good father.

"After I got off drugs, I got into the Rock Machine. I did not want you around all the drugs and guns. In fact, I did not want you to see anything of the world I was living in. I was just trying to get my life in order, not thinking about anyone but myself. I'm just so sorry."

He had many questions about what drugs did to me, and whether many friends of mine in the Rock Machine had died. I looked at him to see what he was thinking. His expression was so serious.

"Is everything going to be OK now?" he asked.

"I can't change what I've done in the past, but there is nothing stopping us from being a family and having fun in the future. If you let me."

Nothing mattered to me at that moment but his response.

"Cool."

I was so relieved he still wanted me as his dad. He didn't waste any time, pulling out a new plastic-model kit of a Porsche to build together.

"Where's the glue?" I asked him.

"Glue for what?" he responded. Things had changed since I was young. The cars now snap together. We made it, and then had to take it apart to put in the steering wheel we had left out.

When he left for school after a lunch of tacos, it was my turn with Brigitte. As the cops sat in the living room, we headed to the bedroom. My son came back after school and we had a family dinner of steak and potatoes.

When my handlers took me back to jail, my son turned to Brigitte.

"Ma, my father has really changed," he said. "Will he stay like that?"

"That's for sure," she replied. "Or I'll kick his ass."

EPILOGUE

Boring. That's how I would describe the story you just read. You might find my life different, but it seemed nothing special to me at the time. It began as fun with all the money, partying, women, and drugs. The end was harrowing, full of terror, nightmares, and explosive violence. Sometimes it felt like a childhood game of cowboys and Indians that went terribly wrong. Someone replaced our plastic bows and arrows with submachine guns and dynamite. But in time, all that fun and fear became commonplace. Boring.

The war goes on without me and I feel no regrets for that. At one point, the police thought they had decimated the Rock Machine. That allowed the Hells to flourish. Then their top leaders were jailed in a spectacular raid in the spring of 2001. Next, the Rock Machine became full-fledged Bandidos and began blowing up many bars in my old neighborhood while in the midst of a recruitment drive. My own brother is now a full patch. I learned that by seeing his patches on TV at the funeral for my old drug supplier, Toute-Toute. That gentle man was gunned down at the same chalet he let me use to heal the holes in my body so long ago.

Then, in the spring of 2002, it was the Bandidos' turn to be targeted by the law. Police arrested lots of my old friends and even my brother. Robert's arrest unleashed a turmoil of emotions in me, all very personal. So here you now have a tale of two brothers, very close since they were children, separated on two different sides of the law. We will both have to live with the decisions we made as adults. The only good point of his arrest is he will be safe behind bars.

The body count goes on. Not only bikers, but ordinary citizens also seem to be more and more in the line of fire. A bar owner in the town of Terrebonne north of Montreal was beaten to death with baseball bats in front of his home because he refused to let a gang affiliated with the Hells sell drugs in his place. A 17-year-old boy was fatally shot while waiting in line to get into a Montreal bar. The man accused of firing numerous shots at the club's entrance is a Rocker who supposedly was kept from barging to the front of the queue. Then a suburban father mistaken for a biker was gunned down at a gas station.

At the core of this war are the huge profits from drugs. If it wasn't biker gangs, it would be the Mafia or any other organized-crime group. They attract the miserable to their ranks like bugs flocking to lightbulbs. No father or functional family? Well, a biker gang can make a good substitute, full of fake camaraderie and good times. No money? Not for long. No women? They can be bought or impressed with the violent biker lifestyle. No emotions? Perfect, because whatever feelings you have before joining will have to be buried in a cave to protect that stereotypical fearless image. In the end, though, everything is artificial. You get no love from a biker gang.

The police can stop individual criminals, but not the process. There will always be another Peter Paradis sucked in by money, power, an eagerness to impress his gang and boost his ego by striking fear in ordinary citizens. That is the beginning. The end result is emptiness, a dead soul, self-hatred. That's the only moral I can draw from my lost years in crime. My life is testimony to how the whole process is all a sham. I estimate I made a couple of million dollars in my days pushing drugs. Not one cent stayed in my pockets.

I hurt many people, most of whom didn't deserve it. This whole subject is difficult for me to deal with. There is so much guilt there. My victims include Brigitte and my son, friends who became hooked on my drugs, and all the strangers who were terrorized by my bombs or who saw a family member destroyed by blow. I can't do anything about that now. Before, I would write it off by saying the junkies would just get their blow from someone else, or it was the war that made me brutal. Saying sorry now would be ridiculous.

I would just like to say I realize all the bad I did. I expect I'll be dealing with that guilt for a long time.

Brigitte and my son will make it easier for me to mellow out, to become anonymous, to live a normal family life. Without them, I would have been very alone. Seeing them every day will remind me why I want to change. I've had second thoughts about leaving behind a life I knew, however destructive, and jumping into the unknown. Those doubts come and go for various reasons, especially when I feel out of control, having to rely on police and the government—my past enemies—for my safety, sanity, and future. I rail constantly at the things in jail I find stupid. Brigitte often reminds me I had done some violent things in the past, even had people killed, and the system isn't there to make my life easy, no matter how much I felt I'd helped by testifying against my former gang. I was in jail, not a spa.

But let's go back to Bordeaux jail's C Wing for a moment, when I was there in 1996. I felt in control. It was a time to regroup, to recruit, to make contacts, to socialize. Isn't it a joke that I had a harder time behind bars as an informant than as a hardened gang member?

Despite my doubts, I can't go back, as a judge said when I pleaded guilty.

"You have walked through a door and it is obvious you cannot decide to return," Quebec Court Judge Serge Boisvert told me. "Good luck."

Recently, I was talking with a visitor in jail about certain sentences handed down to dealers for the Hells Angels.

"What they got is fucking ridiculous," I said. "Those guys will do so little time."

"Watch out," my visitor said, smiling. "You are starting to sound like a fine, upstanding citizen."

I laughed. I knew what he meant. He was joking, knowing full well I had a bit of work to do on that. I still feel for the Rock Machine in this war, and that probably won't change for many years, if ever. Which leads to the question in everyone's mind, mine included. Can I stay straight after this? Even my police handlers tell me the odds are against informants.

The public has the impression that a criminal takes the easy way out by becoming an informant. They are paid, pampered, and given special privileges in jail. But people seem to forget something. Is it really easy to change every aspect of the only life you know, to abandon one set of morals, however skewed, for an untried set while going from pure criminal to regular citizen? Let me tell you, it is terrifying.

I feel like a newborn, grappling with how to eat, walk, and talk. When I'm out, I will be in a new city, with no experience making real friends and a 15-year gap in my résumé. I will take my schooling soon—the courses I fought hard to get. I won't tell you what I'll be learning since that would give clues to finding me. I will tell you, though, that I want my new life to work. I just have no idea if it will.

Before that life can start, I have to testify over and over again. I was begrudgingly persuaded to be an expert witness of sorts at the megatrials of all those Hells Angels arrested in the spring of 2001. That could delay my life for years. But Brigitte helped convince me it could be a good way of repaying my debt to society. Prosecutors also used that argument, and dangled a little more money in front of me to compensate for putting my life on hold and in danger.

But I'm left frustrated because I want to start my new life, to work, to see if I can make it as an honest man. And I'm terrified the government will take away whatever remains of my soul by forcing me to testify against my own brother.

If you never hear of me after that, that means all is fine. If my name does pop up in the news, then I'm back behind bars. Or my new life is over, because one of my old friends has found me.